English grammar: an outline

English grammar:
an outline

RODNEY HUDDLESTON

Department of English
University of Queensland

CAMBRIDGE
UNIVERSITY PRESS

Published by the Press Syndicate of the University of Cambridge
The Pitt Building, Trumpington Street, Cambridge CB2 1RP
40 West 20th Street, New York, NY 10011-4211, USA
10 Stamford Road, Oakleigh, Melbourne 3166, Australia

First published 1988
Reprinted 1988, 1990, 1991, 1993, 1995, 1996

Printed in Great Britain at
the University Printing House, Cambridge

British Library cataloguing in publication data

Huddleston, Rodney
English grammar: an outline.
1. English language – Grammar – 1950–
I. Title
428.2   PE1112

Library of Congress cataloging in publication data

Huddleston, Rodney D.
English grammar.
Bibliography
Includes index.
1. English language – Grammar – 1950–
I. Title
PE1106.H76   1988   428.2   87-34124

ISBN 0 521 31152 7 paperback

For James and Alexandra

Contents

Preface

This book is intended as an introductory text for courses in English grammar at tertiary level. It offers an outline account of the most important and central grammatical constructions and categories in English. I have assumed only minimal prior familiarity with the structure of English: all the grammatical terminology used is systematically explained. The analysis draws on the descriptive and theoretical advances made in modern linguistics, and for this reason the book could be used for an elementary course on English within a linguistics programme. It is, however, intended for a wider audience: for any course aiming to present a descriptive overview of the structure of English. Significant departures from traditional grammar in analysis or terminology are pointed out, normally in footnotes.

One distinctive feature of the book is that it discusses the major grammatical categories at both a language-particular and a general level. The language-particular account gives the distinctive grammatical properties of the various categories as they apply to English: it thus provides the criteria for determining whether some word is a noun, verb, adjective, adverb or whatever, whether some verb-form is a past participle, a past tense form, etc., whether some clause is declarative, interrogative, imperative, exclamative – and so on. Analysis at the general level is concerned with what is common to the categories across languages, thus providing criteria for the application of the same terms in the grammars of different languages. For this reason the book could also be used as a reference work on English for a course in linguistic typology.

I should like to record here my deep gratitude to Bernard Comrie, who was good enough to read the book in draft form and make numerous suggestions for improvement. Thanks are due also to Steve Johnson for helpful comments on several chapters. Neither, of course, is to be blamed for the faults that remain. Finally, I would express my thanks to Julie Lyons and Pauline O'Neill, who typed the book through several versions.

Symbols and notational conventions

Bold face italics indicate lexemes (see 1.2).

Ordinary italics are used for citing sentences, words and other forms (in orthographic representation).

/ / obliques enclose phonological representations, indicating the pronunciation as opposed to the spelling.

/ oblique is used to abbreviate examples: *He allowed/refused me a second go* is an abbreviation of *He allowed me a second go* and *He refused me a second go*.

( ) parentheses enclose optional items: *I know (that) she is here* indicates that the *that* may be present, *I know that she is here*, or absent, *I know she is here*.

[ ] square brackets enclose relevant context for an example: *[I wonder] if it is true* represents the form *if it is true* considered as occurring in the context '*I wonder*

⟨ ⟩ angle brackets enclose letters representing different speakers in a conversational exchange: ⟨A⟩ *What are you doing?* – ⟨B⟩ *Testing the chlorine level* cites an exchange where *What are you doing?* is said by one speaker, *Testing the chlorine level* by another.

* asterisk indicates that what follows is ungrammatical – at least in the construal under consideration.

? indicates that the grammaticality (or, if followed by *, the ungrammaticality) of what follows is questionable.

' ' single quotation marks are used as 'scare quotes', e.g. for technical terms not previously introduced.

" " double quotation marks are used to represent meanings.

ROMAN SMALL CAPITALS are used for emphasis.

Roman bold face is used for important technical terms when explained.

xi

The following abbreviations are used for syntactic classes, functions and other categories:

Adj	adjective	O^i	indirect object
AdjP	adjective phrase	P	predicator
Adv	adverb	PC	predicative
AdvP	adverb phrase	PC^o	objective predicative
Cl	clause	PC^s	subjective predicative
Comp	complement	PP	preposition phrase
Dep	dependent	Periph-Dep	peripheral dependent
Detnr	determiner	Pers	person
Detve	determinative	Pl	plural
DetveP	determinative phrase	PossP	possessive phrase
Fem	feminine	Pred	predicate
Masc	masculine	Prep	preposition
Mod	modifier	S	subject
N	noun	Sg	singular
NP	noun phrase	TDC	tensed declarative clause
Neut	neuter	V	verb
O	object	VP	verb phrase
O^d	direct object		

Phonological symbols

Consonants

/p/ as in *pie*	/dʒ/ as in *jaw*	/ʒ/ as in *pleasure*
/t/ *tie*	/f/ *few*	/h/ *hill*
/d/ *die*	/θ/ *thigh*	/m/ *meat*
/k/ *car*	/s/ *see*	/n/ *neat*
/g/ *go*	/z/ *zoo*	/ŋ/ *wing*
/tʃ/ *chew*	/ʃ/ *shy*	/r/ *run*

Vowels

/ɪ/ as in *pit*	/ʌ/ as in *putt*	/ɛə/ as in *paired*
/e/ *pet*	/ɒ/ *pot*	/ə/ *sofa*
/æ/ *pat*	/əʊ/ *pole*	

" precedes a syllable carrying 'nuclear' stress (main stress within an intonation group)

↓ indicates intonation with falling terminal, ↑ with rising terminal

Cross-references

Cross-references to another section of the same chapter take the form '... §3 above/below', while cross-references to a section in a different chapter take the form '... 4.3' (i.e. section 3 of Ch. 4).

1

Preliminaries

The description of a language comprises three major components: **phonology**, **grammar** and **lexicon**. The phonology describes the sound system: consonants, vowels, stress, intonation, and so on. The two most basic units of grammar are the word and the sentence: one subcomponent of grammar, called **morphology**, deals with the form of words, while the other, called **syntax**, deals with the way words combine to form sentences. The lexicon – or dictionary, to use a more familiar term – lists the vocabulary items, mainly words and idioms (such as *red herring*, *give up*, and so on), specifying how they are pronounced, how they behave grammatically, and what they mean. In this book we will confine our attention to the grammar, with only occasional passing mention of phonological and lexical matters.

On another dimension we can distinguish between the study of linguistic form and the study of meaning: all three of the major components are concerned with aspects of both. The special term **semantics** is applied to the study of meaning, and we can accordingly distinguish phonological semantics (covering such matters as the meanings expressed by stress and intonation), grammatical semantics (dealing with the meanings associated with grammatical categories such as past tense, interrogative clause, and so on) and lexical semantics (the meanings of vocabulary items).

The relation between form and meaning in grammar is by no means straightforward. This is one of the issues we shall need to consider in this introductory chapter, where the aim is to explain briefly the model or framework of grammatical description that we shall be using in the book and the methodological approach adopted. We begin with the question of how we can go about defining the various grammatical categories that will figure in the description – categories such as noun, subject, imperative clause, past tense, and so on: there will inevitably be a considerable number of them.

1. Grammatical categories: definitions and prototypes

It is important to distinguish two levels at which our grammatical categories need to be defined: the **language-particular** level and the **general** level. At the language-particular level we are concerned with the properties that characterise the category in the particular language under consideration, which in our case of course is English but which might equally well be French, Urdu, Vietnamese or whatever. At this level we investigate, for example, how nouns, verbs, adjectives, etc., behave differently in English sentence structure, how English distinguishes between the subject and object of a verb, and so on. At the general level, by contrast, our concern is with the properties that are common across different languages to categories such as noun, verb, adjective, subject, object.

To make the distinction more concrete, consider the part-of-speech analysis of the underlined words in the following sentences:

(1) i   *The boss had watched the secretary destroy the files*
     ii *The boss had witnessed the destruction of the files*

At the language-particular level we will give the criteria that lead us to put all the words with solid underlining (*boss, secretary*, etc.) into one part-of-speech, and all those with broken underlining (*had, watched*, etc.) into a second. At the general level we will give the criteria that lead us to call the first class 'noun' and the second 'verb'. We do not devise a fresh set of terms for each new language we describe but draw, rather, on a large repertoire of general terms: definitions at the general level provide a principled basis for applying these terms to the various categories that need to be differentiated in the grammatical description of particular languages.

Considerable confusion arises when this distinction of levels is not made, when what is really a general definition is in effect presented as though it were a language-particular definition – and this happens quite frequently in traditional grammar, especially traditional school grammar. For example, the standard traditional definition of a noun as 'the name of a person, place or thing' is commonly presented as though it provided the criterion for deciding which words in English are nouns (i.e. as though it provided a language-particular definition), whereas it should be construed as providing a criterion for deciding which word class in English should be called 'noun' (i.e. as part of a general definition). For when it is construed at the language-particular level, the definition is clearly unsatisfactory. Suppose we take 'thing', as it appears in the definition, as equivalent to 'concrete object'. By this criterion *destruction* would be excluded from the class of nouns, as it obviously does not denote a concrete object; but in fact all grammarians include it in the noun class – because in terms of the way it enters into the structure of grammatical sentences it behaves like *boss, secretary*, etc. Nor does the definition fare any better if we say that 'thing' is to be interpreted in some abstract sense, since this simply makes it circular and unworkable. For we would have no way of determining whether a word was the name of a thing in this more abstract sense which did not presuppose that we already knew whether it was a noun. Thus the way we decide to assign *destruction* in (ii) and *destroy* in (i) to different classes is by noting, not that *destruction* denotes a thing while *destroy* does not, but rather that they differ in their grammatical behaviour.

In the first place, the verb *destroy* takes as 'complement' an expression like *the files*, but nouns do not take complements of this kind: *destruction* takes a complement introduced by *of*. Secondly, *destruction*, like other nouns, enters into construction with the 'definite article' *the*, but we could not add *the* before *destroy* in (i). Thirdly, if we wanted to add a modifier, we would use an adjective with the noun *destruction* (e.g. *the surreptitious destruction of the files*) but an adverb with *destroy* (e.g. *surreptitiously destroy the files*). And so on. It is properties of this kind that must figure in our definitions of nouns and verbs at the language-particular level. At the general level we will reformulate the definition to avoid misinterpretation, saying that 'noun' is the part of speech which contains among its most elementary members those words that denote persons, places or concrete objects. Because it is a general definition, the fact that not all nouns in English denote persons, places or concrete objects does not invalidate it. *Boss, secretary, files, destruction* belong to the same part of speech in English because they are alike with respect to the kind of grammatical property mentioned above; this part of speech we then call noun because this is the one to which words denoting persons, places and concrete objects belong – words like *boss, secretary, files*.

As a second example, consider the category 'imperative clause'. Imperative contrasts with 'declarative' and 'interrogative', as illustrated in (2):

(2)   i   *Be generous!*   Imperative
     ii   *You are generous*   Declarative
     iii   *Are you generous?*   Interrogative

An imperative clause is commonly defined as one that is used to issue a command or request. But it is easy to see from examples like (3) that this will not work as a language-particular definition.

(3)   i   *Have a good holiday*   Imperative
     ii   *Passengers are requested to remain seated*   Declarative
     iii   *Would you mind speaking a little more slowly?*   Interrogative

The imperative (i) would normally be used to express a hope or wish rather than a request, and conversely (ii) and (iii) would normally be used as requests but are not imperative clauses. A language-particular definition of imperative clause for English will have to refer to the grammatical properties that distinguish clauses like (i) in (2) and (3) from declaratives like (ii) and interrogatives like (iii). Note, for example, the form of the verb in (2): *be* in (i), but *are* in (ii) and (iii) – and again it is *are* that we find in (3ii). Another difference is that the imperatives here have no subject, whereas the declaratives and interrogatives do (*you* or *passengers*). On the basis of such differences – which we will need to specify with a good deal more care and precision – we will assign clauses like (2i) and (3i) to a distinct clause class at the language-particular level, and we can draw on the fact that members of this class are CHARACTERISTICALLY used as commands/requests to apply the general term 'imperative' to the class that we have established.

Again, then, we will need to reformulate the traditional definition so as to make clear that it is to be interpreted at the general level: the term 'imperative clause' will be applied to a grammatically distinguishable class of clauses whose members are characteristically used as commands/requests. The fact that examples like (3i) are analysed as imperative clauses is now no longer a problem: they are assigned to the same clause class as (2i) because they are like (2i) in respect of their grammatical form, and this class is called 'imperative' because the great majority of its members are like (2i) in that they would most naturally be used as commands or requests.

'A noun is the name of a person, place or thing' and 'An imperative clause is one that is used as a command or request' are both examples of what are commonly called **notional** definitions – definitions based on the SEMANTIC properties of expressions, i.e. their meaning, rather than on their grammatical FORM. Notional definitions are unsatisfactory at the language-particular level because the relation between categories of grammatical form and categories of meaning is normally too complex for us to be able to define the former in terms of the latter. A central task for the grammarian is precisely to show how categories of grammatical form are related to categories of meaning: a notional definition at the language-particular level thus confuses the very things that we need to distinguish and relate.

Notice, moreover, that we will recognise a grammatical category in analysing a given language only if it is grammatically distinguishable from other categories in the language. To take a very obvious example, we will not recognise 'pointed noun' as a subclass of nouns containing words like *pin* or *spire* which denote pointed objects, because there is nothing grammatically special about such words: they are not grammatically distinguishable from words like *circle* or *bed*. A satisfactory definition or explication of a grammatical category must thus surely make reference to the kind of properties that justify its inclusion in our analysis, properties based on its distinctive grammatical behaviour; this a notional definition completely fails to do.

These objections to notional definitions apply, however, only at the language-particular level. At the general level we are concerned with naming and identifying across languages categories that have already been established by language-particular criteria, and here it is perfectly legitimate to make use of notional definitions. This is not to say that general definitions will be based exclusively on meaning, but normally they will be expected to include some reference to meaning. Although we do not find a one-to-one relation between categories of grammatical form and categories of meaning, we do not expect to find grammatical categories that have no connection at all with semantic categories. Rather they will have their basis in semantics, and a general definition will need to indicate what is the semantic basis for a given category. The grammatical distinction between declaratives, interrogatives and imperatives in English, for example, clearly has its basis in the semantic distinction between statements, questions and requests/commands; we can regard the former as arising through the **grammaticalisation** of the latter, the process of grammatical differentiation on the basis of semantic differences.

Some general categories are universal: all languages, for example, distinguish between nouns and verbs. Many, however, belong in only a subset of languages.

We contrasted (2ii) and (2iii) above as declarative vs interrogative, but the latter belongs more precisely to the category of closed interrogative, as opposed to an open interrogative like *Where are they going?* – and these categories of closed and open interrogative clause are not found in all languages. They apply to clause constructions whose members are characteristically used to ask questions where the set of answers is respectively closed and open: for *Are you generous?* the answers are *Yes* and *No*, whereas *Where are they going?* has an indefinite number of possible answers: *To Canberra, To New York*, and so on. All languages enable their speakers to ask these two kinds of question, but they do not all have distinctive clause constructions based on them. The distinction between statements and closed questions is grammaticalised in English by the different positions of the subject, but there are languages where it is expressed by a difference in intonation rather than by a difference in grammatical construction, and this type of language therefore has no grammatical category of closed interrogative clause. And similarly there are languages which have no grammatical distinction (as opposed to an intonational one) corresponding to that found in English between the open interrogative *Where are they going?* and the declarative *They are going somewhere*, and here the grammatical category of open interrogative clause will likewise not be applicable. It is for this reason that our general definitions incorporate a condition of grammaticalisation. Thus the general term closed interrogative will be defined as applying to a grammatically distinct clause class whose members are characteristically used to ask closed questions: the reference to a grammatically distinct clause class ensures that the definition will be satisfied only in languages where the semantic category is grammaticalised – grammaticalised more specifically in the structure of the clause. As we have observed, the grammaticalisation condition is in this example satisfied in English, but there are other categories – including one or two that figure in traditional grammars of English – where it is not. Thus we shall see in Ch. 5, for example, that English has no future tense; we can, of course, refer to future time in English, but the semantic category of future time (unlike that of past time and present time) is not grammaticalised in the tense system of English.

A second important distinction we must make is between **prototypical** and **non-prototypical** examples of a grammatical category. We very often find for a given category a central core of examples sharing a number of grammatical properties, with other examples exhibiting some but not all of these properties: the core of examples having the full set of properties we will then regard as the prototypical examples. For example, *secretary, friend* and *idea* are prototypical nouns, whereas *perseverance* and *wetness* are not: they differ from the prototype in not entering into contrasts of 'number', singular vs plural. Thus *secretary* contrasts with *secretaries* but there is no plural for *perseverance*. *Perseverance* and *wetness* certainly have enough properties in common with *secretary, friend, idea* to justify their assignment to the same part of speech, but the lack of number contrast makes them non-prototypical. A good deal further removed from the prototype is an example like *umbrage* "offence": this is now restricted to the idioms *take umbrage* and *give umbrage*, so that it is unable to enter into many of the grammatical relations that are characteristic of prototypical nouns. Not only is there no contrasting form *umbrages*, but we cannot have *this umbrage, *my umbrage, *the umbrage that had impressed us so much, and so on. (The asterisk, here and henceforth, indicates that what follows is ungrammatical, at least in the interpretation under consideration.) An example of a non-prototypical verb might be *beware*, as in *Beware of the new boss*. It is very different from a prototypical verb inasmuch as it does not enter into contrast with past and present tense forms – we do not have *He bewares/bewared of the new boss*; there is nevertheless no doubt that it belongs to the part of speech 'verb' rather than to any of the others.

What such examples show is that grammatical likeness is often not an all-or-nothing matter but a matter of degree, and that we cannot expect to be always able to give a language-particular definition of a category in the form of a set of sufficient and necessary conditions for inclusion in the category – i.e. a set of properties such that an item will be included if and only if it has all the properties in the set. Instead we will often begin with definitions of the prototype and consider then how far beyond the prototype the category should be allowed to extend – and there may be a certain amount of indeterminacy or arbitrariness over precisely where the boundary should be drawn.

2. Words and lexemes

Syntax deals with combinations of words, we have said, morphology with the form of words. The term 'word', however, is used in a variety of senses, so that it will be helpful to begin with some clarification of how it will be used here. Consider then the sentences *This tooth needs attention* and *These teeth need attention*. Are *tooth* and *teeth* instances of the same word or of different words? In one sense they are clearly different: they differ in pronunciation, spelling, meaning and in their grammatical behaviour. In another sense, however, they are manifestations of a single element, and indeed they are traditionally said to be 'forms of the same word'. We thus have two distinct concepts here, the second more abstract than the first: I will use **word** in the less abstract sense and introduce the term **lexeme** for the more abstract one. Thus I will say that *tooth* and *teeth* are different words, but forms of the same lexeme. Words will be represented in ordinary italics, lexemes in bold italics: *tooth* is the singular form of the lexeme *tooth*, while *teeth* is its plural form.

More precisely, we will say that *tooth* and *teeth* are different **inflectional forms** of *tooth*, and will speak of 'singular' and 'plural' here as **inflectional properties**. Similarly with verbs: *sang* and *sung*, for example, are respectively the past tense and past participle forms of the lexeme *sing*. The set of inflectional forms of a lexeme constitutes an inflectional **paradigm**: the paradigm for *tooth* contains the two forms *tooth* and *teeth*, while that for *sing* contains *sang, sung, sing* and various others: verb inflection is a good deal more complex than noun inflection and we will be looking at it in detail in Ch. 3 – at this point it is sufficient to be aware of the concept of inflection.

The distinction we have drawn between word and lexeme makes our concept of word more precise, but there remains one further point to be clarified. Consider the pairs [*The window was*] *clean* vs [*I'll*] *clean* [*the window*] and [*She drew some cash from the*] *bank* [*by the post office*] vs [*She lay on the*] *bank* [*of the river*]. The two *clean*'s are forms of different lexemes: the first is a form of the adjective **clean**, which has *cleaner* and *cleanest* as its other forms, whereas the second is a form of the verb **clean,** which has *cleaned*, *cleans*, etc., as its other forms. The difference between the two *bank*'s is lexical rather than grammatical: they are different lexical items – i.e. different items of the vocabulary. I will distinguish between the term **word** used without qualification and **lexicogrammatical-word** in such a way that the former does not presuppose any lexical or grammatical analysis while the latter does. Given this terminology, the two *clean*'s or the two *bank*'s will be instances of the same word but of different lexicogrammatical-words. I shall have more occasion to talk simply of words than of lexicogrammatical-words and it will not be necessary for our purposes to investigate in detail the far from straightforward question of what kinds of grammatical and lexical criteria establish a difference between lexicogrammatical-words.

3. Constituent structure, classes and functions

Syntax is concerned with the way words (strictly, lexicogrammatical-words) combine to form sentences. The sentence is the largest unit of syntax, the word the smallest. But we need also to recognise units of intermediate size: instead of analysing a sentence immediately into a sequence of words we will assign it a hierarchical or layered structure. For example, the sentence *The boss made a bad mistake* may be broken down step-by-step as shown in (4):

(4)

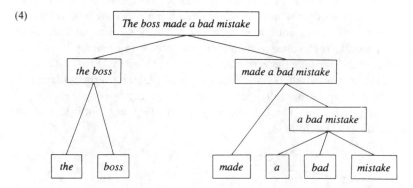

All the boxed units other than the topmost one are said to be **constituents**: a constituent is a part of some unit higher in the hierarchy. More specifically, we say the *the boss* and *made a bad mistake* are the **immediate constituents** of the sentence, those that it is first divided into; similarly, *made* and *a bad mistake* are the immediate constituents of *made a bad mistake*, and so on. (4) is said to be a representation of the **constituent structure** of the sentence.

Complementary to the concept of constituent is that of **construction**. All the boxed units in (4) other than the lowest ones, the words, are constructions: con-structures are made up of units lower in the hierarchy. *Made a bad mistake*, then, is both a constituent (by virtue of being part of the sentence as a whole) and a construction (by virtue of being analysable into the constituents *made* and *a bad mistake*); analogously for *the boss* and *a bad mistake*. The words, by contrast, are not syntactic constructions because they are the minimal units of syntax, and the sentence is not a constituent because it is the maximal unit of syntax. An equivalent but typographically simpler way of representing constituent structure is shown in (5), and this is the form that we shall use henceforth:

(5)

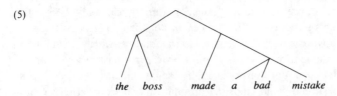

the   boss   made   a   bad   mistake

The constituent structure analysis identifies all the syntactic units in the sentence: we must next consider how they are to be further described. In the first place, we will assign them to **syntactic classes** on the basis of properties shared with other expressions in the language. The traditional parts of speech are special cases of such classes, namely word classes.[1] Thus *boss* and *mistake* in (4) are analysed as nouns because they have the properties sketchily mentioned in §1 above as characteristic of that class. Similarly, *made* is a verb and *bad* an adjective; *the* and *a* are traditionally called the definite and indefinite articles respectively: here we will treat them as belonging to a class of 'determinatives', which also includes words like *my*, *some*, *this*. The classification of the larger units is for the most part derivative from that of the words. *The boss* and *a bad mistake* are 'noun phrases' because they each have a noun as their major or 'head' element, and similarly *made a bad mistake* is classified as a verb phrase because (for reasons we will go into in due course) we take the verb *made* as the head element. Finally, the topmost unit, the sentence itself, is classified as a 'clause'. All these terms will need of course to be explained more fully, but for the moment we are using them simply for illustrative purposes. The classificatory information just outlined can be incorporated into (5) as follows:

(6)

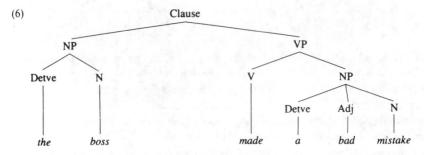

¹ Strictly speaking, the parts of speech cover both word classes and lexeme classes: we will take up this point in 2.3.

This of course is only a start: a more detailed analysis will need to recognise subclasses of various kinds. For example, *boss* and *mistake* are, more specifically, common nouns, contrasting with proper nouns, such as *Mary* or *Paris*.

In addition to assigning the units to classes, we will give an analysis in terms of **syntactic functions**, accounting for the grammatical role of units within the construction immediately containing them. In (6), for example, we say that *the boss* functions as 'subject' of the clause, while *made a bad mistake* is 'predicate'; then within the VP that forms the predicate, *a bad mistake* is 'object' and *made* is 'predicator'. (Note here the terminological distinction between 'predicator', the function of the verb, and 'predicate', the function of the verb phrase.) *The boss* and *a bad mistake* are both noun phrases, but they have different functions in this particular sentence: in *A bad mistake would annoy the boss*, by contrast, *a bad mistake* is subject and *the boss* object.

Syntactic functions make a very obvious contribution to the meaning – so that *Kim shot Pat* (with *Kim* subject and *Pat* object) means something quite different from *Pat shot Kim* (with *Pat* subject, *Kim* object). But as with other kinds of grammatical category, they cannot be defined notionally at the language-particular level. At this level we need to look at the strictly syntactic properties of the subject. In the most elementary kind of clause (what we shall call a 'kernel' clause) the subject precedes the predicator – while the object, if there is one, follows. Secondly, the first verb very often agrees with the subject. For example, in *He likes it* the verb *likes* agrees with the subject *he*: if we change singular *he* to plural *they* we must also change *likes* to *like* (whereas changing the object *it* to *them* would have no effect on the verb). Thirdly, a few pronouns such as *I, he,* **they** have contrasting inflectional forms, with the subject selecting the 'nominative' form, *I, he, they*, and the object selecting the 'accusative' form, *me, him, them*: *I shot him/He shot me*.

'Subject', 'object' and 'predicate' are likely to be familiar from traditional grammar, but the latter does not provide a comparable set of terms for the functional analysis of smaller units. The main concepts we will use here are, in the first instance, 'head' for the function of the major element and 'dependent' for the subordinate elements, with various more specific terms then used where appropriate. Thus in *a bad mistake* the noun *mistake* functions as head, while *a* is determiner and *bad* modifier. Predicator and object in the structure of the VP are, as we shall later argue, special cases of head and dependent respectively – and so too indeed are predicate and subject in the structure of the clause.

Incorporating such functional information into (6) gives (7), overleaf, as the representation of the structure of our sample sentence. No function is assigned to the topmost unit because the question of what function an element has arises only when that element is part of a construction at the next higher layer in the constituent structure: the clause which forms the sentence as a whole in (7) has no function precisely because it is not part of any other syntactic unit.

The head position in a given class of phrase is always filled by the same class of smaller units: the head position in an NP is always filled by a noun, the head (predicator) position in a VP by a verb, and so on. But very often a dependent posi-

(7)

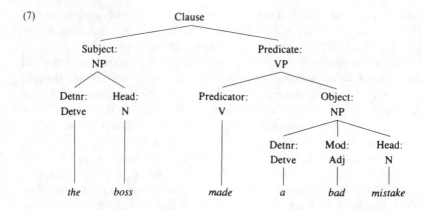

tion can be filled by expressions from different classes. For example, such a verb as ***know*** can take as object either an NP, as in [*They*] *knew the result*, or a subordinate clause, as in [*They*] *knew that it had failed*. The same goes for the subject of a verb like ***surprise***: compare *The decision surprised everyone* (subject position filled by the NP *the decision*) and *That he was allowed to stay on surprised everyone* (subject position filled by the subordinate clause *that he was allowed to stay on*). This complex relation between function and classes reinforces the need to keep them conceptually and terminologically distinct.

Before concluding this section, it is worth observing that many sentences are ambiguous and very often the ambiguity is attributable to the fact that the same sequence of words has two (or more) analyses of the kind we have been discussing. An elementary example is *Liz attacked the man with a knife*, whose constituent structure (simplified slightly) can be as shown in (8) or (9).

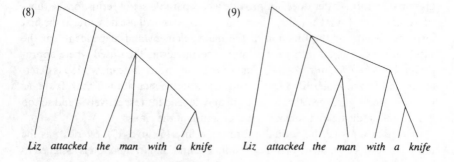

In (8) *with a knife* enters into construction with *the* and *man*, so that *the man with a knife* forms a single constituent (an NP functioning as object of *attacked*): under this analysis the meaning is "Liz attacked the man who had a knife". In (9), by contrast, *attacked the man with a knife* has three immediate constituents, *attacked* (predicator), *the man* (object) and *with a knife* ('adjunct'): there is here a direct structural relation between *with a knife* and *attacked*, so that *with a knife*

specifies the means of attack – hence the meaning "Liz used a knife in her attack on the man".

Although there are two interpretations, we have a single sentence – it is, precisely, an ambiguous sentence. Like the unqualified term 'word', then, 'sentence' is used in such a way that it does not presuppose any lexicogrammatical analysis. Further, we will use **utterance** as a technical term that is neutral between speech and writing, so that we can have spoken and written utterances of the same sentence. We then distinguish between the **verbal** and **non-verbal** components of an utterance, where the verbal component consists of the words, and the non-verbal component consists of what is, as it were, overlaid upon the words: in speech the non-verbal component includes prosodic properties (intonation and sentence stress), loudness, tempo, tone of voice, etc., whereas in writing it covers punctuation, typeface (roman vs italic, bold vs ordinary), and so on. And sentence identity will depend solely on the verbal component. Thus *Kim shot Pat* can be pronounced with main stress on any of the three words and with either falling intonation (indicating a statement) or rising intonation (typically indicating a question), but we will regard these simply as prosodically different utterances of the same sentence – and similarly *Kim shot Pat*, and *Kim shot Pat?* will be punctuationally different utterances of the same sentence.

4. Kernel and non-kernel clauses

In the last section we introduced the concepts of constituent structure, class and function by reference to the analysis of particular sentences. The analysis of particular sentences interacts, of course, with the grammar for the language as a whole: the latter specifies what are the grammatically possible sentences and what their grammatical structure is. The primary justification for the concepts of constituent structure, class and function is that they enable us to simplify the overall grammar. Instead of attempting to specify the set of grammatical sentences immediately in terms of permitted sequences of words, we make our task more manageable by breaking it down into separate stages: we first specify the range of sentence constructions in terms of clauses (a sentence may have the form of a simple clause or of a sequence of clauses related in various ways), then deal with the permitted clause constructions, then the different classes of phrase, and so on.

In this section we will introduce an important distinction between two kinds of clause, **kernel** and **non-kernel**, which likewise permits a significant simplification of the grammar.[2] Consider:

(10) i *He sliced it with a knife*   Kernel
    ii *Did he slice it with a knife?*
    iii *[The knife] he sliced it with [was extremely sharp]*   } Non-kernel

(Material in square brackets is relevant context but not part of the expression

---

[2] The terms 'kernel' and 'non-kernel' are not used in traditional grammar, though the concepts are to some extent implicit. I have borrowed the terms from the first version of transformational-generative grammar, adapting them, however, to the much more informal framework within which I am working.

under consideration itself, so that in (iii) we are concerned with the clause *he sliced it with* as it occurs in the context *The knife   was extremely sharp*.) We can greatly simplify the grammar if instead of attempting to treat all clauses as of equal syntactic status we assign descriptive priority to kernel clauses and then handle the non-kernel clauses derivatively, in terms of the way they differ from the kernel patterns. Thus for the above examples we take (i) as basic: it can be described quite straightforwardly in terms of the kinds of concept introduced in §3 above. (ii) is an interrogative clause, and the grammar will contain rules for forming interrogatives from their declarative counterparts: in this case we derive it from (i) by adding the verb *do* before the subject and transferring to it the tense inflection which in the declarative is carried by *slice*. Clause (iii) is subordinated so as to function as modifier to the noun *knife*; it is one type of 'relative clause', and in the process of subordination the complement of *with* is lost altogether, which leaves a clause that could not stand alone as a sentence. Note that although (iii) contains fewer words than (i) there is a clear sense in which (i) is more elementary or basic, for (iii) is dependent on the context for its interpretation and is itself structurally incomplete by virtue of lacking a complement for *with*.

For the most part we will focus our attention in the first half of the book on kernel clauses, leaving the systematic description of non-kernel clauses until Chs. 9–13. It will be helpful, however, to present here a summary overview of the grammatical properties distinguishing kernel from non-kernel clauses. A kernel clause has all of the following properties:

(a) It forms a sentence on its own – i.e. it is not part of some larger syntactic unit. Thus a kernel clause is neither coordinate with, nor subordinate to, some other clause. For example, in

(11) i   *Either he is ill or he has overslept*
    ii   *I know that he is ill*

the coordinate clauses *either he is ill* and *or he has overslept* and the subordinate clause *that he is ill* are all non-kernel by this criterion. Coordination and subordination are not always reflected in the internal structure of the clause concerned: in *He is ill or he has overslept*, for example, the first of the two coordinate clauses contains no overt marker of coordination and in *I know he is ill* the subordinate clause *he is ill* contains no overt marker of subordination. Nevertheless, we will still regard such clauses as non-kernel and simply allow that the process of coordination or subordination may or may not lead to structural change. In coordination – for which the most common markers are *and, but* and (*either* [. . .]) *or* – the clauses are of equal syntactic status: one is not embedded as a constituent within another; (11i) thus does not itself have the structure of a clause. In subordination, by contrast, one clause, the subordinate one, is embedded within another, superordinate, clause – as *that he is ill* is embedded as object within the superordinate *I know that he is ill* or as *he sliced it with* is embedded as modifier within the NP subject in *The knife he sliced it with was extremely sharp*. The superordinate clause in both these examples does satisfy the criterion of forming a sentence on its own and is (as all the other criteria are satisfied too) a kernel clause: a kernel clause can thus contain a non-kernel clause within it. There is no special name for a clause that is not coordinate, but one which is not subordinate is called a **main** clause; thus only a non-coordinate main clause can be a kernel clause.

(b) A kernel clause is structurally complete, not reduced by **ellipsis**, the omission of one or more elements that can be recovered, understood, from the linguistic or situational context. Some kinds of ellipsis result from coordination as in *Kim went by bus and Pat by train*, where *and Pat by train* lacks a predicator (we understand "went") or from subordination, as in *Kim is taller than Pat is*, where the subordinate *Pat is* is elliptical by virtue of lacking a 'predicative' (we understand "tall" or rather something like "tall to such and such a degree"). In other cases, however, we find ellipsis unaccompanied by coordination or subordination:

(12) ⟨A⟩ *What are you doing?*   ⟨B⟩ *Testing the chlorine level*

B's reply here is neither coordinate nor subordinate, but it still does not have the form of a kernel clause, lacking as it does a subject and a 'tensed' verb (a verb carrying a present or past tense inflection) – compare the non-elliptical and kernel *I am testing the chlorine level.*

(c) A kernel clause is **declarative** as opposed to **imperative** or **interrogative** so that in our earlier example (2), *You are generous* qualifies as a kernel clause but *Be generous!* and *Are you generous?* do not.

This dimension of clause contrast is known as **clause type**: we say that declarative, imperative, interrogative (and we shall in fact add a fourth term, **exclamative**, as in *How generous you are!*) are terms in the system of clause type, where a **system** is a set of mutually exclusive classes contrasting grammatically on a single dimension. The most elementary, or **unmarked**, term in the system is declarative: clauses belonging to any other term in the system are for that reason non-kernel.

(d) A kernel clause is **positive** (e.g. *They were helpful*), not **negative** (*They weren't helpful*). These categories contrast in a system of the clause known as **polarity**, with positive the unmarked term, negative the marked.

(e) Finally, a kernel clause is unmarked in respect of all **thematic** systems of the clause. The major thematic systems of the clause are illustrated in (13)–(17), where the clause numbered (i) is in each case the unmarked, i.e. structurally more basic, member of the pair. Except in (13), no special name is applied to the unmarked member; the terminology will of course be explained in due course (Ch. 12).

(13) i   *My father wrote the letter*   Active (voice)
     ii *The letter was written by my father*   Passive (voice)

(14)	i	*They invited John*	[Unmarked]
	ii	*It was John they invited*	Cleft
(15)	i	*Two policemen are at the door*	[Unmarked]
	ii	*There are two policemen at the door*	Existential
(16)	i	*That he should be so late is annoying*	[Unmarked]
	ii	*It is annoying that he should be so late*	Extrapositioned
(17)	i	*He has known her father for three years*	[Unmarked]
	ii	*Her father he has known for three years*	Thematically reordered

These systems are alike in that they provide alternative ways of saying what is in some intuitive sense (which we shall clarify in the next section) 'the same thing'. It would nevertheless be a mistake to think that the choice between them is of no communicative significance. The grammar makes available a variety of different ways of saying 'the same thing', so that at a particular point in a spoken discourse or written text we can select a form that is appropriate in the light of our assumptions about what information the addressee(s) will already possess, of what parts of our message we wish to emphasise or focus upon, of the contrasts we wish to draw, and so on. The thematic systems of the clause are those where the paired clauses always or normally differ in this kind of respect. And again we exclude from the set of kernel clauses any clause belonging to the marked, structurally less elementary, term in one or more of these systems.

5. Some basic concepts in semantics

Most of what is said in this book about the meanings associated with grammatical categories does not depend on an understanding of any theoretical concepts in semantics, and we thus have no need for extended preliminary discussion in this area. We will confine our attention in this section to drawing a distinction between sentences and propositions and to explaining what is meant by the basic semantic relation of entailment.

We need to distinguish between sentences and propositions in order to clarify how the concepts true and false can be applied to utterances. If we take an elementary declarative sentence like *Peter is in the kitchen* and consider it simply as a sentence of English, in abstraction from its use on any particular occasion, then it does not make sense to ask whether it is true or false: we cannot divide declarative sentences into two sets, those that are true and those that are false. This, of course, is because most of them can be used now to say something true, now to say something false. We accordingly introduce the concept of **proposition** to denote the abstract entities to which the terms true and false have their primary application. We will say that *Peter is in the kitchen* can be used to express an indefinite number of different propositions and it is these propositions that can be said to be true or false. What proposition it expresses on a given occasion of its utterance depends on who is being referred to as *Peter*, or which room is being referred to as *the kitchen* and on the time of the utterance (i.e. on what time is being referred to by means of the present tense verb *is*). If we apply the terms true and false to sentences, it can only be derivatively, relative to their use in a particular context to express a true or false proposition.

Just as the same sentence can be used in different circumstances to express different propositions, so the same proposition can be expressed by different sentences. One case of this is where the sentences belong to different languages: English *Peter is in the kitchen* and French *Pierre est dans la cuisine*, for example. An example where the sentences are from the same language is provided by *I had chicken-pox*, as uttered BY a certain individual, and *You had chicken-pox*, as uttered TO that same individual (assuming reference to the same time).

In this last example the sentences had to be used in different circumstances – the utterer of the first had to be the addressee of the second. More important for our purposes, however, is where two sentences would express the same proposition if used in the SAME circumstances. Examples (13)–(17) above are of this kind. *My father wrote the letter* can be used to express indefinitely many different propositions depending on the reference of *my father*, *the letter* and the past tense, but assuming the reference was kept constant *The letter was written by my father* would express the same proposition. We suggested earlier that they provide alternative ways of saying what is in some intuitive sense the same thing; now that we have introduced the concept of proposition we can reformulate this: they provide alternative ways of expressing the same proposition. For this reason we will say that the two sentences have the same **propositional meaning** – they are alike with respect of that part of their meaning which is a matter of the propositions they can be used to express. There is more to meaning than propositional meaning: we are not saying that these two sentences are semantically identical, that the choice between them is of no communicative significance. Nevertheless, propositional meaning is arguably the most central part of meaning – and very often the part which can be most precisely and rigorously described, by specifying the conditions under which a sentence could be used to express a true proposition.

One important relation between sentences deriving from their propositional meaning is **entailment**. *Pat killed Kim*, for example, entails *Kim died*. Provided we bear in mind that truth applies to sentences only derivatively, as explained above, we can define entailment thus:

(18) S_1 entails S_2 = If S_1 is true, then necessarily S_2 is true

Thus if the proposition expressed by *Pat killed Kim* under given circumstances is true, then that expressed by *Kim died* under the same circumstances (i.e. with *Kim* and the past tense having the same reference) must be true too. It would therefore be contradictory, logically inconsistent, to assert the first and deny the second – to say *Pat killed Kim but Kim didn't die*. In this example the entailment relation holds in one direction only: *Kim died* clearly does not entail *Pat killed Kim*. In other cases we find mutual entailment. This arises where the sentences have the same propositional meaning: *My father wrote the letter*, for example, entails and is entailed by *The letter was written by my father*. If a sentence is ambiguous, its entailments will be relative to particular interpretations: the example of §3, *Liz attacked the man with a knife*, entails *The man had a knife* under the interpretation "Liz attacked the man who had a knife" but not under the interpretation "Liz used a knife in her attack on the man".

As (18) makes clear, we speak of entailment only when the truth of S_2 follows NECESSARILY from that of S_1. This distinguishes entailment from the looser relation between, say, *Kim used to live in Berlin* and *Kim does not now live in Berlin*. It is very likely that the first would be said in a context where the second was also true, that in saying the first I would, other things being equal, be taken to have implied the second. Nevertheless, there is certainly no entailment here, for it would not be inconsistent to say *Kim used to live in Berlin and it may be that she still does*. For S_1 to entail S_2 there must be no context where S_1 is true and S_2 false (assuming, as always, that we keep the reference constant): S_2 must follow directly from the propositional meaning of S_1.

6. Morphology

Morphology is concerned with the structure and derivation of words. The morphologically most basic words have the form of **simple stems** – *cat*, *kind*, *window*, etc. Other words, such as *cats*, *unkindness*, *window-sill*, etc., have the form of non-simple stems and will be described in terms of the various **morphological processes** by which they are derived from more elementary stems. For example, *cats* is formed from *cat* by adding the suffix *-s*; *unkindness* is formed from *unkind* by suffixation of *-ness*, while *unkind* is itself formed from *kind* by prefixation of *un-*; *window-sill* is formed by putting together the two simple stems *window* and *sill*.

The three main morphological processes are **compounding**, **affixation**, and **conversion**. Compounding involves adding two stems together, as in the above *window-sill* – or *blackbird*, *daydream*, and so on. In English, affixes are of just two kinds: prefixes, added before the stem, and suffixes, added after it. Affixation may or may not result in a change of class: if we prefix *be-* to *calm* to derive *becalm* we change from adjective to verb, and in suffixing *-ness* to *rude* to derive *rudeness* we change from adjective to noun; but adding *un-* to *kind* or *-ish* to *green* yields the stems *unkind* and *greenish*, which belong to the same class, adjective, as *kind* and *green* themselves. For the most part, affixes attach to **free** stems, i.e. stems that can stand alone as a word. Examples are to be found, however, where an affix is added to a **bound** stem – compare *perishable*, where *perish* is free, with *durable*, where *dur* is bound, or *unkind*, where *kind* is free, with *unbeknown*, where *beknown* is bound. Similarly with compounding: the stems are generally free, as *black* and *berry* in *blackberry*, but may occasionally be bound, as the *bil* of *bilberry*. Stems (in English) are prototypically free: bound elements are then allowed as stems when their position within the structure of the word is like that of a prototypical stem.

Conversion is where a stem is derived without any change in form from one belonging to a different class. For example, the verb *bottle* (*I must bottle some plums*) is derived by conversion from the noun *bottle*, while the noun *catch* (*That was a fine catch*) is converted from the verb. The direction of conversion depends on which meaning is more basic: the meaning of the verb *bottle* is derivative from that of the noun, and vice versa with *catch*. Conversion achieves the same results as affixation commonly does. Thus the conversion of *bottle* is comparable to the affixation which gives *hospitalise* from *hospital*: both derive a verb from a noun (a 'denominal verb'). Similarly the conversion of *catch* is comparable to the affixation which gives *appointment* from *appoint*: both derive a deverbal noun. It is this similarity to affixation that leads us to treat conversion as a morphological process. But it is also important to recognise the difference between conversion and affixation – that conversion does not produce any overt change in the stem itself. From this point of view conversion may be regarded as a special case of a more general and not specifically morphological process, the extension in the range of use of a word; such extension may involve either its use with a new sense (as when *memory*, say, is extended to apply to computers as well as humans and animals) or its use in a different grammatical construction.

Morphological processes vary in their **productivity**, which is a matter of the range of stems to which they apply. Processes of low productivity apply to a small number of items: for example, suffixation of *-th* to form a de-adjectival noun applies to only a handful of adjectives, such as *warm*, *long*, *wide* (the last two illustrate how a morphological process may be accompanied by phonological modification of the stem). By contrast, prefixation of *un-* to an adjective stem is of very high productivity: a high proportion of 'gradable' adjectives (those denoting a property that can be possessed to varying degrees) take this prefix. Full productivity is where the process can apply freely to any member of a given stem class, and notably to any new addition to the class. Thus the process for forming past tense verbs by adding the phonologically appropriate variant from the suffixes /ɪd/ (or /əd/), as in *waited*, /t/, as in *jumped*, or /d/ as in *robbed*, is fully productive, so that we do not have to specify individually the verbs to which it applies (see 3.3 for the rules). Rather we specify only the **irregular** verbs to which various other processes of low productivity apply (such as the vowel change in *take → took*): the fully productive process can then apply to any regular verb, including new ones introduced into the language.

Morphology divides into two sub-branches: **inflectional morphology** and **lexical morphology**. Inflectional morphology is concerned with the processes which yield the various inflectional forms of a lexeme from its 'lexical stem' – the past tense rule just referred to is inflectional because it yields a particular inflectional form of verbs. Other processes are lexical in that they yield a different lexical item from the source, a new item of vocabulary: *hospital* and *hospitalise*, *warm* and *warmth* or *kind* and *unkind* are different lexical items, while *wait* and *waited* are not. The point of the division is that inflectional morphology is just one aspect of inflection, the other being syntactic: inflectional properties are morphosyntactic. The rules of syntax give the conditions under which a lexeme may or must carry a given inflectional property, while the rules of morphology specify what the actual form will be. Take, for example, the passive construction illustrated in *The letter was written by my father*. It is a matter of syntax that the verb following **be** (here **write**) carries the past participle inflection in the passive construction, whereas it is a matter of morphology that the past participle form of **write** is *written*, and so on. Lexical morphology does not interact with syntax in this way. The set of denominal verbs in *-ise*, for example, is not a syntactically distinctive class: syntactically, *hospitalise*, say, does not behave differently from a morphologically simple verb like *cure*. Prototypically, inflections apply to large classes or subclasses of stems: almost all verbs have past participles, for example, and the great majority of nouns have plurals. Moreover, the morphological processes yielding the past participle and plurals of regular verbs and nouns are fully productive – and the meaning of the resultant plural is almost always quite straightforwardly predictable. Lexical processes, on the other hand, tend to be of more restricted productivity, and the meaning of the resultant stem is often at least partially idiosyncratic. For example, the meaning of the compound *greenhouse* is not predictable from the meanings of the parts, but has to be learnt or recorded individually, and the semantic relation of, say, *payable* to *pay* is not quite the same as that of *attestable* to *attest*, for *payable* has the meaning "must be paid" as well as "can be paid".

7. Descriptive and prescriptive grammar

The final issue we need to consider in this preliminary chapter concerns the distinction between descriptive and prescriptive grammar. The difference is essentially one of goals: the descriptivist aims to present the grammar that underlies actual usage, whereas the prescriptivist tells us how we *ought* to speak and write.

This book is purely descriptive. For practical reasons it confines its attention to standard English (and makes only occasional reference to the proportionately rather small amount of regional variation found therein). Standard English is to be understood, however, as covering a range of variation in style; for our purposes it will be sufficient to distinguish three styles – formal, informal and neutral, illustrated in

(19) i   [*He knew more about it*] *than I*   Formal
     ii   [*He knew more about it*] *than me*   Informal
     iii [*He knew more about it*] *than I did*   Neutral

(i) is most characteristically used in contexts of some social formality, (ii) in more relaxed, informal contexts, whereas (iii) is quite neutral with respect to this contrast. Most speakers of standard English will have both (i) and (ii) in their repertoire as well as (iii), though they will differ quite considerably in where they draw the line, as it were, between formal and informal contexts.

Many prescriptive manuals classify examples like (ii) which contain features of informal style as 'grammatically incorrect', but this is a very unsatisfactory term to apply. There is no reason to restrict the term 'correct' to expressions that are appropriate in formal contexts, and it is positively harmful to do so if this is taken to imply – as it often is – that one really ought to avoid constructions like (ii) altogether. (ii) no less than (i) is, of course, constructed in accordance with systematic rules of grammar – they just happen to be different rules from those underlying formal style. (i) is not inherently any better than (ii), and indeed use of (i) in an informal context may well have the effect of making the speaker appear somewhat cold, unrelaxed, unfriendly, distant. Modern manuals of usage are tending to be more enlightened, more ready to accept informal style as a valid variety of the language perfectly appropriate in a wide range of social contexts – but the older attitudes are still quite deeply ingrained in our society.

EXERCISES

I. Lexemes and inflectional forms

For each lexeme in the following examples, say which inflectional form or forms of the lexeme are grammatically allowable in the context given by the example. For (20) the answer would be: *have* – *has, had, hasn't, hadn't*; *be* – *been*; *look* – *looking*; *key* – *key, keys*. Thus we can have *Tom has been looking for the key* but not (as a complete sentence) **Tom having been looking for the key*, and so on. Note that an inflectional form is always a single word; thus while *has* and *hasn't* are forms of *have*, *to have, has not, was having*, and so on, are not.

(20) [*Tom*] **have be look** [*for the*] **key**
(21) [*I*] **be** [*the*] **one he** [*meant*]
(22) [*The*] **boss** [*is*] **be question** [*by the police*]
(23) **This copy** [*seem much*] **clear** [*than*] **that** [*one*]
(24) [*Both members had*] **difficulty** [*in*] **understand** [*the*] **long** [*version*]
(25) [*Tom's answer*] **be** [*the*] **bad** [*of*] **they** [*all*]

II. Constituent structure: notation and interpretation

Examine the following constituent structure analysis, and then answer the questions below (working on the assumption that the analysis is correct).

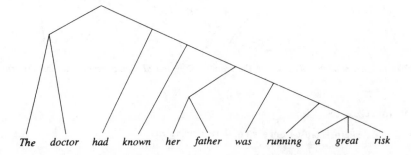

(α) Is *the doctor had known* a constituent? (β) Is *running a great risk* a constituent? (γ) What are the immediate constituents of *was running a great risk*? (δ) Does *her father* enter into construction with *known* (i.e. are they immediate constituents of the same construction)?

III. Constituent structure ambiguities

In each of (26)–(28), two constituent structures are given for an ambiguous sentence. Explain the ambiguity of the sentences, saying which meaning corresponds to which constituent structure.

(26) i    ii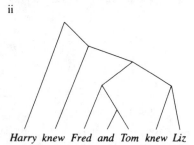

Harry knew Fred and Tom knew Liz   Harry knew Fred and Tom knew Liz

(27) i 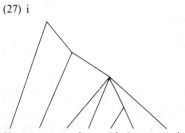   ii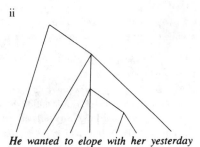

He wanted to elope with her yesterday   He wanted to elope with her yesterday

(28) i 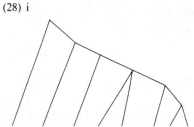   ii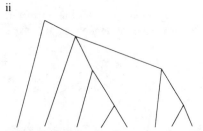

They talked about the disaster on the train   They talked about the disaster on the train

IV. Kernel clauses

Pick out the kernel clause from each of the following sets:

(29) i   *The vase was broken by Pat*
ii   *The vase wasn't broken by Pat*
iii   *Pat broke the vase*
iv   *It was Pat who broke the vase*
v   *Was the vase broken by Pat?*

(30) i   [*One son was studying law,*] *the other dentistry*
     ii *The other son was studying dentistry*
     iii *Wasn't the other son studying dentistry?*
     iv [*She says*] *that the other son was studying dentistry*
(31) i   *It is obvious that he was lying*
     ii *That he was lying is obvious*

V. Non-kernel clauses

Give the kernel counterparts of the following non-kernel clauses:

(32) *Have you seen the other chapters?*
(33) *I can't understand most of what she says*
(34) [*The money*] *he hadn't spent* [*he was allowed to keep*]
(35) [*The first lecture was given by Professor Jones,*] *the second by Dr Smith*
(36) *All the others we considered perfectly satisfactory*
(37) *It remains a mystery why she married him*

VI. Entailments

For each of the following pairs, say whether (i) entails (ii) and whether (ii) entails (i):

(38) i   *Max had forgotten that Jill was an orphan*
     ii *Jill was an orphan*
(39) i   *He sold his VW after he bought the Volvo*
     ii *He bought the Volvo before he sold his VW*
(40) i   *Liz had intended to revise her will*
     ii *Liz did not revise her will*
(41) i   *She almost managed to win the race*
     ii *She didn't win the race*

VII. Morphological processes

Give a step-by-step morphological analysis of the following words: *handwriting, pinned, actresses, denationalisation, soundproof* (as in *I'd like to soundproof my room*). For *ungentlemanly* the answer would be:

Step 1. Compounding of *gentle* (Adj) + *man* (N) → *gentleman* (N)
Step 2. Class-changing suffixation of *-ly* → *gentlemanly* (Adj)
Step 3. Class-preserving prefixation of *un-* → *ungentlemanly* (Adj)

2

The parts of speech: a preliminary outline

1. Introduction

A major problem in presenting the grammar of a language is that the various categories are closely interrelated: one cannot give a definition of one category, at the language-particular level, without making reference to other categories. For example, it is a crucial property of nouns that they head phrases functioning as subject or object in clause structure – and so on. We are dealing, that is to say, not with a set of independent categories but with a highly structured network of interlocking categories. The problem is then to describe such a network in step-by-step fashion. As suggested in the last chapter, the concepts of kernel clause and prototype are of major importance in this respect: they enable us to begin with the central and relatively straightforward cases, providing a base from which we can work progressively outwards. In similar vein I shall in this chapter present a quick overview of the parts of speech, aiming to give simply a preliminary and inevitably rough idea of the categories, one that will then be considerably refined in the more detailed chapters to follow.

At the primary level – i.e. before we embark on subclassification – I shall distinguish eight parts of speech,[1] illustrated in

(1) i   *[She] will [perhaps] say [it] is [hers]*   Verb
     ii   *Tom [bought a] bottle [of] sherry*   Noun
     iii   *[The] new [captain was very] good*   Adjective
     iv   *[She] usually [says they are] very [useful]*   Adverb
     v   *[A thick carpet] of [snow lay] on [the ground]*   Preposition
     vi   *The [boss had] a [chance to get] his [revenge]*   Determinative
     vii   *[You can have fish] and [chips] or [stew]*   Coordinator
     viii   *[He says] that [he asked] whether [it was free]*   Subordinator

---

[1] Strictly, we should recognise a ninth, the interjection (*hello, goodbye, blast, hurrah, shh*, etc.). Interjections can, however, be omitted from an outline treatment: they are very peripheral to the language system and are not tightly integrated into the structure of sentences – they very often stand alone or have something of the character of an interpolation.

22

In the first instance, we take the parts of speech to be word classes – in the sense of 'class' introduced in 1.3. It should be emphasised at the outset, however, that many words belong to more than one class. For example, *better* is an adjective in *The film was better than I'd expected*, an adverb in *He played better than ever*, and a verb in *She's trying to better her time for the 5000 metres*. Similarly, to take a commonly cited example, *round* can occur as any one of five different parts of speech: an adjective in *They cut a round hole in the side*, an adverb in *She'll soon come round*, a verb in *Let's round it up to $100*, a noun in *She bought a round of drinks*, and a preposition in *She disappeared round the corner*. A glance at a few pages of a dictionary will give some idea of how widespread this phenomenon is.

It follows that we cannot classify a given instance of a word by considering it in isolation: we need to examine how it is being used in that particular instance. Normally, as in the examples given above, the context provided by the rest of the sentence will be sufficient to determine which part of speech the instance belongs to. But not always: *Kim looked hard*, for example, is ambiguous, with *hard* either an adjective ("Kim appeared to be hard") or an adverb ("Kim looked intently").

Both words and lexemes can be assigned to part-of-speech classes. In *You should take more care, I took the bus, It takes too long*, the words *take, took* and *takes* are verbs, and we likewise classify the lexeme of which they are inflectional forms, namely **take**, as a verb. As far as English is concerned, there are grounds for giving priority to the classification of words, with the classification of lexemes derivative therefrom. We will see that for the most part inflection provides at best only a subsidiary criterion of classification. It is only for verbs that inflectional contrasts constitute the most salient defining property. For the rest, greater weight will be attached to 'combinatorial' properties, the way items combine to form larger units, ultimately sentences – and in the first instance it is words that combine to form sentences: the lexeme is an abstraction from a set of words. Many words, moreover, are not forms of lexemes at all, because they carry no inflectional property – words like *beautiful, quickly, there, in, and*, etc. The great majority of lexemes are verbs, nouns or adjectives; the preposition, coordinator and subordinator classes apply exclusively to words, while the adverb and determinative classes apply predominantly to words: there are just a handful of adverb lexemes and one or two determinative lexemes.

We will take the view (again restricting our attention to English) that the inflectional forms of any lexeme all belong to the same part of speech, so that there is no conflict between the word and lexeme classification: for example *short, shorter*, and *shortest*, the three forms of the adjective lexeme **short**, all belong to the word class adjective, and analogously for the other parts of speech.

2. Open and closed classes

The parts of speech can be divided into two major sets, commonly called **open** classes and **closed** classes. The open classes are verb, noun, adjective and adverb, the closed classes the rest: preposition, determinative, coordinator and subordinator. The open classes have very large membership, while the closed ones have relatively few members; a large grammar could be expected to list all members of the closed classes, whereas for the open ones we would be referred to the lexicon.

The distinction between open and closed applies not just to primary classes but also to subclasses. For example, we shall subclassify nouns as common nouns, proper nouns or pronouns – so that in *Tom gave her the keys*, for example, *keys* (*key*) is a common noun, *Tom* (*Tom*) a proper noun, and *her* (*she*) a pronoun. Of these three subclasses the first two are clearly open, while the third, the pronoun, is closed.

Open classes are so called because they readily accommodate the addition of new members as the vocabulary of the language adapts itself to the changing needs of its speakers. New members may arise through the application of various morphological processes to existing words (as with the verb *hospitalise* derived from the noun *hospital* by suffixation – see 1.6), through borrowing from another language (as with the noun *sputnik*, from Russian) or, though this is very much rarer, through creation of a new word from the phonological resources of the language, as with the noun *nylon*, coined in the 1930s. Closed classes, by contrast, are highly resistant to the addition of new members – though the term 'closed' should not be taken to imply that such expansion is strictly impossible.

As far as grammatical analysis is concerned, the open classes (and subclasses) are a good deal more straightforward than the closed. The set of closed primary classes proposed here differs quite considerably (in ways that will be pointed out) from that found in traditional grammars, and numerous other schemes can be found in the literature. But it is scarcely conceivable that anyone could propose a grammar that did not contain classes corresponding fairly closely to our verb, noun, and adjective. Differences will be found in the treatment of adverbs, but this reflects the fact that the traditional adverb class covers a number of subclasses of which some are closed: the differences tend to be associated with these rather than with the central open subclass containing words like *carefully*, *quickly*, *surreptitiously*, etc.

3. Words and phrases

We are taking the parts of speech categories to be classes of words (or, in certain cases, of lexemes): we will not apply them to expressions larger than a word.[2] Thus in keeping with the conception of constituent structure outlined in 1.3, we will make a systematic distinction between the classification of the minimal syntactic units, the words, and that of the units higher in the constituent hierarchy.

The classification of phrases, however, reflects that of the word functioning as head. In our original example, *The boss made a bad mistake*, the phrases *the boss* and *a bad mistake* are classified as noun phrases by virtue of having a noun, *boss* or *mistake*, as head, while *made a bad mistake* is a verb phrase as its head is the verb *made*. Corresponding phrase classes are found for all four of the open word

---

[2] Except for certain fixed and syntactically unanalysable expressions like *each other*, which is best treated as belonging to the class of nouns (more specifically, the subclass of pronouns).

classes verb, noun, adjective and adverb, and also for preposition and determinative among the closed classes. The correspondence is shown in the following examples, where the unbracketed expression is the phrase under consideration and the head word is underlined:

		Phrase	Head Word
(2)	i [*Tom*] <u>*used*</u> *the wrong method*	VP	V
	ii *Several new <u>cracks</u>* [*had appeared in the wall*]	NP	N
	iii [*They were*] <u>*kind*</u> *to her*	AdjP	Adj
	iv [*She spoke*] *too <u>slowly</u>*	AdvP	Adv
	v [*They presented her*] <u>*with*</u> *a magnificent bouquet*	PP	Prep
	vi [*He had*] *very <u>little</u>* [*patience*]	DetveP	Detve

Coordinators and subordinators, by contrast, do not function as heads of phrases, and there are accordingly no phrase classes corresponding to them.

The head is the syntactically dominant element in the phrase, while the dependents are subordinate. This difference in status is reflected in the following ways:

(a) Dependents are often syntactically optional, whereas the head is obligatory (except in the special case of ellipsis). In (ii), for example, we could omit the dependents *several* and *new* without loss of grammaticality to give *Cracks* [*appeared in the wall*]. Similarly in (iii), (iv) and (vi). But not in (i) and (v), where the dependents *the wrong method* and *a bouquet* are not omissible: optionality is not a necessary condition for dependent status but (again leaving aside ellipsis) it is a sufficient one. The qualification concerning ellipsis is needed to cater for examples like [*He gave me a glass of red wine but I'd have preferred*] *white wine*, where *white wine* could (and more often than not would) be reduced to *white*, with ellipsis of the head *wine*. Omission through ellipsis is quite different in kind from that illustrated above for the missing element is understood, recovered from the context, even though not overtly expressed; elliptical constructions will be described derivatively, in terms of their differences from corresponding 'complete' constructions (cf. 1.4), whereas *Cracks appeared in the wall*, for example, is grammatically perfectly complete as it stands.

(b) The head is dominant in determining the combinatorial potential of the phrase as a whole. In cases like (ii) this simply reinforces point (a): *several new cracks* can occur as subject (as in (ii) itself), as object (as in *I found several new cracks*), as complement of a preposition (*He was pointing towards several new cracks*), and so on: it is easy to see that its ability to occur in these positions is attributable to the presence of the noun *cracks*, because *cracks* can stand alone in these positions. But we can apply this criterion also in cases like (i) where neither element in the phrase is optional. *Used the wrong method* is functioning as predicate to the subject *Tom* and although the verb *used* cannot occur alone in this function, there are many other verbs that can – compare, for example, *Tom disappeared*. In kernel clauses at least, the phrase functioning as predicate always contains a verb and, if it is a verb of the appropriate kind, may contain just a verb – this justifies our taking the verb to be the syntactically most significant element in the phrase, the head. Similarly we might compare (iii), where *kind* is shown to be head by the optionality of *to her*, with [*They were*] *fond of her*, where *of her* is not omissible. We take the adjective *fond* to be head here because the phrase as a whole has the potential to enter into construction with verbs like **be**, **become**, **remain**, **seem**, etc., a function characteristically filled by adjectival, not prepositional, expressions. In (v) we cannot relate *with a bouquet* to a PP where the preposition can stand alone, for PPs (in kernel clauses) always have a complement as well as a head. Nevertheless, we can still see that the preposition *with* is head by the present criterion, because it is the *with* that determines that the phrase can occur as complement to *presented*: *present* in this construction requires a *with* phrase.

A consequence of this property is that it is very often possible to replace a dependent by a functionally equivalent expression of another class without affecting the combinatorial potential of the phrase as a whole, whereas this is not possible with the head. In [*She*] *knew the outcome*, for example, we can replace the NP *the outcome* by a subordinate clause such as *that he was guilty*, whereas we cannot replace the head *knew* by a non-verb. Similarly, in [*You're dealing with*] *a man without scruples* the dependent *without scruples*, a PP, is replaceable by a clause such as *who has no scruples*, but no comparable replacement is possible for the head *man*.

The concept of 'phrase' adopted in this book differs somewhat from that found in traditional grammar. A phrase is to be understood as a type of construction containing a head element optionally accompanied by one or more dependents. Because the dependents are very often optional, the head may stand alone. The head-based concept of phrase, unlike the traditional one, thus allows for a phrase to consist of a single word. In *John made a bad mistake* for example, we will say that the subject position is filled by a noun phrase consisting of a noun (functioning as head of the phrase): *John* is analysed as both a noun phrase and a noun. It is simpler to handle the choice between *the boss* and *John* (or between *another John* and *John*) at just one place in the grammar, that dealing with the structure of the noun phrase, than to have to account for it in the description of all the various constructions in which such expressions occur – than to say, for example: (α) the subject can be either an NP (*The boss made a bad mistake*) or a noun (*John made a bad mistake*); (β) the direct object can be either an NP (*I saw the boss*) or a noun (*I saw John*); (γ) the complement of a proposition can be either an NP (*He threw it at the boss*) or a noun (*He threw it at John*); – and so on for all the other functions that can be filled by such expressions. For the same reason we will slightly revise our analysis of *The boss made a bad mistake* in 1.3 in such a way that *bad* will be an AdjP as well as an adjective.

The head-based concept of phrase also allows for a phrase to have another phrase, rather than a word, as its head. Thus in a subject + predicate construction, we take subject to be a special case of dependent, and predicate of head. Note, with respect to the criteria introduced above, that while the predicate of a kernel clause is always filled by a VP the subject can be either an NP or a subordinate clause (recall the earlier contrast between *The decision [surprised everyone]* and *That he was allowed to stay on [surprised everyone]*) – with the possibility of a subordinate clause being dependent on the selection of an appropriate VP (compare **That he was allowed to stay on ceased*). A clause is accordingly a special kind of phrase.[3] But not all syntactic constructions are phrases. In particular, coordinative constructions are not. In *Either he is ill or he has forgotten the appointment*, for example, *either he is ill* and *or he has forgotten the appointment* are of equal syntactic status: neither is superordinate to the other, so that neither is head and the whole is for this reason not a phrase.

4. The open classes

We will turn now to an outline account of the properties that characterise the eight parts of speech, beginning in this section with the four open classes verb, noun, adjective and adverb. For each of these four, we will give the properties under four headings: (α) FUNCTION: what are the characteristic functions within a phrase of the words belonging to a given class, and what are the functions within larger constructions of the phrases they head? (β) DEPENDENTS: what kinds of dependents do they take within the phrases they head? (γ) INFLECTION: what inflectional systems apply? (δ) LEXICAL MORPHOLOGY: what are the most salient morphological processes for deriving lexical stems of one class from those of another?

The last two are 'internal' properties: they have to do with the make-up of the word itself, its inflectional properties or derivational affixes and the like; the first two, by contrast, are 'external': they have to do with the way the word combines with others in larger constructions. Although we will consider each open class under all four headings, we will vary the order somewhat so as to reflect the variation in the relative importance they have: inflection, for example, is of prime significance for the verb but of very minor significance for the adverb.

4.1 Verbs

(a) Inflection. The great majority of verb lexemes have a paradigm containing six inflectional forms, illustrated for **take** in

(3)   i   *[He/They] took [great care]*   Past tense
      ii   *[He] takes [great care]*   3rd pers sg present tense
     iii   *[They] take [great care]*   General present tense
     iv   *[He/They should] take [great care]*   Base form
      v   *[He is/They are] taking [great care]*   Present participle
     vi   *[He has/They have] taken [great care]*   Past participle

---

[3] Again this departs from the much more restricted use of the term 'phrase' found in additional grammar.

The verb paradigm will be explained in detail in Ch. 3; here we will confine our-selves to a few initial observations.

It will be noted that the word *take* occurs twice in (3): as the general present tense form and as the base form. Where two or more inflectional forms are pro-nounced and spelled the same, we say that there is **syncretism** between them (or that they are syncretised). Syncretism between the base form and the general present tense is found in the paradigm of virtually all verbs: only for *be* (which in fact has more than six forms in its paradigm) do we find such a contrast as between [*They*] *are* [*very careful*] (present tense) and [*They should*] *be* [*very care-ful*] (base form). *Walk* and all other regular verbs, together with a good number of irregular ones, such as *buy*, also have syncretism between the past tense form (*They walked there, He bought it*) and the past participle (*They had walked there, He had bought it*). A small handful of verbs like *shut* have syncretism between four inflectional forms: past tense, past participle, general present tense and base form are all *shut*.

The main division within the paradigm is between the tensed and non-tensed forms. It is the tensed forms that are most distinctively verbal and we may regard the prototypical verb word as tensed. With the single exception of *beware*, all verb lexemes have tensed forms, whereas there are a number of very frequent verbs – the 'modal operators' *can, may, must, will*, etc. – which lack non-tensed forms. All kernel clauses contain a tensed verb as predicator.

(b) Function. Tensed verbs have the distinctive property of functioning as the ultimate head of kernel (and many kinds of non-kernel) clauses; as head, they re-strict the range of other elements in the clause, so that we have, for example, *He took it* but not **He arrived it, He seemed anxious* but not **He used anxious*, and so on. Base forms head VPs functioning as head (predicate) in various kinds of non-kernel, often subjectless clauses – for example, imperative clauses (*Open the door, Be careful*), clauses functioning as complement to the modal operators *can, may*, etc. ([*She may*] *be here soon*), clauses marked by the infinitival particle *to* ([*It is important*] *to read both versions*),[4] and so on. Participles likewise head VPs in predicate function in non-kernel clauses – for example, after 'progressive' *be* ([*She was*] *working*), 'perfect' *have* or 'passive' *be* ([*They had*] *seen us*, [*He was*] *seen by the guard*). This we will call the 'predicator' use of participles, contrasting with their 'attributive' use, where the VP functions as modifier in NP structure ([*the*] *fiercely boiling* [*kettle*], [*a*] *rarely heard* [*work by Purcell*]). Participles are not as clearly distinct from adjectives and nouns as are the other forms of verbs.

(c) Dependents. Verbs take a wide range of dependents. They differ from the other open classes, for example, in that a subclass of them – transitive verbs –

---

[4] Verb lexemes are traditionally cited by means of this *to* plus the base form – thus *take* as 'to take', *be* as 'to be', etc. Infinitival *to*, like the *to* of *I went to Paris*, is traditionally analysed as a preposition, but this reflects its historical origin, not its behaviour in Modern English; it differs syntactically from other words so much that it cannot be illuminatingly assigned to any of the parts of speech.

take objects as dependents: recall the contrast drawn in 1.1 between [*The boss had watched the secretary*] *destroy the files*, with *destroy* a verb, *the files* its object, and [*The boss had witnessed*] *the destruction of the files*, with *destruction* a noun and thus requiring a preposition before *the files*.

(d) Lexical morphology. Many verbs, nouns and adjectives have simple lexical stems, but it is a measure of the importance of the distinction between them that there are numerous morphological processes for deriving stems of one class from those of another. The most productive verb-forming affix is *-ise* as in de-adjectival *nationalise*, or denominal *hospitalise*; among the less productive ones are *-ify*, *-en*, *be-*, as in de-adjectival *beautify, sadden, becalm*.

4.2 Nouns

(a) Function. Nouns most characteristically function as head in NP structure; NPs in turn occur in a variety of functions, notably subject, object, predicative (complement of verbs like *be, seem, become, remain*, etc.) and complement of a preposition (such as *of, to, with, at, by*, etc.):

(4)	i	*A dog* [*was barking*]	Subject
	ii	[*She bought*] *a dog*	Object
	iii	[*That's*] *a dog*	Predicative
	iv	[*I was attacked by*] *a dog*	Comp of preposition

NPs also occur in the possessive construction that we will be taking up later in this chapter: *The dog's* [*tail was wagging furiously*].

(b) Dependents. Nouns take a different range of dependents than other parts of speech. Most distinctively, they take as pre-head dependents determinatives like *the, a, some, few, my*, etc., and adjectives: *the table, a cup, some problems, my cousin, good ideas, a big increase, some bad mistakes*. It is also distinctive of nouns that they take 'restrictive relative clauses' as posthead dependents: *the man who came to dinner, the book that he was reading, a box in which he kept his valuables*.

(c) Inflection. Prototypical nouns enter into inflectional contrasts of number, singular (*dog, goose*) vs plural (*dogs, geese*). However, whereas virtually all verbs have contrasting tense forms, there are many nouns without a contrast of number: *equipment, muck, wetness* and the like have no plural counterparts, while a few, such as *alms, dregs, remains*, have no singular counterparts. It is for this reason that we attach greater weight to the external properties of nouns than to inflection.

(d) Lexical morphology. Among the most frequent noun-forming suffixes are *-ness* (of very great productivity) and *-(i)ty*, deriving de-adjectival nouns like *politeness, loyalty*, and *-er, -ee, -ation, -ment*, etc., deriving deverbal nouns like *driver, payee, organisation, abandonment*.

4.3 Adjectives

(a) Function. Adjectives function as head in AdjP structure. The two main functions of AdjPs are predicative in VP structure and pre-head modifier in NP structure, the latter involving what is called the attributive use of adjectives:

(5)   i   [*The coat seemed*] *too large*   Predicative use
      ii [*an*] *unusually large* [*deficit*]   Attributive use

The great majority of adjectives can be used both predicatively and attributively.

(b) Dependents. Most adjectives are 'gradable'. Semantically this means that they denote properties, etc., that can be possessed in varying degrees; syntactically it is reflected in their ability to take degree expressions as dependents: *too large, quite good, very young, rather doubtful*. Degree modification is possible with some verbs and nouns (cf. *I very much liked it, an enormous improvement*) but there are differences in the modifying expressions found with the three classes: notably, *very* (in the sense "to a large degree") and *too* (in the sense "to an excessive degree") do not modify verbs or nouns – compare

(6)   i   [*He was*] *very/too young*   Adj
      ii *[*He had*] *very/too loved* [*her*]   V
      iii *a very/too deficit*   N

By no means all adjectives are gradable, so that the present property is very much secondary to function. Non-gradable adjectives typically denote 'categorical' as opposed to 'scalar' properties – thus *anthropological, female, phonetic*, etc.

(c) Inflection. Many adjectives inflect for 'grade', with a three-term paradigm, as illustrated in (7) for regular **tall** and irregular **good** and **bad**:

(7)   **tall**   **good**   **bad**
         Absolute   *tall*   *good*   *bad*
         Comparative   *taller*   *better*   *worse*
         Superlative   *tallest*   *best*   *worst*

This property is related to the last, comparison being a special case of degree specification. The comparative and superlative degrees may be expressed either inflectionally, as here, or analytically, i.e. by means of separate closed class words, in this case *more* and *most* – *valuable, more valuable, most valuable*. Longer adjectives allow only the analytic construction, while some allow either (cf. *livelier/more lively*, etc.).

(d) Lexical morphology. There are a fair number of suffixes that characteristically derive adjectives from nouns: *-ful* (*careful*); *-less* (*careless*); *-ly* (*friendly*); *-like* (*childlike*); *-al, -ial, -ical, -ic* ([*a*] *professional* [*footballer*], *professorial, philosophical, heroic*); *-ous* (*poisonous*); *-ian, -ese* ([*a*] *Christian* [*burial*], *Japanese* [*literature*]). There are others deriving deverbal adjectives: the most productive is *-able* (*derivable*).

4.4 Adverbs

The adverb is a much less homogeneous part of speech than the other three open classes. Adverbs, or rather the phrases they head, are found in a variety of functions but with very incomplete overlap between the subclasses that occur in the different functions. Thus although it is function that provides the primary defining characteristic of adverbs, the easiest route to an initial grasp of the class is probably through lexical morphology and it is accordingly with this that I shall begin.

(a) Lexical morphology. A high proportion of adverbs are derived from adjectives by suffixation of *-ly*: *careless→carelessly*, *constant→constantly*, *frank-→frankly*, and so on. It is primarily because of the highly productive nature of this process that the adverb is an open class; certainly there are far fewer adverbs with simple lexical stems than there are verbs, nouns and adjectives.

The *-ly* ending is neither a sufficient nor a necessary indication of adverb status. It is not sufficient because there are words of other classes ending in *-ly*, notably adjectives like *beastly*, *cowardly*, *deadly*, etc. It is, however, very easy to recognise these as adjectives by the functional property given above: they can be used attributively and predicatively, whereas *-ly* adverbs cannot – compare:

(8)   i   [*a*] *cowardly* [*decision*]
      ii [*His behavior seemed*] *cowardly*   } Adjective
(9)   i   *[*a*] *carelessly* [*decision*]
      ii *[*His behaviour seemed*] *carelessly* } Adverb

In (9) we need the form without *-ly*, the adjective *careless*, not the adverb *carelessly*. The *-ly* ending is not a necessary indication of adverb status because there are numerous adverbs not derived in this way; virtually all subclasses of adverb, however, contain *-ly* adverbs among their members, so that adverbs without this ending can generally be replaced by a *-ly* adverb without change of grammatical construction – witness [*She was*] *very/exceptionally* [*strong*], [*She drove*] *well/carefully*, [*She decided*] *therefore/consequently* [*to reject it*]. This is a factor which gives some unity to the set of functions where adverb phrases are found.

(b) Function. Adverbs generally occur as head in AdvP structure. AdvPs often function as dependent of the verb, especially as modifier/adjunct. In *He behaved carelessly* and *She drove carefully*, for example, *carelessly* and *carefully* modify the verbs *behaved* and *drove* respectively. AdvPs can also modify adjectives or other adverbs – so that verbs, adjectives and adverbs characteristically take adverbial modifiers, while nouns take adjectival ones: compare adverbial *sufficiently* with adjectival *sufficient* in

			Head
(10)	i	[*She*] *loved him sufficiently*	V
	ii	*a sufficiently long delay*	Adj
	iii	[*She*] *spoke sufficiently slowly*	Adv
	iv	*a sufficient sum*	N

(c) Dependents. Many adverbs are gradable and take the same range of degree modifiers as adjectives: *rather carelessly*, *too constantly*, *very frankly*. The distinction between adjectives and adverbs is thus primarily a matter not of the dependents they take, but of the functions of the phrases they head: see, especially, the contrast in (8)–(10).

(d) Inflection. Although, as just observed, many adverbs are gradable, most of them enter only into the analytic comparative construction (*carelessly*, *more carelessly*, *most carelessly*). Just a few, however, inflect for grade, like adjectives: *soon*, *sooner*, *soonest* or *fast*, *faster*, *fastest* (as in *He drove fast* – in *the fast car*, by contrast, *fast* is an adjective).

5. The closed classes

For the four closed classes, preposition, determinative, coordinator and subordinator, we will consider only external properties: with the exception of one or two items there is no inflection, and we find no lexical-morphological processes of any significant productivity. Moreover, it is only with prepositions that we carry over the distinction between 'function' and 'dependents': for the others the closed class word does not, for the most part, function as the head of a phrase.

5.1 Prepositions

(a) Dependents. Prepositions generally take NPs or clauses as dependent (more specifically, as complement): *in + the garden*, *because + it was raining*; quite a number of them allow either type of dependent: *after + the meal/they had eaten*, *since + his arrival/he arrived*. The only other class of word taking NPs as complement is the verb, and verbs are easily distinguished from prepositions by their inflectional properties.

(b) Function. Prepositions function as head in PP structure. PPs occur in a variety of functions, most notably dependent of a verb, as in [*She relied*] *on the minister*, a noun, as in [*the author*] *of the book*, or an adjective, as in [*similar*] *to the earlier version*.

5.2 Determinatives

Determinatives function as determiner in NP structure. The most central members are *the*, *a(n)* and words which are mutually exclusive with these: *my*, *your*, ..., *this*, *these*, *that*, *those*, *some*, *any*, *which*, etc. Thus we have *the dog*, *my dog*, etc., but not **the my dog*, **my the dog*, and the like. We also include in the class certain words that can precede the central determinatives, such as *all* or *both* (*all the money*, *both my parents*) or follow them, such as *every*, *many*, *few* (*her every gesture*, *the many mistakes*). However, these last two – *many* and *few* – lie very much at the boundary between the determinative and adjective classes: both are gradable and *few* inflects for grade.

5.3 Coordinators

The main coordinators are *and* and *or*. They can join units at all levels in the constituent hierarchy – notably clauses, phrases and words:

(11) i   *It was raining and I didn't have an umbrella*   Clauses
     ii *John and his father [were quarrelling as usual]*   Phrases
     iii *[You can go] with or without [a guide]*   Words

There is no grammatical limit to the number of units that may be linked by a single coordinator – cf. *Tom, Bill, Ed, Max, ... and Liz*. Less central coordinators are *but, both, either, neither, nor, not*. They are more restricted than *and* and *or* with respect to the above properties – and these words belong to the coordinator class in only some of their uses. The coordinator use is illustrated in *[I asked them] but [they refused]*, *Both [Ed and Pat signed the letter]*, *[She's arriving] either [tomorrow or on Tuesday]*, *Neither [Tom] nor [his father was at home]*, *[I bought it] not [for myself] but [for you]*. *And*, *or* and *but* can occur as the sole marker of a coordinative construction, but the others cannot: *both, either, neither* and *not* require a following *and, or, nor* and *but* respectively, while *nor* is a coordinator only when paired with a preceding *neither*.

5.4 Subordinators

The central subordinators are *that*, as in *[I know] that it is possible*, and *whether*, as in *[I wonder] whether it is possible*. Their function is to mark a clause as subordinate: *that it is possible*, for example, is the subordinate counterpart of kernel *It is possible*. *That* is the declarative subordinator, while *whether* is interrogative – the non-subordinate counterpart of *whether it is possible* is *Is it possible?*. Subordinators have some affinities with prepositions, but an important difference is that *that* is freely omissible in many environments (compare *I know it is possible*): it is for this reason that it is not analysed as head of a 'subordinator phrase'.

There are two less central subordinators: *if* and *for*. *If* is a subordinator when it is equivalent to *whether*, as in *[I wonder] if it is possible*, but a preposition in its conditional use, as in *I'll be furious if they're late*. *For* is a subordinator when it introduces an infinitival clause (one where the VP contains *to* + a verb in the base form), as in *[It is necessary] for the water to be boiling*; elsewhere *for* is a preposition, as in *[I made it] for you*.

6. Possessive expressions

To conclude this chapter we must consider briefly the various types of possessive expression, whose analysis presents a number of problems. Let us begin with examples like *the king's daughter* or *the King of Spain's daughter*. Both of these are NPs with the head position filled by the noun *daughter* and the determiner position filled by a possessive expression – *the king's* and *the King of Spain's*. The *'s* element is what is known as a **clitic**, something which from a grammatical point of view is a word but which merges phonologically with an adjacent word as it lacks itself the normal phonological properties of a word – all ordinary words in English contain a vowel. The possessive *'s* is not the only clitic in English, but it is the only one which is not a reduced version of some ordinary word; the clitic *'ve* of *I've finished it*, for example, is a reduced version of *have* and the non-possessive clitic *'s* of *He's working* and *He's finished it* is reduced from *is* and *has* respectively: what is peculiar about possessive *'s* is that it is inherently clitic. The reason for saying that *'s* is a word, not an affix, is that it enters into construction with a phrase, not a stem.[5] The immediate constituents of *the King of Spain's* are *the King of Spain* and *'s*: clearly *Spain's* is not a complete unit on its own, so that *'s* cannot be taken as entering into construction with the stem *Spain*. Semantically *'s* is similar to *of*; grammatically it differs in that it follows its NP whereas *of* precedes (cf. [*the daughter*] *of the King of Spain*), but is otherwise similar, and we accordingly take it as head of the phrase *the King of Spain's* just as (the first) *of* is head of *of the King of Spain*. *Of* is a preposition: *of the King of Spain* is therefore a PP; possessive *'s* by contrast is unique (so that we have not allotted it to any part of speech), and we will accordingly classify *the King of Spain's* simply as a possessive phrase (PossP). Thus we have the structure:

(12)

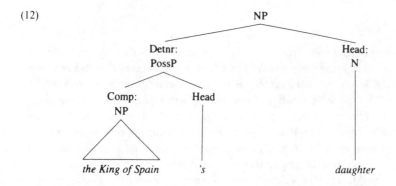

(The triangle notation used here and in several later diagrams indicates that the structure of the element in question, here the NP *the King of Spain*, is left unspecified as it is not relevant to the point being made.) *The king's daughter* is similar: here the NP complement is simply *the king*.

Where the complement of the possessive element is an NP ending with a regular plural noun such as *the kings* (and under certain other conditions too – cf. *Socrates' death*), the possessive element has no separate phonological expression: cf. *the kings' wives*; orthographically, however, it is expressed by the apostrophe,

---

[5] In traditional grammar, however, it is treated as an affix, *king's* being then analysed as the possessive, or 'genitive', inflectional form of **king**.

and we will still analyse the possessive expression as a PossP: it is simply a matter of the possessive element merging phonologically with the last consonant of the NP complement.

Not all possessive expressions are PossPs, however. The *my* of *my daughter*, for example, differs from *the King of Spain's* or *the king's* in two respects. In the first place, it is not found in all the grammatical positions where the latter occur – in some we find *my*, in others *mine*: *the king's/my/*mine daughter*, but *This is the king's/*my/mine*. In the second place, *my* is evidently not phonologically analysable into an ordinary word plus a clitic – compare informal style *the man opposite me's facial expression*, where possessive *'s* is phonologically attached to *me*. *My* is thus a single word; it is not analysable into an NP as complement plus a possessive element as head – and hence it is not analysable as a PossP. Rather we will treat *my*, *your*, etc., as a subclass of determinatives (possessive determinatives) and similarly *mine*, *yours*, etc., as a subclass of pronouns (possessive pronouns). *His*, of course, belongs in both sets.

By virtue of its role as the ultimate head of a clause, the verb is syntactically the most important of the parts of speech, and for this reason we shall be examining it first in the chapters that follow. Ch. 3 deals with the verb itself and Ch. 4 with the kernel constructions of which it is head, while Ch. 5 takes up the categories of tense, aspect and modality, which are primarily associated with the verb. The noun is the next most important part of speech after the verb and accordingly occupies second place (Ch. 6) in the main part of our outline. Its syntactic importance is reflected in the fact that all simple kernel clauses contain at least one noun, just as they contain at least one verb, but need not contain any other part of speech (cf. *People laughed, He snores, Kim arrived*); moreover, the complexity of phrases headed by nouns approaches that of phrases headed by verbs, while other phrase classes are much simpler. Chs 7 and 8 then deal with the other parts of speech that function as head in phrase structure. Those that do not – subordinators and coordinators – are left until we come to take up non-kernel constructions: they are discussed in the chapters on subordination (Ch. 11) and coordination (Ch. 13) respectively.

EXERCISES

I. Overlap between the parts of speech

From each of the following sets of words pick out those belonging to both of the classes specified for the set in question; for those that do belong to both, construct example sentences illustrating the two uses. (α) Noun and verb: *father, mother, son; head, eye, nose, cheek, neck, shoulder, arm, elbow, wrist, hand, palm, finger, thumb; cat, dog, fox, horse;* (β) Adjective and verb: *big, calm, despise, dry, humble, open, smooth; lower, upper; blue, green, red, yellow, grey, black, white;* (γ) Adjective and adverb: *hard, heavy, slow; poor, poorly; good, well, worse; early, late, soon.*

II. Closed classes

Pick out from the following list those words that belong to a closed class or subclass: *you, ewe, lick, tick, in, inn, to, too, up, pup, ban, can, have, halve, fat, hat, who, do, wheel, will, this, miss, either, neither.*

III. Heads and dependents

The unbracketed phrases in (13)–(21) have been divided into their immediate constituents by vertical lines: label them as head or dependent.

(13) [*She was looking for*] *the* | *secretary* | *of the Bushwalking Club*
(14) *The* | *enemy* | *commander* [*had been captured*]
(15) [*A*] *quite extraordinarily* | *careless* [*blunder had gone unnoticed*]
(16) *Something* | *strange* [*was happening to me*]
(17) [*He was*] *loath* | *to admit defeat*
(18) *Everyone* | *who knew her* [*admired her*]
(19) [*He made*] *surprisingly* | *few* [*mistakes*]
(20) [*We*] *enjoyed* | *it*
(21) [*I cut it*] *with* | *a razor blade*

IV. Elementary part-of-speech analysis

Give a part-of-speech classification of the words in (22)–(26), using the eight classes we have distinguished: verb, noun, adjective, adverb, preposition, determinative, coordinator, subordinator.

(22) *John tried hard but nevertheless couldn't finish it*
(23) *These things always look worse than they really are*
(24) *I don't anticipate having any difficulty with the Russian visitors*
(25) *They were very glad that the new version was so much cheaper*
(26) *While he was checking the final proofs he found several serious mistakes*

V. Possessive expressions

Suggest a constituent structure analysis for the phrase *a friend of mine's husband.*

3

Verbs

1. General definition

At the general level, 'verb' is applied to a grammatically distinct word class in a language having the following properties:

(a) It contains amongst its most central members the morphologically simplest words denoting actions, processes or events; in predications of these types at least, the word functioning as head of the predicate expression will normally belong to the class we call verb.

(b) Members of the class carry inflections of tense, aspect and mood if the language has these as inflectional categories.

Reference to morphological complexity is needed in (a) because we find countless verb/noun pairs denoting the same action, etc. – cf. the earlier example of *destroy*/*destruction*: what we are saying in (a) is that with such examples the noun will normally be derived from the verb rather than the other way round. Compare also pairs like $catch_V$/$catch_N$, where on semantic grounds we take the verb to be more basic. Many verbs in English and other languages denote states (cf. *know*, *like*, etc.) and traditional definitions of the verb generally use some such formula as 'action or state'; given the concept of general definition that we have introduced, however, it is better to omit states: 'state' will figure, rather, in the general definition of adjectives, for with verbs there are more words denoting actions, processes, events than states, whereas with adjectives the situation is very much the reverse.

We outlined in 2.4.1 the main distinctive properties of verbs at the English-particular level. The next six sections of this chapter will take up the description of verb inflection in more detail and Ch. 4 will deal with the function and dependents of verbs; it is not necessary to add anything further to what was said concerning the lexical morphology of verbs.

37

2. The inflectional paradigm

Most verb lexemes have the six-term inflectional paradigm illustrated in:

(1)

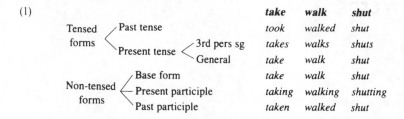

			take	walk	shut
Tensed forms	Past tense		took	walked	shut
	Present tense	3rd pers sg	takes	walks	shuts
		General	take	walk	shut
Non-tensed forms	Base form		take	walk	shut
	Present participle		taking	walking	shutting
	Past participle		taken	walked	shut

The main departures from this pattern are as follows:

(a) An important subclass of verbs called **operators** – *be*, *have*, *do*, *can*, *will*, etc. – have negative as well as positive forms in the tensed part of the paradigm. Thus *have* has *hadn't* as a negative past tense, *hasn't* and *haven't* as negative present tense forms; non-operator *take*, by contrast, has no negative forms: **tookn't* is ungrammatical and *didn't take* is not a single verb, thus not a form of *take* (see §7 below).

(b) A subset of the operators – we will call them the **modal operators** – have only tensed forms and only a single positive present tense form. *Will*, for example, has just four forms: positive *would* and negative *wouldn't* for the past tense, *will* and *won't* for the present tense. The central modal operators are *can*, *may*, *must* (which has only present tense forms), *will* and *shall*; see §7 below.

(c) The verb *be* has extra person–number contrasts in the past and present tenses.

3. Inflectional morphology

(a) Base form. This is in all cases identical to the lexical stem.

(b) General present tense form. This is syncretised with the base form; only for *be* are all the present tense forms distinct from the base.

(c) 3rd person singular present. This is normally formed by adding a suffix to the lexical stem. The suffix has three main variants, depending on the phonological properties of the stem:

(2) i   If the stem ends in a 'sibilant' (/s, z, ʃ, ʒ, tʃ, dʒ/) it is /ɪz/ or /əz/ as in *kisses*, *watches*, etc. The choice between /ɪz/ and /əz/ is a matter of the regional or social accent.

ii   If the lexical stem otherwise ends in a 'voiceless consonant' (thus after /p, t, k, f, θ/) it is /s/, as in *hops*, *walks*.

iii   Otherwise it is /z/, as in *lobs*, *runs*, *sees*.

There are only four irregularities. For **be** and **have** the forms are /ɪz/ and /hæz/ (or reduced versions thereof), while for **do** and **say** there is a change in the quality of the vowel (not reflected in the spelling): /dʌz/ and (for most speakers) /sez/.

(d) Past tense form. Regular verbs add to the lexical stem a suffix which again has three main variants, phonologically conditioned:

(3) i If the stem ends in an 'alveolar stop' (/t/ or /d/), it is /ɪd/ or /əd/ as in *wanted, landed*. The choice between /ɪd/ and /əd/ depends again on the regional or social accent.
   ii If the stem otherwise ends in a voiceless consonant (thus after /p, k, f, θ, s, ʃ, tʃ/) it is /t/, as in *pushed, laughed*.
   iii Otherwise it is /d/, as in *killed, died, robbed*.

With irregular verbs, the past tense generally involves a change in the stem vowel – alone (*sang, knew, met*, etc.) or accompanied by the suffixation of either /d/ (*sold*) or more often, and even after voiced consonants, of /t/ (*lost, crept, felt*). Other types of irregularity are illustrated in *taught, burnt, cut*, etc.: there is not space to cover the two hundred or so irregular verbs in detail.

(e) Past participle. For regular verbs and the majority of irregular verbs too, the past participle is syncretised with the past tense form. Where it is not syncretised, the past participle generally ends with the suffix /ən/ or (less often) /n/, as in *taken, broken, forbidden, fallen, grown, drawn*, etc. Examples of a distinct past participle form without the /ən/ suffix are *begun, drunk, swum*, etc.

(f) Present participle. This is always formed by adding to the lexical stem the suffix /ɪŋ/ – or its regional/social variants /ɪn/, /ɪŋg/.

(g) Negative forms. These are normally formed by adding /nt/ to the corresponding positive; when following a consonant, /nt/ constitutes a separate syllable. There are a few irregularities: *won't, shan't, can't, don't* (/dəʊnt/).

4. The inflectional categories

(a) Tense. The primary use of the past and present tenses is to locate in past and present time respectively the state, action, process, or whatever described in the clause: *Kim lived in Berlin* (past tense, past time) vs *Kim lives in Berlin* (present tense, present time). The relationship between tense and time is, however, not always so simple, and we will examine the uses of the tenses in more detail in Ch. 5.

(b) Person and number. For most verbs, we have noted, there are two present tense forms: 3rd person singular and general (= 'not 3rd person singular'). The categories of person and number are primarily nominal rather than verbal: they apply in the first instance to NPs and then derivatively to verbs. In *He takes it ser-*

iously, for example, *he* is inherently 3rd person singular and *takes* is derivatively classified as 3rd person singular because it occurs with such a subject. An NP is 1st person if its head is a form of *I* or *we*, 2nd person if its head is a form of *you*, 3rd person otherwise; the contrast between singular NPs like *the dog* and plural NPs like *the dogs* needs no commentary at this stage. Most present tense verbs, then, agree with the subject with respect to the combined property '3rd person singular': there is one verb form occurring with a subject having this property and another occurring with a subject not having it.

The two departures from this agreement pattern have already been noted: the modal operators do not enter into agreement with the subject and *be* has more person–number distinctions than other verbs.

(c) Polarity. Polarity is the dimension contrasting positive and negative. The system applies not just to the verb but to the clause, and we shall be considering it in that larger context in Ch. 10. At this point we need note only that negative verb forms are usually avoided in formal written style, which prefers analytic negatives, marked by the adverb *not* – thus *They are not well* rather than inflectional *They aren't well*.

(d) Non-tensed forms. The **base** form is so called on account of its morphology rather than its characteristic meaning: it is the form that is identical with the lexical stem and hence is the morphologically most basic form.

The general term **participle** applies to a form which has characteristics of both verbs and adjectives – it is in 'part' like a verb, in part like an adjective. Take *sung*, for example. In its predicator use, more specifically after perfect *have*, as in *She had sung the aria splendidly*, it has much in common with a prototypical verb: it takes just the same range of dependents as a tensed verb – in this example, an object (*the aria*) and a manner adjunct (*splendidly*). In its attributive use, however, as in *a splendidly sung aria*, it has certain affinities with an adjective, inasmuch as it heads a phrase modifying a noun, a function prototypically filled by an adjective – cf. *a truly remarkable aria*. Whether participles are to be analysed as verbs or adjectives or as a distinct word class altogether will depend on their more specific properties in the particular language under analysis: as far as English is concerned we will include them in the verb class, but will take up the issue further in our discussion of 'adjectivalisation' in 7.3.

The appropriateness of the term 'participle' for the present participle is a good deal more problematic than it is for the past participle, which is the one we have just used to explain the concept. The present participle does occur in constructions where it has affinities with an adjective, as in *a peacefully sleeping child*; but it also occurs in constructions where it has affinities with a noun. Thus in *Sleeping in so late made me miss the train*, for example, *sleeping* is head of the expression functioning as subject of *made me miss the train* – and the subject position is prototypically filled by a phrase headed by a noun. There is then another general term, 'gerund', which is used for forms sharing the characteristics of verbs and nouns. Ideally we would have a higher order term available, subsuming participle and gerund and applicable to forms sharing characteristics of verbs, adjectives and nouns; in the absence of any such term in the standard repertoire, however, I will follow the practice of employing the term 'participle' for this form of the verb.

The distinction of the participles as 'past' and 'present' derives from their use in such constructions as *Ed has written a novel* vs *Ed is writing a novel*: although the superordinate verbs, perfect **have** and progressive **be**, are both in the present tense, in the first we understand the composition of the novel to be in past time whereas the second characteristically locates it in present time. Two points, however, must be emphasised. First, the use of the terms 'past' and 'present' does not imply a contrast of tense: the participles belong with the non-tensed forms. Second, the past participle occurs not only in the perfect construction just illustrated (*Ed has written a novel*) but also in the passive construction (*The replies are always written by the secretary*); the past time component is found only in the former case – but since virtually all verbs occur in the perfect construction while many are excluded from the passive, it is appropriate to base the name on the perfect use.

5. The resolution of syncretism

We have seen that there is a good deal of syncretism in the inflectional system of the verb. The two most frequent cases involve on the one hand the past tense and past participle forms, and on the other the general present tense and base forms. How can we 'resolve' syncretism? How, for example, can we tell that in (4) *rejected* is a past tense form in (i), a past participle in (ii)–(iii)?

(4) i   *[They] rejected [it]*   Past tense
    ii   *[They] had rejected [it]*   ⎫
                                                              ⎬ Past participle
    iii *[Those] rejected [were of little value]* ⎭

There is a very simple test that can be applied: replace the lexeme by one which does not exhibit the syncretism concerned, and see which form the construction requires. Suppose we replace **reject** by **take**, which has *took* as its past tense form and *taken* as its past participle. Then we can see that construction (i) requires past tense *took* (*They took/*taken it*), while (ii)–(iii) require past participle *taken* (*They had taken/*took it, Those taken/*took were of little value*).

In applying this test we must bear in mind that verbs may differ in respect of what we shall be calling their 'complementation': they may take different types and combinations of 'complements'. For example, **use** requires an object, while **disappear** excludes an object: *He used a stick, *He used, He disappeared, *He disappeared a stick*. The complements, however, have no effect on the inflectional form (**use** and **disappear**, for example, have the same six forms as in the normal paradigm). It follows that, when we substitute one lexeme for another, we can – and may have to – change the complementation. Thus in *He had blamed the misunderstanding on Peter* we do not need to search for a verb taking the same complements as **blame** (an NP as object plus a PP headed by *on*) but can again show the *blamed* to be a past participle, as opposed to a past tense form, by substituting **take**, as in, say, *He had taken/*took the misunderstanding lightly*. Of course one will quickly be able to dispense with explicitly applying the test, knowing immediately, for example, that perfect **have** takes a past participle after it, not a past tense form – but the rule that perfect **have** takes a past participle is in effect based on the data deriving from such substitution tests.

Consider now the syncretism between the general present tense form and the base form:

(5) i   [*They*] *open* [*at 8.30*]   General present tense
     ii   [*They will*] *open* [*at 8.30*]
     iii *Open* [*it carefully*]   } Base form
     iv   [*They wouldn't let us*] *open* [*it*]

As we have noted, the only verb whose base form is distinct from all present tense forms is **be** and this is the lexeme we must therefore use in our substitution test. As its complementation is different from that of **open** we will need to make adjustments to the material following the verb; (i)–(iv) then correspond respectively to *They are at school at 8.30* (with present tense *are*), *They will be at school at 8.30*, *Be careful with it*, and *They wouldn't let us be present during the interrogation* (with base form *be*).

This result is confirmed by two other more specific tests that we can use to resolve the base vs general present tense syncretism. They derive from the different positions of the two forms within the classification of the inflectional forms given in paradigm (1).

(a) The general present tense form is tensed and as such contrasts with the past tense form, whereas the base form does not enter into contrasts of tense. We note then that (5i) contrasts with *They opened at 8.30*, whereas there are no corresponding contrasts for (ii)–(iv): *They will opened at 8.30*, *Opened it carefully*,[1] *They wouldn't let us opened it*.

(b) The general present tense form likewise contrasts with the 3rd person singular, the choice being determined by agreement with the subject. In the case of (5i), therefore, we find that if we replace *they* by a 3rd person singular NP we must change *open* to *opens*: *He opens/*open at 8.30*. In (ii), by contrast, the *open* remains unchanged, for the base form does not agree with the subject: *He will open/*opens at 8.30*. Similarly if we replace *us* by *him* in (iv): *They wouldn't let him open/*opens it*. (There is no expressed subject in (5iii), so the test could be applied here only in a much more indirect way, which we need not explore.)

[1] This might occur in certain styles as an elliptical version of *I opened it carefully* (e.g. in a postcard: *Received your parcel. Opened it carefully ...*) but that would involve a crucial change in the clause construction, for (5iii) is imperative.

6. Verb inflection, finiteness and clause subordination

Except in their attributive use, verbs function as the ultimate head of a clause, and the inflectional distinctions found in the verb correlate to a significant extent with syntactic distinctions we need to make between different classes of clause. We need, for example, to distinguish between **tensed clauses** (e.g. *They are ill*), present-participial clauses ([*Those*] *going by bus* [*should assemble at 6*]) and past-participial clauses ([*Those*] *arrested last night* [*have been released on bail*]) – clauses whose ultimate head is respectively a tensed form, a present participle form or a past participle form of verb.

The base form of verbs is found, however, in a somewhat heterogeneous set of clause constructions; we shall accordingly not have use for a category of 'base form clauses', but will work instead with the following more narrowly defined classes:[2]

(6) i   *Be careful*   Imperative jussive
    ii [*It is essential*] (*that*) *they be present*   Non-imperative jussive
    iii [*They want*] *to be with her*   *To*-infinitival
    iv [*They may*] *be right*   Bare-infinitival

As a first approximation (we will look more carefully at jussive clauses in Ch. 9 and at infinitivals in Ch. 11) we can distinguish these as follows. Imperatives – which, as we have noted, are characteristically used to issue requests/commands – are virtually always main clauses, whereas the other three classes are virtually always subordinate. Subordinate jussives are distinguished from infinitivals by the actual or potential presence of the subordinator *that*, and by the fact that a case-variable pronoun in subject function appears in the nominative form – thus *they* in (ii), not accusative *them*. The two types of infinitival are distinguished by the presence or absence of the special marker *to* before the verb: *to*-infinitivals are thus quite easy to recognise by means of this *to*.

Although all the clause constructions in (6) contain the same inflectional form of the verb, there are reasons for grouping (i) and (ii) initially with tensed clauses in a class we shall call **finite**, and putting (iii) and (iv) with participial clauses in a non-finite class. This gives us the following classification:

(7)

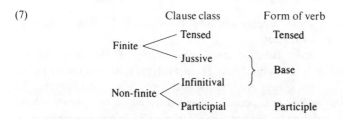

	Clause class	Form of verb
Finite	Tensed	Tensed
	Jussive	Base
Non-finite	Infinitival	
	Participial	Participle

The special properties of jussives are for the most part handled on the clause type dimension. The principal marker of subordination in jussives is *that*, which is also

---

[2] They are not exhaustive: I omit consideration of the slightly archaic construction involving a base form in conditional and similar clauses – *if that be so*, . . .

found in tensed declaratives – compare [*I know*] *that he leaves this evening* (declarative) and [*I insist*] *that he leave this evening* (jussive); it is for this reason, precisely, that it is useful to recognise a clause class, the one we are calling 'finite', which groups the jussives with tensed clauses. It is more usual in languages for the category of finiteness to apply in the first instance to verbs, with a finite clause then being defined derivatively as one containing a finite verb: what has happened in English is that coalescence of formerly distinct inflectional forms into a single base form has yielded a situation where the significant clause classes are not fully definable in terms of verb forms. The meaning of 'finite' as a general term in grammar is related to that of 'finite' in its everyday sense: "limited, bounded". Thus a finite verb is one that is 'limited' by properties of person, number and tense. In English, as we have seen, the categories of person and number apply to verbs to only a relatively small extent: leaving aside *be* and the modal operators we simply have a two-way contrast in the present tense, but not the past, between 3rd person singular and general forms. For English, therefore, 'tensed' is a more appropriate term than 'finite' for the verb-inflection category, and this then leaves 'finite' for application to a clause category: since this is the clause class where the verb inflections of person, number and tense are found, the class falls within the scope of a general definition of finite clause.

With only a very narrow range of exceptions (such as bare-infinitival *Why bother?*, etc.), main clauses are all finite: such exceptions apart, therefore, it is in subordination that we have a contrast of finite vs non-finite. Non-finite subordinate clauses differ more sharply in form from kernel clauses than do finite ones. Indeed with the latter, subordination may not be overtly marked at all in the internal form of the clause – compare subordinate [*He thinks*] *she likes him*, [*I know*] *who broke it* with main *She likes him* (declarative) and *Who broke it?* (interrogative). Non-finite constructions are thus more peripheral members of the clause category than finites.[3]

Finite subordinate clauses fall into three major classes – relative clauses, comparative clauses and content clauses:

(8) i   [*I found the book*] (*that*)/*which he had recommended*   Relative
     ii [*She is more talented than*] *he is*   Comparative
     iii [*They said*] (*that*) *you had done it*   Content

We will be examining these categories in some detail in Ch. 11: here we attempt only a rough first approximation.

Relative clauses usually function as dependent in NP structure: (i), for example, is dependent to the noun *book*. The prototypical relative clause differs structurally from a main clause in either of two ways. The type illustrated by *which he had recommended* has a special relative word – *which, who, whom, whose, when, where, why* – 'relating to' the noun head: thus *which he had recommended* is comparable to the main clause *He had recommended the book*. The type illustrated by (*that*) *he had recommended* has an actual or potential *that* as subordinator and a missing element understood as likewise relating to the noun head: in

---

[3] Some grammars restrict the term 'clause' to finite constructions.

(*that*) *he had recommended* the verb *recommended* has no overt object, but there is one understood, so that the relative clause is again comparable to the main clause *He had recommended the book*.[4]

Comparative clauses function as complement to *than* or *as*, and all are, in varying degrees, elliptical. Thus *he is*, (ii), is understood as "He is talented (to such-and-such a degree)".

Content clauses constitute the unmarked category among the three classes: they lack the special distinctive properties of relatives and comparatives, and accordingly tend to differ less sharply in structure from main clauses. The main clause counterpart of (iii), for example, is simply *You had done it*. The system of clause type (Ch. 9) applies to content clauses: (8iii) is declarative, (6ii) above is jussive, [*I wonder*] *what he wants* is interrogative, and [*I remember*] *what a struggle it was* is exclamative.

7. Operators

There are four non-kernel constructions in English which require the presence of a verb from a small subclass called operators: *be*, *have*, *can*, *may*, *must*, *will*, *do*, etc. Compare

(9) i   *She isn't/is not the captain*   ⎱
     ii **She likesn't/likes not the captain*   ⎰   Tensed verb negated

(10) i   *Had he read it?*   ⎱
     ii **Read he it?*   ⎰   Tensed verb precedes subject

(11) i   *She "can swim*   ⎱
     ii **She "knows him*   ⎰   Polarity emphasised

(12) i   [*I'm not sure he'll go*] *but he may*   ⎱
     ii **[We enjoyed it] and Ed enjoyed too*   ⎰   Post-verbal ellipsis

In each case (ii) is ungrammatical because the verb – *like*, *read*, *know*, *enjoy* – is not an operator. The examples can be corrected by inserting *do* as a 'dummy' operator: *She doesn't/does not like the captain*, *Did he read it?*, *She "does know him*, [*We enjoyed it*] *and Ed did too*. *Do* is a dummy operator in the sense that it is semantically empty, satisfying a purely syntactic requirement. The syntactic rules that derive these four non-kernel constructions from their more basic counterparts (*She likes the captain*, *He read it*, *She knows him*, and *Ed enjoyed it too*) say that if there is not already an operator present, then *do* must be inserted.

The construction in (9) involves either inflectional or analytic negation of the tensed verb. The tensed verb + subject order illustrated in (10) is found most often in interrogative main clauses, but the inversion takes place under certain other conditions too – after an initial negative (*At no time had he read it/did he read it*) or *so* ([*She had read it*] *and so had he*, [*She read it*] *and so did he*). (11) involves emphasis that applies to the positive or negative polarity: (i) is understood

---

[4] The *that* introducing relative clauses is commonly analysed as a relative pronoun like *which*, *who*, etc.: under such an analysis, *that he had recommended* would have *that* as object.

as an emphatic denial of "She can't swim", but (ii) cannot be similarly used as an emphatic denial of "She doesn't know him" (though it can be used in other ways – cf. *He "knows her but I'd hardly say he was a friend of hers*). Post-verbal ellipsis is ellipsis of material following the verb, immediately or with intervening subject and/or *not*: in (12i) *go* is omitted immediately after *may*, whereas in [*She has resigned*] *and so have I* there is ellipsis of *resigned* after *have* plus subject *I*.

The rule requiring the presence of an operator in these constructions is very idiosyncratic to English: closely comparable rules are not found in other languages. For this reason the term 'operator' that we have introduced is chosen ad hoc for English: it is not a general term.[5] Its language-particular definition, of course, is that it is the class of verbs allowed in constructions (9)–(12).

The operator class contains the following verbs:

(a) *be*

(b) *have*, in certain uses: 'perfect' *have* (see 5.2.3) is always an operator (*She hasn't arrived*), while the dynamic *have* of *have a dinner/a shower/a swim* and the like never is; 'possessive/obligational' *have* (replaceable by the idiom *have got*, which contains perfect *have*) can behave either as an operator (*Have you any money?, Have we to go?*) or a non-operator (*Do you have any money?, Do we have to go?*)

(c) *do*, in the 'dummy' use illustrated above; it is, by contrast, a non-operator in *She did her best, They did so, They did something terrible*, etc., as is evident from the fact that these require the addition of dummy *do* in the four operator constructions (*She didn't do her best, Did they do so?*, etc.)

(d) the modal operators: *can, may, must, will, shall, should,*[6] *ought, need* and *dare*. Besides having the properties common to all operators, these lack non-tensed forms (and indeed all but *can, may, will* and *shall* lack past tense forms too), and they show no person–number variation in the present tense. There is also a non-operator *need* and *dare* having the normal six-form paradigm – compare operator *She need/dare not tell them* and non-operator *She does not need/dare to tell them*. (As operators they take a bare-infinitival complement like all the other modal operators except *ought*, and they are restricted to interrogative, negative and other 'non-affirmative contexts' – cf. 10.2.)

(e) *use* in its 'aspectual' sense, as in *She used to like them*; this is a very marginal member, partly because it occurs as an operator only in the first two operator constructions (*He usedn't to like them, Used she to like them?*), partly because

---

[5] Some grammars use the term 'auxiliary' instead, and this is a general term. It is not used here for reasons given in footnote 7 of Ch. 4.
[6] The status of *should* as a lexeme is somewhat problematic. The *should* of examples like *I should be very surprised if he won* is analysable as a form of *shall* (compare *I shall be very surprised if he wins*) but in *You should try harder* and the like it is arguable that the connection with *shall* has been lost and that *should* ought to be assigned to a distinct lexeme.

even here many speakers treat it as a non-operator (*She didn't use(d) to like them,
Did she use(d) to like them?*).

EXERCISES

I. Paradigms

Give the six inflectional forms of the following verb lexemes, following the model for *take*,
etc. set out in (1): *drive, find, go, hit, run, sing, want*.

II. Syncretism: past tense vs past participle

(a) Pick out the verb lexemes in the following list which have syncretism between their past
tense and past participle forms: *buy, catch, come, do, draw, eat, fall, find, forbid, hang, lose,
play, ring, see*.

(b) Is the unbracketed verb in the following examples a past tense form or a past participle?

(13) [*He may simply have*] made [*a mistake*]
(14) [*It is time he*] made [*his mind up*]
(15) [*If you*] caught [*the earlier plane, you'd have more time*]
(16) [*If he*] caught [*the earlier plane, he should be here by now*]
(17) [*He had been*] caught [*photocopying a confidential report*]
(18) [*Anyone*] caught [*trespassing will be severely dealt with*]

III. Syncretism: base form vs general present tense form

Is the unbracketed verb in the following examples a base form or a general present tense
form?

(19) [*Don't*] make [*me laugh*]
(20) [*If they*] want [*it, they can have it*]
(21) [*It is necessary that she*] refund [*it in full*]
(22) [*I think you*] know [*what I mean*]
(23) [*They*] do [*their best*]
(24) [*You can only*] do [*your best*]
(25) *Do* [*your best!*]
(26) [*What do you*] want [*?*]

IV. Verb inflection: analysis

For each verb in the following sentences, say which one of the six major inflectional categories it belongs to: past tense, 3rd pers sg present tense, general present tense, base form,
present participle, past participle.

(27) *Is Kim still working or has she finished?*
(28) *They have been endeavouring to contact him*
(29) *Stop pretending you understand it*
(30) *He could not get her to agree, though he tried very hard to do so*

V. Operators

Change the following declaratives into their closed interrogative counterparts and in the light of your answer say whether the first verb of the declarative is an operator.

(31) *He needn't have gone with them*
(32) *He needs to get his hair cut*
(33) *We ought to notify the landlord*
(34) *We have enough time for one more game*
(35) *He has got a reasonable place to live*
(36) *She had a talk with the director*
(37) *We had better finish it tomorrow*

4

The structure of kernel clauses

A verb, we have seen, functions as head of a VP, which prototypically enters into construction with a subject to form a clause. In this chapter we will deal with these two layers of structure: the VP and the clause. As both are headed, immediately or ultimately, by the verb, it is convenient to take the two together – and for simplicity we will subsume both under the heading of clause structure; indeed, as we shall see towards the end of the chapter, it is arguable that we need more than two layers of structure with the verb as ultimate head. We will confine our attention, apart from the occasional aside, to kernel clauses.

1. Subject and predicate

The first division we make in the analysis of kernel clauses, then, is into subject and predicate. Thus in an elementary example like

(1) *Your father washed the car again*

your father functions as the subject of the clause and *washed the car again* as the predicate.

We will initially consider the subject function at the language-particular level: its general definition will be discussed in §4, along with that of the object and predicative. In English the **subject** is distinguished grammatically from other functions in the clause by a whole cluster of properties, most notably the following:

(a) Form class. The prototypical subject is an NP: there is no predicate that cannot take an NP as subject. In kernel clauses virtually the only other form of subject we find is a subordinate clause, such as *that he was guilty* in *That he was guilty was now clear to everyone*. Thus in (1), the only candidates, as it were, for subject function are the NPs *your father* and *the car*: this first property excludes the verb *washed* and the AdvP *again*.

(b) Position in declarative clauses. In declarative clauses the normal position for the subject is before the verb – immediately as in (1), or with an intervening

49

AdvP, as in *Your father very often loses his temper* (where the AdvP *very often* comes between the subject *your father* and the verb *loses*). Only in certain thematically marked non-kernel clauses is this order departed from. Thus in (1) *your father* and *the car* are most easily distinguished as subject and object respectively by virtue of their linear position.

(c) Position in interrogative clauses. In main clauses containing an operator (cf. 3.7) the simplest kind of interrogative clause is derived from its declarative counterpart by moving the operator to the left of the subject. Thus declarative *Your father is washing the car again* yields interrogative *Is your father washing the car again?*. If the declarative's verb is not an operator, then the interrogative is formed by introducing dummy **do** in that position: the interrogative of (1) is *Did your father wash the car again?*. In either case the subject ends up following the tensed verb, so that *your father* is immediately identifiable as subject by its position after tensed *is* and *did*. But we can also use the present criterion indirectly for the declaratives: *your father* is seen to be subject of the two declaratives precisely because it is the element whose position relative to the tensed verb is changed when the interrogative is formed.[1]

(d) Subject–verb agreement. Person–number properties of the verb are determined by agreement with the subject. In *Your father likes it*, for example, *likes* agrees with 3rd person singular *your father*: if the latter is replaced by *your parents*, then *likes* must also be replaced by *like*. Modal operators and past tenses of verbs other than **be** have no person–number properties, but we can apply the agreement criterion indirectly in such cases by changing the verb and/or the tense. Thus in *Tom wouldn't help me* there is no agreement, but if we replace past modal *wouldn't* by present non-modal *doesn't* we can see that it is *Tom* that selects *doesn't* in contrast to don't. Similarly, with *Your father knew them*: if we replace *knew* by a present tense, it is easy to see that the 3rd person singular form *knows* is required, so as to agree with *your father*.

(e) Case in personal pronouns. A handful of pronouns, we have noted, have contrasting case forms: nominative *I, he, she, we, they* vs accusative *me, him, her, us, them*. In finite clauses the subject requires a nominative form, while the object takes an accusative. Thus in *They shot him* we have nominative *they* as subject, accusative *him* as object. (The 'predicative' – see §4 below – allows either nominative or accusative, according to style: compare formal *It was I* with informal *It was me*.) In analysing a clause where the NPs do not carry any case inflection we can again usually apply the case criterion indirectly by making appropriate sub-

---

[1] Note that there is no comparable interrogative for *That he was guilty was now clear to everyone*: **That he was guilty now clear to everyone*. We can of course have *Was it now clear to everyone that he was guilty?*; this, however, is the interrogative of the extrapositioned counterpart *It was now clear to everyone that he was guilty*. Subordinate clauses cannot in general follow the tensed verb in interrogative or analogous structures: this is one reason for saying that they make less prototypical subjects than NPs.

stitutions: in (1), for example, *your father* is replaceable by nominative *he*, while *the car* is replaceable by accusative *them*.

(f) Conditions on omissibility. In kernel clauses the subject is an obligatory element, along with the predicator: the minimal kernel construction consists of just these two elements, as in *Everyone laughed*. One respect in which a clause may be non-kernel is by virtue of being elliptical, and a number of elliptical constructions specifically involve the subject. One is the imperative, where a second person subject is omissible: (*You*) *be quiet!*. Others are subordinate non-finites, such as the infinitival [*Ed remembered*] *to take his key* (compare the finite main clause *Ed took his key*) or present-participial [*Liz married Ed before*] *hearing of this incident* (compare *Liz heard of this incident*). Notice that these particular non-finite constructions require a double reference to the subject: firstly, the subordinate clause lacks a subject, and secondly, the missing subject is recoverable from the superordinate clause subject (so that, we understand "Liz married Ed before she heard of the incident", not ". . . before he heard of the incident").

In kernel clauses the subject is very easily identifiable by the criteria we have given. Some non-kernel clauses, as just noted, lack a subject, but for the rest, most of the processes deriving non-kernel clauses leave the subject intact. For example, if we coordinate, subordinate or negate (1) the subject will remain *your father* (cf. [*Tom mowed the lawn*] *and your father washed the car again*, [*He says*] *that your father washed the car again*, *Your father didn't wash the car again*). There are, however, some processes which change the subject – notably some of those yielding thematically marked clauses. Thus when we change active (1) into its passive counterpart *The car was washed again by your father* the original object *the car* takes over the subject function – as can be verified by applying criteria (b)–(f). In examining the thematic processes in Ch. 12, we will take up the question of which ones are like passivisation in effecting such a reassignment of the subject function.

The **predicate** we can deal with very quickly. At the language-particular level it is in fact most easily defined negatively by reference to the subject: as a first approximation, the predicate is what is left of the clause when we remove the subject (together with any coordinator and/or subordinator introducing the clause). For example, in *I realise that he is ill* the predicate of the superordinate clause is *realise that he is ill* (what is left after the removal of the subject *I*), while that of the subordinate clause is *is ill* (what is left after the removal of the subject *he* and the subordinator *that*).

As a general term, predicate applies to the function of a constituent, prototypically having a main verb as its ultimate head, that enters into construction with the subject and characteristically serves semantically to ascribe to the person or thing referred to by the subject some property or a role in some relation, action, event, etc. In *John is tall*, for example, the predicate *is tall* ascribes the property of tallness to John, in *Your father washed the car* the predicate *washed the car* ascribes to your father the role of actor with respect to the action of washing the car, and so on.

2. Predicator, complements and adjuncts

The predicate position is filled by a verb phrase. Leaving aside cases of ellipsis, a VP contains a verb as head optionally accompanied by one or more dependents. A more specific term for the head of a VP in predicate function is **predicator**. Thus in (1), for example, *washed* is predicator, *washed the car again* predicate; in *Kim washed*, just as *Kim* is both a noun and an NP, *washed* is both a verb and a VP, hence both predicator and predicate.

The dependents of the predicator within the VP are of two main kinds, **complements** and **adjuncts**. Illustrating again from example (1), *the car* is a complement (more specifically an object), while *again* is an adjunct. Complement is a function that we shall be using in the analysis of other constructions than the VP (for example, we analyse the dependent following a preposition as its complement, and indeed we shall take the subject in clause structure to be a complement of the predicate), but it will be convenient to explain it initially with reference to VP structure – which is where it has its application in traditional grammar. Complements are distinguished from adjuncts in VP structure, then, by the following properties:

(a) Non-omissibility. Complements are sometimes obligatory, whereas adjuncts are always omissible. Thus if a dependent of the verb is obligatory it will be a complement, if it is omissible its status will have to be determined by other criteria. In *He became ill* or *He used a drill* the dependents *ill* and *a drill* are both obligatory and hence complements. By 'obligatory' we mean that dropping the element yields either ungrammaticality, as in these examples, or else a significant change in the meaning of the verb, as in *Kim fell ill*, where dropping *ill* leads to a clear change in the meaning of *fell*.

(b) Verb lexeme classification. The selection of a complement of a particular type depends on the presence of a verb lexeme of an appropriate class, whereas the selection of adjuncts is not lexically controlled in this way. Take example (1) once more. There are lots of verbs which exclude the selection of a dependent with the function of *the car*: *Your father hoped/disappeared/relied the car* and thus *the car*, although it is not obligatory, is identifiable as a complement. *Again*, by contrast, can occur with any verb and is accordingly an adjunct.

(c) Form class. The most central complements are NPs or AdjPs, while the most central adjuncts are AdvPs. All the examples given have followed this pattern, but the form class criterion is very much subsidiary to the others, so that in the case of conflict priority will be given to criteria (a) and (b). To a very large extent, however, the correlation does hold. The main exception involves temporal NPs like *this morning*, *last week*, etc., which, although they can function as complement (as in *I wasted this morning*), more often function as adjunct (as in *I arrived this morning*).

All three properties are relevant at both the general and language-particular levels. The etymology of the term 'complement' relates to the first property. Verbs like **become** and **use** are traditionally said to be 'verbs of incomplete predication' – i.e. they cannot form a predicate by themselves: they require a dependent element to 'complete' the meaning or, in other words, to 'complement' them. In many languages there is a closer match between complements and obligatoriness than there is in English, where property (b) provides the main distinguishing criterion. It does not yield an absolutely sharp boundary between complements and adjuncts, but again we will follow our policy of concentrating on the clear cases.

3. Objects and predicatives

The two most central types of complement are objects and predicatives. We will see in due course that they can occur together, but initially we will confine our attention to clauses containing a single complement of one or other of these two types – more specifically a 'direct' object (O^d) or a 'subjective' predicative (PC^s: the 'C' distinguishes PC, a complement, from P, the predicator). Prototypical examples are given in

(2)   i   *Her son shot the intruder*   S   P O^d
     ii   *Her son was brilliant/a genius*   S   P PC^s

The construction in (i) is called 'transitive', that in (ii) 'copulative' – and these terms likewise apply to the verbs appearing in the two constructions, so that **shoot** in (i) is a transitive verb, **be** in (ii) a copulative verb.

At the language-particular level, **direct object** and **subjective predicative** are distinguished grammatically in English by the following properties.

(a) Form class. While both PC^s and O^d positions can be filled by an NP, only a PC^s can be filled by an AdjP. In (ii), for example, we have either an AdjP (*brilliant*) or an NP (*a genius*), whereas in (i) only an NP is possible. With some verbs the PC MUST be adjectival: *He went mad/*a lunatic*. Note similarly that with **get** an adjectival complement will be predicative (e.g. *He got angry*), with **get** meaning "become", while a nominal one will be an object (e.g. *He got a good seat*), with **get** meaning "obtain".

(b) Passivisation. Transitive clauses can normally undergo the thematic process of passivisation, with the object of the active becoming the subject of the passive, whereas copulative clauses can never be passivised. Thus (i) can be transformed to *The intruder was shot by her son*, with *the intruder* now subject, but performing the corresponding operation on (ii) yields the completely ungrammatical **Brilliant/A genius was been by her son*.

(c) Number. With an NP object, number is selected quite independently of the subject, so that in the transitive construction we usually have all four combinations of singular and plural NPs: Sg + Sg in (2i), Sg + Pl in *Her son shot the intruders*, Pl + Sg in *Her sons shot the intruder*, Pl + Pl in *Her sons shot the intruders*. Here we have a semantically significant contrast between a singular object and a plural object, just as we do between a singular subject and a plural subject. With an NP predicative, however, number is normally not semantically contrastive in this way. In the simplest cases, the predicative agrees in number with the subject: *Her son was a genius/*geniuses* but *Her sons were geniuses/*a genius*. But very often the predicative is non-contrastively singular: *Kim and Ed had both been a strange colour/a pain in the neck/President of the Union*. The most distinctive semantic role of NPs, the one most characteristically associated with subject and object function, is to refer and it is in this role that number is typically found to be contrastive. The predicative role is shared with AdjPs, to which the category of number does not apply, and it is accordingly not surprising that number in predicative NPs should be less significant than in referential ones. The only construction of any generality where we find a plural PC with a singular subject is illustrated in *The only solution is more frequent patrols*. This belongs to what we will call the 'identifying' *be* construction, where the complement differs significantly from a prototypical predicative; apart from its independently selected and contrastive number, it has the property that it can be switched to subject function (cf. *More frequent patrols are the only solution*), a property bearing some resemblance to the potential of an object to be switched to subject function by means of passivisation: see 12.3.

(d) Pronominal case. A case-variable pronoun in object function takes accusative form, whereas one in PC[s] function takes nominative or accusative depending on style (as we noted above in discussing the case of the subject): *Ed saw me/*I* but *The only one they didn't notice was I/me*. The *I* of the latter belongs to relatively formal style. Personal pronouns, however, are far from prototypical predicatives (semantically they are chiefly used to refer, not to predicate), and they do not occur with all copulative verbs (cf. *The victim seemed he/him*): they are virtually restricted to the identifying *be* construction mentioned in (c) above.[2]

4. Subject, object and predicative as general terms

At the general level the subjective predicative may be defined as a grammatically distinct function usually filled by an AdjP or an NP, prototypically in construc-

---

[2] There is a good deal of variation in terminology with respect to what I am in this book calling 'predicative' (and have elsewhere called, more fully, 'predicative complement'). Some grammars do not employ 'complement' in the broad sense adopted here but restrict it to the predicative: a subjective predicative is then called a 'subject complement' and an objective predicative (to be introduced in §5 below) an 'object complement'. The contrast between object and predicative is sometimes made in terms of 'extensive' complement vs 'intensive' complement. A further term quite widely used is 'predicate nominal': this applies to predicatives in the form of an NP.

tion with the verb "be" and characteristically denoting some property that is predicated of the person(s) or thing(s) referred to by the subject. By "be" I mean *be*
or its equivalent in other languages. In prototypical examples like (2ii), however,
be can hardly be said to have any independent meaning: it serves syntactically to
carry the tense inflection that is required in kernel clauses. The main semantic
content of the predicate lies in the complement – hence the term 'predicative'
complement. The *be* thus serves as what is called a **copula**, i.e. a 'link' between the
complement and the subject – which again is why the term copulative is applied
to the construction, and by extension to other verbs that are syntactically substi-
tutable for *be*, such as *appear*, *become*, *get*, *remain*, *seem*, etc., in some of their
uses.

Semantically the subject and the direct object, unlike the predicative, prototypically refer to persons or things involved in the situation described in the clause
– to 'participants' in the situation. Thus (2i), for example, describes a situation
involving two participants, her son and the intruder. In (2ii), by contrast, there is
only one, her son: *brilliant/a genius* does not refer to a second participant but
gives a property of the sole participant in the situation.

Normally the participants in a two-participant situation have different semantic 'roles'. In (2i) her son has the role of 'actor', the performer of the action, while
the intruder has the role of 'patient', the undergoer of the action. What the roles
are will depend on the type of process: *Her son knew the intruder*, for example,
does not describe an action (to know someone is not to perform an action) and
hence it would be inappropriate here to speak of her son as the actor and the
intruder as the patient. Nevertheless we will take action clauses as a starting-
point for an explication of subject and object at the general level, for actor and
patient are clear, salient and sharply differentiated roles in a large range of
examples. We will apply the labels 'NP$_A$' and 'NP$_P$' to the two NPs in a kernel
action clause which refer to the actor and patient respectively. Thus in (2i) *her son*
is NP$_A$ and *the intruder* NP$_P$. (The restriction to kernel clauses serves to exclude
passives, such as *The intruder was shot by her son*.) In a one-participant situation
the issue of differentiating roles does not arise, and we will apply the label 'NP$_S$'
(mnemonic for 'single participant') to the NP in a kernel clause describing such a
situation – most straightforwardly in clauses consisting of just an NP and a verb,
such as *Her son fainted*.

In English NP$_S$ behaves grammatically like NP$_A$: both have the language-
particular properties of the subject set out in §1 above. Not all languages are like
this, however, for it is also possible for NP$_S$ to be grouped grammatically with
NP$_P$. The general term subject is applicable only in languages (the majority)
where there is significant syntactic resemblance between NP$_A$ and NP$_S$: its definition is that it is a grammatically distinct function subsuming NP$_A$ and NP$_S$.[3]

A further semantic property of the subject in many languages is that it is the
element correlating most closely with the 'topic' of the clause, i.e. with the per-

---

[3] The literature on subject and object as general categories uses A, P (or O) and S instead of
NP$_A$, NP$_P$ and NP$_S$ respectively.

son(s) or thing(s) that the message expressed in the clause is primarily about. Leaving aside examples like *As for Tom, he was too ill to join us* or *As regards health insurance, they're proposing to retain the present scheme*, where *as for* and *as regards* serve to encode the topic status of Tom and health insurance, the grammar of the English clause does not explicitly mark one element as identifying the topic, and this inevitably makes the category of topic a somewhat elusive one – more so, for example, than that of actor. What the topic is (if indeed there is one) normally has to be inferred from the larger context. For example, an utterance of a clause like *He shot her*, with *he* referring, let us say, to Ed and *her* to Liz, could be construed as being primarily about Ed (e.g. in response to *What did Ed do?*) or as being primarily about Liz (e.g. in response to *What happened to Liz?*). Nevertheless we can say that, other things being equal, the subject is the element that is most likely to identify the topic. Compare, for example, active *Kim struck Pat across the face* (with *Kim* as subject) and passive *Pat was struck across the face by Kim* (with *Pat* as subject). The two clauses describe the same event – and the most likely reason for selecting the non-kernel passive rather than the kernel active would be to present the message as being primarily about Pat rather than Kim. This broad correlation with topic constitutes a significant general property of the subject, but it will be clear that the correlation is not remotely close enough to provide an identifying criterion at the language-particular level for English. For it is easy to find examples where it would be quite implausible to claim that the subject picked out the topic: *Nothing will satisfy you* (with *nothing* as subject) would characteristically be used to say something about you, *There's a fallacy in that argument* (with *there* as subject: see 12.5) to say something about that argument, and so on.

5. The complex-transitive and ditransitive constructions

This section introduces two constructions containing not just a single complement like those in §3, but two. A **complex-transitive** clause contains both an object and a predicative:

(3)   *Everyone considered Pat an imposter*   S   P   O^d PC^o

The relation between *an imposter* and *Pat* here matches that holding between them in the copulative (single-complement) construction *Pat was an imposter*; in the latter *Pat* is subject and *an imposter* subjective predicative, in (3) *Pat* is object and we therefore analyse *an imposter* as **objective predicative** (PC^o). Thus the relation between PC^o and O^d in the complex-transitive construction is the same as that between PC^s and S in the copulative construction, and an objective predicative is definable derivatively as like a subjective one except that it relates to the object rather than the subject. Consider it then with respect to properties (a)–(c) of §3 (we need not take up (d) because personal pronouns do not occur in PC^o function, which reinforces the point that they do not make prototypical predicatives).

(a) Form class. An objective predicative can be an AdjP or an NP: *an imposter* in (3), for example, is replaceable by the AdjP *dishonest*.

(b) Agreement. The number of an NP in PC° function is again prototypically determined by agreement – this time with the object. Note then that in (3) singular *an imposter* matches singular *Pat*, and if we replace *Pat* by *them* then we will need a corresponding change in PC°: *Everyone considered them imposters*.

(c) Passivisation. An NP in PC° function cannot become subject through passivisation: the only passive counterpart of (3) is *Pat was considered an imposter by everyone* (with the object *Pat* becoming subject), not **An imposter was considered Pat by everyone*.

A second double-complement construction is the **ditransitive** clause, containing two objects:

(4)   *The woman gave Kim the money*   S P O^i O^d

(For the clause containing just one object we will use the term **monotransitive**; 'transitive', as introduced earlier, applies to a clause containing at least one object.) The first object in (4), *Kim*, is the **indirect object** (O^i), while the second, *the money*, is the direct object. We have already dealt with the latter, so it remains just to examine the general and language-particular properties of the indirect object.

At the general level it is definable as a grammatically distinct function usually filled by an NP and characteristically referring, in a kernel clause describing an action, to the 'recipient' – recipient, that is, of what is referred to by the direct object. (As usual with semantic correlations, we need the qualification 'characteristically': Kim is the recipient of the money in (4) but in *He forgave Kim her indiscretion* she did not receive the indiscretion, and in *They charged Kim $10* she did not receive the $10 – quite the reverse.) It will be noted that 'recipient' is explained by reference to the direct object and this reflects the fact that in kernel clauses an indirect object normally occurs only if there is also a direct object: if there is just one object it will normally be direct. Subject, direct object and indirect object are similar functions in that they characteristically refer to what we have called a 'participant' in the situation, the semantic differences having to do primarily with the role of that participant. The grouping together of the direct object and indirect object as different kinds of object in contrast to the subject reflects the fact that the subject is often set apart semantically by its special association with the topic and syntactically by the constituent structure, where (in quite a number of languages, including English) the clause is first divided into subject and predicate, with direct and indirect objects then both being functions within the predicate. Typically there are also more specific syntactic resemblances between the two kinds of object; in English, for example, both require accusative case for case-variable pronouns (though languages with richer case systems than English will usually have different cases for them), the indirect object is like the direct in its ability to become subject through passivisation (compare (4) with *Kim was given the money by the woman*) and whereas all kernel clauses must contain a subject, they do not all contain an object. The terms 'direct' and 'indirect' are based on the idea that the referent of the direct object is characteristically more directly involved in the action than that of the indirect object – in (4), for example, it is the money that the woman most immediately acts upon: she takes it and passes it then to Kim.

Turning now to the language-particular level, the indirect object in English has the following properties:

(a) Position relative to direct object. In kernel clauses O^i normally occurs with a following O^d, as in (4). Hardly any verbs allow an O^i as sole object and we do not find the order S–P–O^d–O^i,[4] so that the indirect object is prototypically identifiable as the first of two NP objects. Consider, for example, the ditransitive clause *He sent them some flowers.* We can drop the O^i *them* without changing the function of *some flowers*: it remains O^d in *He sent some flowers*. But in *He sent them* the syntactic and semantic role of *them* is different: *them* is O^d and refers not to the recipient but to the patient (more specifically the entity that is caused to go somewhere). Thus **send**, like many other verbs, can occur with $O^i + O^d$ or O^d alone, but not with O^i alone.

(b) Association with prepositional construction. Very often a ditransitive clause is paraphrasable by one containing the preposition *to* or *for*:

(5) i   *Tom lent Kim the binoculars*
     ii *Tom lent the binoculars to Kim*
(6) i   *Tom bought Kim some binoculars*
     ii *Tom bought some binoculars for Kim*

It is thus characteristic of the indirect object to correspond to the complement of *to* or *for* in pairs of this kind. Notice, however, that although the most frequent ditransitive verbs also enter into the corresponding prepositional construction, there are quite a few others that do not – **allow/permit, refuse; bet/wager; bid, charge, fine; begrudge/envy; forgive/pardon; hit/strike; reach; shout** (as in **shout** *someone a drink*); **spare**; and so on (thus *He allowed/refused me a second go*, but not **He allowed/refused a second go to/for me*). Conversely there are verbs entering into the prepositional construction but not the ditransitive – cf. *He said some terrible things to her* vs **He said her some terrible things* (contrast **tell**). It is doubtful whether the correspondence is systematic enough to justify deriving one construction from the other, and I shall accordingly treat both as kernel. Only the (i) example in pairs (5) and (6) contains an indirect object. In (5ii), for example, the NP *Kim* is not a complement of the verb *lent* but of the preposition *to* – and although *to Kim* is a complement of the verb, it is not an object by virtue of being

---

[4] Some dialects do allow this order when O^d is a personal pronoun: *I'll give it you, You must give them Dr Smith.*

a PP rather than an NP: notice that one clear respect in which PP complements differ from objects is that they can never become subject through passivisation (cf. **To Kim was lent the binoculars by Tom*).[5]

(c) Resistance to fronting. The indirect object cannot, or cannot readily, be moved to the front of the clause by the rules which reorder the elements of structure in various non-kernel constructions. Compare kernel (5i) and (6i) with

(7) **Who(m) did Tom lend the binoculars?*   Closed interrogative
(8) **[the one] whom Tom bought some binoculars*   Relative

Instead of (7) we could of course say *Who(m) did Tom lend the binoculars to?* or *To whom did Tom lend the binoculars?*; these, however, are based not on the ditransitive construction of (5i) but on the prepositional (5ii), where neither the NP *Kim* nor the PP *to Kim* is an indirect object. The fact that either the PP as a whole or the NP within it can be fronted is indeed a major reason for distinguishing them syntactically from the indirect object in spite of the equivalence of semantic role.

6. Five major patterns of complementation

We have now introduced two constructions containing a single complement, O^d or PC^s, and two with a pair of complements, $O^d + PC^o$ and $O^i + O^d$. Adding the construction where there is no complement at all gives us the five patterns of verb complementation shown in (9).

(9)	Structure				Name	Example
I	S	P			Intransitive	*Kim arrived*
II	S	P	PC^s		Copulative	*Kim became ill/a teacher*
III	S	P	O^d		Monotransitive	*Kim saw the accident*
IV	S	P	O^d	PC^o	Complex-transitive	*Kim considered him foolish/a fool*
V	S	P	O^i	O^d	Ditransitive	*Kim told him the truth*

Specification of the syntactic properties of a given verb (such as, ideally, one would expect to find in a comprehensive lexicon matching up with the grammar) will say, among other things, which of these constructions, and others that we have not yet introduced, it can enter into – it is of course for this reason that the post-verbal elements are complements, not adjuncts. For example, **remain** appears in I (*Many problems remain*) or II (*He remained conscious/an agnostic*); **drink** in I (*Pat drank*), III (*Pat drank beer*), IV (*Pat drank himself unconscious*) or V (*They drank us a toast*); **use** only in III (*It uses a lot of fuel*); **get** in II (*Tom's condition got worse*), III (*He got a surprise*), IV (*They got him drunk*) or V (*They got me a drink*). The names given in (9) apply to the clause construction and to the

---

[5] In traditional grammar the *Kim* (or *to Kim*) of (5ii) is analysed as an indirect object, just like the *Kim* of (i) – and analogously for other pairs; the position taken in this book, however, is that the similarity between the *Kim* of (ii) and that of (i) is a matter of semantic role rather than syntactic function.

corresponding (use of the) verb; thus *Kim considered him foolish* is a complex-transitive clause and **consider**, as used here, is a complex-transitive verb.

The indirect object is in general an optional element: all verbs that can enter into construction V can also enter into III (though not vice versa, of course).[6] The great majority of monotransitive verbs also belong to the intransitive class; here, however, we find two main kinds of relation between constructions III and I, as exemplified in (10)–(11):

		III	I
(10)	**eat**	*She ate an apple*	*She ate*
(11)	**stop**	*She stopped the car*	*The car stopped*

In the first kind, the participant role of the subject-referent remains constant and the intransitive clause simply leaves unexpressed the second participant: *She ate* entails that she ate something but doesn't specify what. In the second kind the subject of the intransitive corresponds to the object, not the subject, of the transitive: both clauses in (10) describe a situation in which the car changed from a state of motion to one of rest. Some of the verbs that are found with this second kind of relation normally occur in the intransitive construction only in combination with a manner adverb, a negative or the like. With **iron**, for example, we will not find **The shirt ironed* (matching transitive *He ironed the shirt*), whereas *This shirt irons well* is perfectly natural.

A somewhat higher proportion of predicatives are obligatory than is the case for objects – but we still find examples of both II and IV where the predicative is omissible. Compare, for **die**, II *He died a pauper* and I *He died* and, for **paint**, IV *She painted the fence blue* and III *She painted the fence*. Note, by contrast, that the predicative is not omissible, in the sense we have given to that term, in examples like *She went mad* or *She found him intolerable*, for dropping *mad* and *intolerable* results in a significant change in the meaning of the verb. This is evident from the fact that while *He died a pauper* and *She painted the fence blue* entail *He died* and *She painted the fence*, respectively, *She went mad* and *She found him intolerable* do not entail *She went* and *She found him*.

This concludes our survey of the most central and straightforward complements within the VP: objects with the form of NPs and predicatives with the form of AdjPs or NPs. In the next section we will introduce, more briefly, a range of constructions that depart in various ways from these central patterns.

7. Other types of complement

(a) Place, direction and time complements

(12) i   [*My driving licence is*] *in the car*   Place

---

[6] This is not to say that O[i] can be freely dropped from all clauses containing it – only that all ditransitive verbs also have monotransitive uses. **Give**, for example, is used monotransitively in *Tom gave $5* (with the recipient not expressed but recoverable from the context), but the O[i] could hardly be dropped from a clause like *I must give the door another coat of paint.*

ii [*Ed went*] *into the garage*   Direction
iii [*The meeting is*] *at 5 o'clock*   Time

Place and direction both have to do with space: the difference is that place is static, while direction involves movement (and various subtypes of direction could be distinguished according as the movement is basically to(wards), from or via). We will see that place and time expressions can also function as adjuncts; in (12), however, *in the car* and *at 5 o'clock* qualify as complements because they are not omissible. The directional PP *into the garage* in (ii) is omissible, but its occurrence is dependent on the presence of an appropriate verb, such as *go* in this example. The most frequent form for the three types of complement is a PP, as in (12); they can, however, also take the form of AdvPs (*Ed is here; Ed went upstairs; The meeting is afterwards*) or, to a very limited extent, NPs (*Ed is/went next door; The meeting is this evening*).

(b) Complements of prepositional verbs. A considerable number of verbs take PP complements where the preposition is fully determined by the verb itself and thus does not have any identifiable independent meaning of its own (such as can be ascribed to the prepositions in (12)):

(13) i *Many people referred to her article*
ii *They charged him with perjury*

Whereas the *to* of, say, the complement of direction in *He walked to the cemetery* is replaceable by *from, within, towards*, etc., that in (13i) is not. Lexically it belongs with **refer**: the entry in the lexicon for **refer** must specify that it takes a complement headed by *to*. Syntactically, however, it belongs with *her article*, for *to her article* forms a constituent; this is evident from the fact that *to* can accompany its NP complement to the front of the clause in such constructions as the relative [*the article*] *to which many people referred*.

Verbs that enter into the construction of (13) are called **prepositional verbs** (though there is no standard term for the PP complement itself). There are a great many such verbs – compare intransitive **apply for, approve of, attend to, decide on**, transitive **accuse** ... **of, confine** ... **to, interest** ... **in, protect** ... **from**, and so on. They include verbs such as **lend** ... **to, buy** ... **for** which can also occur in the ditransitive construction: see (5) and (6). A number allow more than one preposition but still without any independent meaning assignable to it. Thus the difference in meaning between **call for** [*an inquiry*] and **call on** [*a friend*] is not derivable from the meanings of the prepositions, but will still have to be dealt with in the lexical entry for **call**. Similarly, the entry for **blame** will specify that the preposition can be *for*, as in *He blamed Kim for the accident*, or *on*, as in *He blamed the accident on Kim*, depending on which semantic role is associated with the direct object and which with the complement of the preposition.

In the examples considered so far the complement of the preposition has some affinities with an object – it might be regarded as an 'oblique object', i.e. one which is not related to the verb immediately but via a preposition. And in the construction where there is no object proper – i.e. in (13i) as opposed to (ii) – the oblique object can often become subject through passivisation: *Her article was referred to by many people.* There are also a few prepositional verbs, however, where the complement of the preposition is an 'oblique predicative': *That counts as wrong/a hit, They took him for dead/a foreigner*; compare also **pass for, describe/recognise/regard** ... *as*, and so on.

(c) 'Particles' as complement

(14) i   *Kim came to*
      ii   *He turned the light off*

The complements *to* and *off* here are 'particles'. These are traditionally regarded as a subclass of adverbs, but they lie very much at the periphery of the adverb class (see 8.1); most words that are used as particles also have uses as prototypical prepositions (cf. *He went to London, He fell off the roof*). Particles may combine with other types of complement – with an object in (ii), a predicative in *It turned out green/a great success*, a PP complement of a prepositional verb, as in *They are looking forward to their holiday* (where *forward* is a particle, *to their holiday* a PP), and so on.

The particles given above are parts of the idioms **come to, turn off, turn out, look forward to**: these will have to be listed in the lexicon, for the meanings are not systematically derivable from the meanings of the separate words. It is a characteristic of English that it contains an enormous number of verb + particle idioms (and also verb + preposition idioms of the type dealt with in (b) above). Particles, however, are not restricted to idioms: most of them can function also as complements of direction (or, less often, place), as in *Ed jumped off, He brought the clothes in*, etc. Indeed, there is no sharp dividing line between idiomatic and literal uses of the particles.

When the particle combines with an object, it is generally possible to reverse the order of the two complements. Thus (14ii), for example, has *He turned off the light* as a thematically marked variant. Note that this construction is to be distinguished from that containing a single complement with the form of a PP. Compare, then:

(15) i   *[He turned] off the light*   Particle + NP
      ii   *[He turned] off the main road*   PP

There are several clear syntactic differences between them: (α) In (i) the two complements can occur in either order as we have noted, but in (ii) there is only one complement and hence no possibility of reordering – cf. **He turned the main road off.* (β) Where the NP object is an unstressed personal pronoun it cannot follow a particle: *He turned it off* but not *He turned off it (*it* = "the light"); an unstressed personal pronoun can of course function as complement of a preposition, so an alternative to (15ii) is *He turned off it* (*it* = "the main road"). (γ) A particle can never be fronted along with a following object (since they do not form a single constituent), whereas a preposition can be fronted along with its complement: compare **[the light] off which he turned* and *[the road] off which he turned.*

(d) Finite clause complements

(16) i   *I knew that he was ill*   S   P O^d
       ii   *The problem is that we can't really afford it*   S   P PC^s

Subordinate clause complements exhibit varying degrees of functional resemblance to NP complements, but finite ones are sufficiently similar for us to be able to assign them the same functions – direct object in (i), predicative in (ii). A direct object with the form of a finite subordinate clause can combine with other complements – with an indirect object (*her*) in *You told her that it was genuine*, with a particle (*out*) in *She made out that she knew him*, and so on. When it combines with PC° in the complex-transitive construction, extraposition is virtually always obligatory; thus instead of **He considers that Liz got the job monstrously unfair* we have non-kernel *He considers it monstrously unfair that Liz got the job* – see 12.4.

(e) Non-finite complements. All four kinds of non-finite distinguished in 3.6 are found as complement to a verb:

(17)	S	P	Non-finite Comp	
i	[*She*	*wants*]	*to leave the country*	*To*-infinitival
ii	[*She*	*must*]	*leave the country*	Bare-infinitival
iii	[*She*	*kept*]	*leaving the country*	Present-participial
iv	[*She*	*has*]	*left the country*	Past-participial

The majority of non-finites contain no subject – and often there is no syntactic possibility of inserting one, which makes them somewhat peripheral to the clause category.

Some non-finites can, like finites, be assigned the same functions as NPs. This applies to the copulative construction (with *be* in its identifying sense): *The only solution is to resign, The first mistake was inviting the boss*. And also to the complex-transitive construction, where extraposition applies with infinitivals (thus *This made it a waste of time to accompany them* rather than **This made to accompany them a waste of time*), but not with present-participials (*She considered attempting it a waste of time*). For the rest, however, non-finites bear too tenuous a functional resemblance to NP or AdjP complements to warrant analysis as objects or predicatives: it is better to treat them as a special kind of complement. There is again no standard term available, but the verbs that take such complements are widely called **catenatives**, and this term we will adopt. Thus *want*, *must*, *keep* and *have* as used in (17) are catenative verbs. The term is derived from 'concatenation', which means "chaining together". The construction is 'recursive', in that one non-finite can occur as complement within another, so that we may end up with a chain of catenative verbs, each followed by its non-finite complement. In *She wants to try to persuade them to stop drinking so much*, for example, the verbs *want*, *try*, *persuade* and *stop* are catenatives; *drinking so much* is the complement of *stop*, *to stop drinking so much* is one of the complements of *persuade*, and so on. Such complements may occur alone, as in (17), or in combination with other complements – a prepositional complement (*upon him*) in *She prevailed upon him to change his mind*, an object (*him*) in *She persuaded him to change his mind*, a particle complement (*up*) in *He ended up changing his mind*, and so on.[7]

It will be evident from the summary survey given in this section that there is a very considerable range of verb complementation patterns; the five with established names, set out in (9) above, are merely a selection from the most elementary and frequent patterns.

8. Adjuncts

Grammars of English (and of languages generally) usually recognise numerous different kinds of adjunct. The following examples are illustrative of the categories to be found, but the list is not intended to be exhaustive.

(18)			Kind of adjunct
	i	[*She spoke*] *very slowly*	Manner
	ii	[*I cut it*] *with the bread-knife*	Instrument
	iii	[*She travelled*] *with her father*	Comitative
	iv	[*We arrive there*] *at midnight*	Time
	v	[*He slept*] *for twelve hours*	Duration
	vi	[*She gets it right*] *more often than not*	Frequency
	vii	[*He left early*] *so as not to miss her*	Purpose
	viii	[*I went home*] *because I had no money left*	Reason
	ix	[*I liked it*] *enormously*	Degree
	x	[*It bounces*] *if you drop it*	Condition
	xi	[*It was a dead loss,*] *from my point of view*	Viewpoint
	xii	[*He took the early train*] *perhaps*	Modal
	xiii	[*He liked her,*] *nevertheless*	Connective

The labels are for the most part self-explanatory: only a few need commenting on. Comitative adjuncts indicate accompaniment – they are prototypically introduced by *with*. Modal adjuncts express various kinds of modality – they have the same kind of meaning as modal operators (see 5.3). Connective adjuncts serve to connect the clause to what has gone before, and constitute one of the devices by which a text is distinguishable by its 'cohesion' from a random sequence of sentences.

---

[7] Many grammars analyse some of the verbs here treated as catenatives as auxiliary verbs; most commonly analysed in this way are the ones belonging to the operator class, such as **must** and **have** in (17). At the general level, **auxiliary verb** may be defined as applying to a syntactically distinct verb class whose members have the following properties: (α) They express meanings or mark grammatical categories of the kind that are often expressed/marked by inflections – e.g. tense, mood, aspect, voice. (β) They function as dependent to the verb they enter into construction with. Analysing *must* in (17ii) as an auxiliary, for example, would imply that it is dependent and *leave* head: *must leave* would then be a constituent (belonging to a class intermediate in the hierarchical structure between verb and VP). There has been a good deal of debate on the issue of whether a well-motivated distinction can be drawn in English between auxiliaries and catenatives; the view taken here is that it cannot, and that we have no class satisfying the general definition of auxiliary verb.

Adjuncts usually have the form of AdvPs, PPs or subordinate clauses but, as noted above, certain kinds (e.g. adjuncts of time) can also take the form of NPs. Thus in *We arrive there this evening* the NP *this evening* has the same function as the PP *at midnight* in (18iv).

Adjuncts are less tightly integrated into the structure of the clause than are complements: their occurrence is less governed by grammatical rule. They are always optional and their selection does not depend on the presence of a verb of a particular subclass (these are the criteria we used to distinguish them from complements); nor can we give grammatical rules excluding particular combinations of different kinds of adjunct or imposing a maximum number of adjuncts for any clause: restrictions of these kinds will depend on considerations of style, comprehensibility and semantic coherence. And indeed the distinction between the kinds of adjunct illustrated in (18) is to a significant extent semantic rather than strictly syntactic. All this is not to suggest that the grammar will have nothing to say about adjuncts: there are grammatical rules concerning some aspects of their position in the linear order of the clause and of their internal form (e.g. the properties of subordinate clause adjuncts).

The boundary between adjuncts and complements is by no means sharply drawn: the manner and instrument categories, for example, lie in the rather fuzzy borderline area. And there are some subcategories, such as place and time as mentioned earlier, that apply to both complements and adjuncts. Thus in *The meeting was this morning* the time element *this morning* is a complement (by virtue of its non-omissibility), whereas in *Ed was absolutely furious this morning* it is an adjunct.

9. Constituent structure

So far we have been working with two layers of structure above the verb: the VP and the clause. Within the clause, we take the VP to be head (predicate). There are two reasons for this. In the first place, the form of the VP plays a major role in determining properties of the clause as a whole: kernel clauses, for example, require a VP with a tensed verb; present- and past-participial clauses, which occupy a distinctive range of positions in larger constructions, are so classified by virtue of the form of their verb; and *to*-infinitivals are likewise marked as such in the structure of the VP. Secondly, the possibility of having a clause rather than an NP as subject depends on the lexical selection made in the VP, usually in the verb. Thus just as there are verbs such as ***believe***, ***know***, ***regret***, which allow a clause as object (*I believe that Kim was guilty*), so there are verbs such as ***annoy***, ***dismay***, ***surprise***, which allow a clause as subject (*That Kim was guilty surprised us all*). I say that it is 'usually' a matter of verb selection because in the copulative construction it depends rather on the predicative (compare *That Kim was guilty was obvious/*weak*),[8] but in either case choice of a clausal subject depends on the

---

[8] This indicates that the predicator + predicative construction is far from a prototypical instance of the head + dependent construction.

presence of an appropriate lexical item within the VP, the head element. As a dependent, the subject belongs to the complement category: in tensed clauses it is obligatory and, as we have just seen, the type of subject allowed depends on lexical selection within the head.

Subject and object are thus both complements, but at different levels in the constituent hierarchy. One major reason for recognising the VP as a constituent (instead of analysing a clause like *I know him* immediately into subject + predicator + object) is that there are various processes that apply to reduce it by ellipsis or substitution. Thus in [*She can speak Dutch but*] *I can't* the predicate is reduced by ellipsis to *can't* (= "can't speak Dutch") and in [*They told him to take a rope but I don't know*] *whether he did so*, it is reduced by substitution to *did so* (= "took a rope", or "did take a rope"): the short forms take the place of a fuller predicate. A second point is that there are various non-finite constructions where no subject is allowed: [*She began*] *to like him*, [*The money*] *belonging to the victim* [*was never returned*], and so on. Such factors lend support, therefore, to the traditional analysis whereby a (kernel) clause is first divided into a subject and a predicate.

We have been more or less tacitly assuming up to this point that adjuncts belong within the predicate – so that the immediate constituents of, say, *I saw her yesterday* will be *I* + *saw her yesterday*. But such an analysis is surely not plausible for all adjuncts: it is, for example, very counterintuitive to say that the immediate constituents of *I saw her, however* are *I* + *saw her, however*. One would want, rather, to divide it into *I saw her* + *however*, with *however* entering into construction with *I saw her* as a whole.

Within the very broad category of adjuncts we will therefore draw a distinction (though again with some fuzziness at the boundary) between **modifiers** and **peripheral dependents**. Modifiers differ from peripheral dependents in that they share with the most central kinds of complement (including the subject) the ability to be brought into contrastive focus by various means, such as the cleft construction – compare

(19)	Thematically unmarked		Cleft
i	*Liz wrote it*	v	*It was Liz who wrote it*
ii	*She wrote the foreword*	vi	*It was the foreword that she wrote*
iii	*She wrote it in France*	vii	*It was in France that she wrote it*
iv	*She wrote it, however*	viii	**It was however that she wrote it*

Thus we can focus the subject *Liz*, the object *the foreword*, the modifier *in France*, but not the peripheral dependent *however*. Just as some categories apply to both complements and adjuncts, so do some apply to both modifiers and peripheral dependents. Thus in *He had gone home early because he felt unwell* (interpreted as giving the reason for his going home early) the reason adjunct is a modifier, but in *He had gone home early, because his light was off* (interpreted as giving the reason why I infer that he had gone home early) it is a peripheral dependent. The first can be cleft (*It was because he felt unwell that he had gone home early*) but the second cannot, under the interpretation given.

Modifiers we will assign to the predicate constituent, the VP, whereas peripheral dependents will be introduced at a higher level in the hierarchy. Thus simplified structures for (19iii) and (iv) are as follows:

(20) i   ii

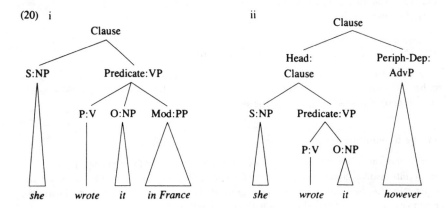

We accordingly allow one clause to function as head within a larger clause – and it will then just be 'minimal clauses' (those which do not have a smaller clause as head) that have a subject + predicate structure.

EXERCISES

I. The subject in non-kernel clauses

Give the unmarked counterpart of each of the following and then determine whether or not the syntactic process deriving the non-kernel construction changes the subject. The unmarked counterpart is in all of these examples a kernel clause, so that its subject will be easily identifiable by reference to the subject properties given in this chapter; use these same properties to identify the subject of the non-kernel clause and hence to determine whether or not it is the same as that of the corresponding kernel clause. In (21), for example, the unmarked counterpart is declarative *Kim wrote the letter herself*, where *Kim* is subject; *Kim* is also subject of (21) and hence the process forming closed interrogatives is not one that changes the subject (though it does change its position).

(21) *Did Kim write the letter herself?*	Closed interrogative
(22) [*The man*] *who came to dinner* [*stole the silver*]	Subordinate: relative
(23) [*The cup*] *that he gave me* [*was cracked*]	Subordinate: relative
(24) *The minister was driven to the station by Liz*	Passive (voice)
(25) *It is a mystery why she puts up with him*	Extrapositioned
(26) *There was only one student present*	Existential construction
(27) *Some of them it completely destroyed*	Marked by thematic fronting

(Answers for (24)–(27) can be checked against the discussion of thematic systems in Ch. 12.)

II. Objects and predicatives

Is the unbracketed expression in the following examples an object or a predicative?

(28) [*That sounds*] *a great idea*
(29) [*The guard sounded*] *the alarm*

(30) [*The inspector looked*] them [*up on his return*]
(31) [*They look*] *decent enough people*
(32) [*She made*] *a first-rate treasurer*
(33) [*She taught*] herself [*Greek*]

III. The ditransitive and complex-transitive constructions

They made him a colonel and *He called her a nurse* are both ambiguous, being analysable as either ditransitive or complex-transitive clauses. Explain the ambiguity, specifying which meaning correlates with which syntactic structure.

IV. Verb complementation

For each of the following verbs, say which of the five patterns of complementation set out in §6 (intransitive, copulative, monotransitive, complex-transitive and ditransitive) it can enter into: **ask, buy, call, elect, find, give, grow, make, run, smile, wish**. Provide illustrative examples consisting of kernel clauses with no adjuncts.

V. Particles and prepositions

Is the unbracketed word in the following examples a particle (forming a complement of the verb on its own) or a preposition (head of a PP in which the following NP is complement)?

(34) [*She looked*] up [*all the references*]
(35) [*He ruled*] out [*any compromise*]
(36) [*It depends*] on [*the time of day*]
(37) [*I didn't take*] in [*the significance of what had happened*]
(38) [*They came*] across [*the meadow*]
(39) [*They came*] across [*a few problems*]

VI. Clause analysis

The following kernel clauses are analysed into their constituents: identify the function of each, selecting from the set S, P, PC^s, PC^o, O^c, O^d, 'C^x' (any other complement), 'A' (adjunct).

(40) *Tom | submits | his tax-return | on time | every year*
(41) *Kim's remark | made | Max | extremely unhappy*
(42) *Everyone | seemed | extraordinarily self-confident | at the time*
(43) *She | remained | an agnostic | all her life*
(44) *They | live | very comfortably | on the income from their shares*
(45) *He | found | it | easy*
(46) *He | found | it | easily*
(47) *They | ordered | all of us | out of the room*
(48) *He | persuaded | them | of his innocence*
(49) *We | sold | them | most of the furniture*
(50) *She | put | up | with his drunkenness | for fifteen years*

5

Tense, aspect and modality

This chapter will be primarily concerned with the semantics of the tense inflections and of certain aspectual and modal catenatives; in addition we will consider, in the light of this semantic discussion and of what has already been said about the grammar, the nature of tense, aspect and mood/modality as general linguistic categories.

1. Tense

We begin with the inflectional category of tense, examining in turn the various uses of the present and past tenses in English.

1.1 Present tense

The following uses of the present tense may be distinguished:

(a) Present time situations

(1)   i   *Kim lives in Berlin*
       ii   *Kim plays defensively forward*
       iii *Kim washes her hair with Zoom shampoo*

The primary use of the present tense is to locate the situation in present time – where 'situation' is to be understood as a general term covering states, actions, processes or whatever is described in the clause, and present time is the time of the utterance. Situations can be classified as either **static** (states of affairs, relations, etc.) or **dynamic** (actions, processes, events, etc.). Static situations will be understood to extend beyond the moment of utterance: Kim's living in Berlin, for example, has much greater duration than an utterance of (1i). Dynamic situations are by contrast understood to be effectively simultaneous with the utterance: (ii), for example, might be used in a running commentary on a cricket match. Notice, however, that (ii) can be interpreted in two ways: as involving either a single instance of playing forward or else repeated, habitual instances (e.g. in response to *What do they do when they get a good length ball?*). In the single instance interpretation we have a dynamic situation, whereas repeatedly playing defensively forward is to be understood as a static situation, a state of affairs characterised by the repeated or habitual behaviour – and again this state of affairs extends beyond the time of utterance, just like the more obviously static situation in (i). Much the more salient interpretation of (iii) is of this habitual kind: a situation where Kim habitually washes her hair with Zoom shampoo and hence one extending beyond the time of utterance. The dynamic, single event reading is less salient because of the difficulty of seeing such an event as virtually simultaneous with the utterance. (It is not altogether excluded, however, and one could perhaps imagine the sentence being so used in a demonstration on a TV commercial for Zoom shampoo.) Thus the use of the present tense for dynamic situations is fairly restricted: it is found mainly in running commentaries, demonstrations (e.g. *I add a pinch of salt* in a cookery demonstration) and for certain kinds of act performed precisely by virtue of uttering a sentence that describes the act (*I promise to be back before six*).

(b) Present time schedules of future situations

(2)   *The match starts tomorrow*

Here we have dynamic situations which are in future time, not present time. There is nevertheless a present time element in the meaning, in that we are concerned with what is presently arranged or 'scheduled' (I use the term in an extended sense, to cover natural events, as in *The sun sets at 6.40 tonight*). This is why (2) is much more likely than, say, *Tom has a heart attack tomorrow*: we don't so readily envisage a heart attack being arranged in advance.

(c) Futurity in subordinate clauses

(3)   [*I want to finish before*] *John gets up*

In certain types of subordinate clause we find a present tense verb for a future situation. This use of the present tense occurs most often after such temporal expressions as *after*, *before*, *until*, and conditional expressions like *if*, *unless*, *provided*. It is thus a non-kernel use: the temporal interpretation of *John gets up* in (3) is different from the one it has when it stands alone as a sentence. These temporal and conditional prepositions do not always induce a future interpretation: it depends on the larger context; compare (3), for example, with *I always leave before John gets up*.

1.2 Past tense

The past tense has the following uses:

(a) Past time situations

(4)   i   *Kim lived in Berlin*

ii *Kim played defensively forward*
iii *Kim washed her hair with Zoom shampoo*

These are the past tense counterparts of (1) and the past tense serves straight-forwardly to locate the situation in past time. Static situations may again extend beyond the time at which they are said to obtain, so that it does not necessarily follow from (4i) that Kim no longer lives in Berlin. Dynamic situations will be wholly in the past – but the past can accommodate longer situations than the present, so that for (4iii), in contrast to (1iii), the single hair wash (dynamic) inter-pretation is at least as salient as the habitual reading (static).

(b) Past time schedule of future situations. The past tense counterpart of (2) is *The match started tomorrow.* There is no change in the time of the starting: what has changed is the time at which the arrangement/schedule is said to hold. Thus a context might be: *At that stage the match started tomorrow, but yesterday they de-cided to postpone it till next week.* This use of the past tense is vastly less frequent than the corresponding use of the present tense. *The match starts on Tuesday* does not allow an interpretation where the event is simultaneous with the time of utterance and hence is readily available for the scheduled future use; *The match started on Tuesday*, by contrast, easily sustains the single event in the past read-ing: for the past schedule meaning one would therefore generally choose a more explicit means of expression, such as *The match was going/due/scheduled to start on Tuesday*.

(c) Factual remoteness. Compare now

(5) i   *If Ed came tomorrow, we could play bridge*
     ii *If her parents were still alive, they would be over eighty*
(6) i   *If Ed comes tomorrow, we can play bridge*
     ii *If her parents are still alive, they will be over eighty*

The subordinate clauses in (6) have present tense verbs; in (i) the time is future, in (ii) present. In (5) we have past tense verbs but the times of Ed's coming and her parents' being alive are still future and present respectively. The tense difference thus signals a difference not in time, but in the speaker's assessment of the likeli-hood of the condition's being fulfilled: the past tense presents it as a relatively re-mote possibility, the present tense as an open possibility. ((5ii) would most often be used when her parents were known or assumed not to be still alive, but it is not restricted to such contexts.) (5) and (6) contrast as **unreal** vs **real** conditional con-structions. An unreal conditional has a past tense in the subordinate clause with this factual remoteness meaning and a modal operator (also in the past tense if it has one) in the main clause. A past tense in the subordinate clause of a real con-dition, by contrast, will serve to locate the state or event in past time in the usual way: *If Ed was at yesterday's meeting, he will have seen her.*

The factual remoteness meaning of the past tense is not restricted to unreal conditional constructions. It is also found in subordinate clauses after *wish* or *it be* time (*I wish/It is time they were here*). In main clauses it occurs only with modal operators. The difference between *He'll be about seventy now* and *He'd be about seventy now*, for example, as responses to *How old do you think he is?*, is that the latter is less assured, more 'hedged', than the former.

(d) Backshifting. Suppose Ed on some occasion utters the sentence *Jill has three children*: I can subsequently report this event in a variety of ways, including

(7)   i   *Ed said that Jill had three children*   Backshifted
      ii *Ed said that Jill has three children*   Non-backshifted

These illustrate what is known as **indirect reported speech**, indirect in that one purports to give only the content expressed, not the actual words used (contrast the direct reported speech in *Ed said: 'Jill has three children'*).

In (i) we have a past tense (*had*) instead of the original present tense (*has*): this shift from present tense to past tense is known as **backshifting**. In (ii), by contrast, there is no backshifting. The difference is then that in (i) the state of Jill's having three children is temporally related to a point in the past, the time of Ed's utterance, whereas in (ii) it is temporally related to a point in the present, the time of my (the reporter's) utterance. The backshifted construction is the more neutral or faithful report, for in Ed's original utterance he was clearly locating Jill's having three children in relation to the time of his own utterance, not my report of it. In using the non-backshifted construction I imply that the change of reference point makes no difference to the validity or significance of what was said: if it was known, for example, that between the time of Ed's utterance and the time of my report Jill or one of her children had died, then it would be out of place for me to use (ii). Similarly, if Ed's utterance has been *I have to leave in a couple of minutes* then unless my report were given immediately I'd have to use backshifting: *Ed said that he had to leave in a couple of minutes*.

The term 'indirect reported speech' is actually too narrow, for backshifting occurs equally in the report of feelings, beliefs, knowledge, etc. It applies, we should also note, to all three of the uses of the present tense outlined above – cf. *I thought Kim lived in Berlin*, *He didn't know the match started tomorrow*, *He wanted to finish before John got up*; in the latter John's getting up is future relative to the time in the past associated with the wanting. Backshifting can be triggered, moreover, by a superordinate past tense expressing factual remoteness: *If I thought it was possible* [*I'd give it a try*].

Backshifting represents a non-kernel use of the past tense. Notice, for example, that in *I knew you'd understand*, the clause *you'd understand* is interpreted quite differently than when it occurs on its own as a sentence.

1.3 Tense as a general term

It will be evident from what has been said that we must distinguish clearly between the grammatical category of TENSE and the semantic category of TIME – and the fairly complex relation between them again shows the importance of distinguishing between language-particular and general definitions. It would clearly be wrong-headed to define the past and present tenses in English as forms used to express past and present time respectively: at the language-particular level they are defined by their place in the verbal paradigm. These forms are then labelled with the general terms past and present tense on the basis of their primary use. We will say that a language has tense if it has a set of systematically contrasting verb inflections (or comparable analytically differentiated classes), where the primary semantic function of the terms is to relate the time of the situation to the time of utterance. Tense thus involves the grammaticalisation of time relations, in the sense of 'grammaticalisation' explained in 1.1 – it is a grammatical category with time relations as its semantic basis.

2. Aspect

2.1 Aspect as a general term

It is unfortunate that the terminological distinction between tense and time has no well-established analogue in the domain of aspect: the one term 'aspect' is widely used both for a grammatical category of the verb and for the type of meaning characteristically expressed by that category. To avoid possible confusion I will not henceforth use the term on its own, but will speak instead of 'grammatical aspect' on the one hand and 'semantic aspect' or 'aspectual meaning' on the other.

There are quite a number of items in English that express aspectual meanings. The majority are catenative verbs: **begin** (*He began looking/to look for it*), **commence**, **start**; **cease**, **finish**, **stop** (*She stopped talking to me*); **continue**, **keep** (*They kept interrupting him*), **be** (*She was resting*); **use** (*I used to like it*: it occurs with the relevant sense only in the past tense); **have** (*You have read it*), and so on. We should also mention the adjective *about* (*The plane is about to land*) and a few idioms: **carry on**, **keep on**, **be going** (*It's going to rain*), *on the point of*, and so on. Aspectual meaning involves not the temporal location of the situation, but rather its temporal flow or segmentation. With **begin** and **stop**, for example, we focus on the initial and final segments; with **keep** the situation is presented as ongoing, usually with repetition (*They kept interrupting him* implies repeated interruptions); with *about* and **be going** (whose meanings fall towards the boundary between the aspectual and temporal location categories) the situation is in prospect; and so on.

Strictly speaking, English does not have grammatical aspect. We will say that a language has grammatical aspect if it has a system of the verb, marked inflectionally or by such analytic devices as auxiliaries, where the primary semantic contrast between the terms is a matter of aspectual meaning. English clearly does not have aspectual inflections and the expressions with aspectual meaning illustrated in the last paragraph are not auxiliary verbs. We can talk of aspectual verbs, i.e. verbs with aspectual meaning, but they do not form a grammatically distinct class and are not dependents of the verbs with which they enter into construction.

As far as English is concerned, then, aspectual meanings are lexicalised (expressed by various lexical items) rather than grammaticalised (expressed by grammatically distinctive dependents or inflections) – and this is reflected in the fact that there are a comparatively large number of aspectual verbs and other expressions.[1]

There is not space here for a comprehensive treatment of these aspectual expressions: instead we will focus on the two most frequent (and difficult) ones, 'progressive' *be* and 'perfect' ***have***.

2.2 Progressive *be*

In its aspectual use, catenative *be* takes a present-participial complement, such as *writing a letter* in *She is writing a letter*. We will investigate its meaning by examining the contrast between the progressive construction, marked by *be* + following present participle, and its non-progressive counterpart – for example

(8)   i   *It was raining*   Progressive
      ii   *It rained*   Non-progressive

(ii) is the non-progressive counterpart of (i) in that they differ only with respect to the presence or absence of *be* + present participle inflection: the inflectional property carried by *be* in (i) – in this case, past tense – is carried by ***rain*** in (ii). For purposes of comparison I will use the term 'situation' in such a way as to exclude the *be* itself, so that in (8) we are in both examples concerned with the situation of its raining: the difference between (i) and (ii) is then a matter of the semantic aspect in which the situation is presented.

Progressive *be* is so called because its basic meaning is that it presents the situation as being 'in progress'. This implies that it is conceived of as taking place, thus as having a more or less dynamic character, rather than being wholly static. The situation is viewed not in its temporal totality, but at some point or period within it. The non-progressive can be used for both static and dynamic situations; in the latter case the situation is, by contrast, presented in its totality.

(ii) above provides an elementary example of the contrast. ***Rain*** denotes a dynamic situation and (ii) accordingly presents it in its totality, as an event; (i), on the other hand, presents it as in progress at some intermediate point or period (as in *It was raining when I woke up*).

Certain more specific contrasts of meaning arise through the interaction of the above basic meaning and the meaning of the following verb and its complements. Consider, for example, progressive *Kim was opening the parcel* vs non-progressive *Kim opened the parcel*. Whereas (8i) entails (ii), there is no such entailment here. Some expressions, such as ***open the parcel*** as opposed to ***rain***, can be used for situations involving some inherent completion point: there is a point at which the opening of a parcel is complete and you cannot go on opening it beyond that

---

[1] As noted in 4.7, many grammars analyse the operators (other than *be* and ***have*** in their non-catenative uses) as auxiliary verbs: in such an analysis English will have aspect as a grammatical category.

point – whereas there is no point beyond which it cannot go on raining. Where the situation has such an inherent completion point, the progressive indicates, then, that it is presented not just as being in progress but as being incomplete.

A different type of special case is illustrated in *Kim is living in Berlin* vs *Kim lives in Berlin*. The progressive here suggests a situation of limited duration, something relatively temporary. Unlike *rain* or *open the parcel*, *live in Berlin* denotes a basically static situation and would thus most neutrally occur in the non-progressive. Use of the progressive requires a dynamic interpretation and this is achieved by viewing the situation as impermanent, as progressing towards its end.

Our discussion of tense in §1 above focused on the non-progressive. We noted that (in the non-progressive) the present tense is less readily used for dynamic situations located in present time than the past tense is for such situations located in past time: with the present tense the dynamic situation has to be short enough to be effectively simultaneous with the utterance. In the progressive, however, there is no such limitation on the use of the present tense: we are here concerned not with the totality of the situation but with some intermediate point or period and it is simply this intermediate point or period that has to be simultaneous with the time of utterance. Thus progressive

(9)   *Kim is washing her hair with Zoom shampoo*

lends itself much more easily than (1iii) above to an interpretation involving a single act of hair-washing rather than repeated acts. It will nevertheless be clear from what has been said that it would be a mistake to analyse the semantic difference between progressive and non-progressive as, say, "single occurrence" vs "habitual". Both (9) and (1iii) allow either single occurrence or habitual readings: this is not a distinction that is expressed by the presence or absence of *be*. For (1iii) we suggested that the single occurrence reading might occur in a commercial demonstration; for (9) the habitual reading would carry an implication of temporariness – Kim might be temporarily using Zoom while her regular shampoo is unobtainable for one reason or another.

Where present or past schedules of subsequent events are involved, as in *Kim is leaving for Sydney tomorrow* vs *Kim leaves for Sydney tomorrow*, the difference in meaning is rather elusive and hardly predictable from the basic meaning of progressive *be* given above; the progressive here seems to allow for a greater element of intention or choice on Kim's part.

Finally we should note that certain verbs denoting clearly static situations are virtually excluded from heading the complement of progressive *be*: *belong*, *consist*, *contain* (as in *contain two pints* as opposed to *contain the enemy*), *possess*, etc. Thus while *It belongs to me* is perfectly natural, *It is belonging to me* is not, and so on.

2.3 Perfect *have*

The verb *have* enters into a variety of catenative constructions: *She had written the report*, *She had to write the report*, *She had her son write the report*, *She had her son writing the report, She had the report written by her son.* We shall be concerned here with just the first of these – that where it has a single complement with the form of a (subjectless) past-participial clause. We will refer to this as the perfect construction, contrasting it with its non-perfect counterpart, differing from it by the absence of **have** and the associated past participle inflection. Thus the non-perfect counterparts of *She had written the report* (with past tense **have**) and *She has written the report* (present tense) are respectively *She wrote the report* and *She writes the report*. Again we will apply the term 'situation' to what is left of the meaning when we abstract away the **have** and the tense – so that the situation in all four of these examples is that of her writing the report.

We need to distinguish two cases of the perfect construction: the 'present perfect', where **have** carries a present tense inflection (*has gone*, [*They*] *have gone*, etc.) and the 'non-present perfect', where **have** either carries the past tense inflection or else is non-tensed (*had gone, to have gone, may have gone, having gone,* etc.).

(a) The present perfect. Like the past tense (in its primary use), the present perfect locates the situation in past time – compare

(10) i   *Kim is ill*   Present non-perfect
      ii   *Kim was ill*   Past non-perfect
      iii *Kim has been ill*   Present perfect

The difference is that the past non-perfect involves a point or period in the past that is exclusive of the present, whereas the present perfect involves a period that is inclusive of the present as well as the past. This is why certain types of temporal expression cannot occur with one or other of them. *Yesterday, last week, three weeks ago* and the like indicate times that are entirely in the past and are hence incompatible with the present perfect: we can have *I arrived here last week* but not **I have arrived here last week*. Conversely, *at present, as yet, so far, since last week* occur with the present perfect but not the past non-perfect: *At present I have written four chapters*, not **At present I wrote four chapters*.

Because the present perfect involves a past inclusive of the present it is well suited to situations beginning in the past and lasting through to the present: *Kim has lived in Sydney since 1975*. Here the situation of Kim's living in Sydney covers the period from 1975 to the present. But it is not of course restricted to such cases, for the present time may be involved in other ways. In *I have lost my key*, for example, the losing took place in the past but the sentence would typically be used when I still don't know where the key is and where the significance of the past event is for the present state of affairs resulting from it. An example like *The New Zealand dollar has been devalued by 20%* might be used in a news bulletin: the present perfect is often used for past events related to the present by their recency and current news value. With *Have you read 'Middlemarch'?* I would typically be concerned not with some specific occasion (contrast *Did you read 'Middlemarch'?*) but simply with whether the event has taken place at any time in the period extending up to the present. In all these examples, the choice of a time period inclusive of the present implies that the situation has some kind of relevance to the present – that it has what is commonly called 'current relevance'.

(b) The non-present perfect. Here the distinction between an inclusive and an exclusive past is 'neutralised' – i.e. the non-present perfect can be used for either. Let us consider first the case where *have* is non-tensed – for example, a base form following a modal operator:

(11) i   *Kim may have been here yesterday*
     ii *Kim may have been here since yesterday*

(i) corresponds to *Maybe Kim was here yesterday*, with past non-perfect *was* necessitated by *yesterday*, while (ii) corresponds to *Maybe Kim has been here since yesterday*, with *since yesterday* indicating a period beginning in the past and stretching through to the present and thus requiring the present perfect *has been*. The contrast between *was* and *has been* is lost in *have been*.

Or take, secondly, the case where *have* carries the past tense inflection:

(12) i   *He had written only one paragraph the previous day*
     ii *He had written only one paragraph so far*

Here we have a double dose of pastness, one expressed by the past tense inflection, one by catenative *have*: the writing is not simply past in relation to the time of utterance, it is past in relation to some contextually given time that is itself past in relation to the time of utterance. Suppose, for example, we have a context where we have been talking about last Tuesday: the writing is then past relative to last Tuesday. In (i) the more distant past is exclusive of the less distant one: Monday is exclusive of Tuesday. In (ii) we have a period beginning in the past relative to last Tuesday but stretching through to include it: the issue is how much he had written in the period up to and including last Tuesday. If the immediate reference point were not last Tuesday but the time of utterance, we would have respectively *He wrote only one paragraph yesterday* and *He has written only one paragraph so far*: again the contrast between past non-perfect and present perfect is lost when the reference point is moved into the past.

The general term 'perfect' is an aspectual label – and like 'aspect' itself is commonly applied to both a grammatical category and a type of aspectual meaning. Perfect aspectual meaning involves a situation resulting from the completion of an earlier situation, and perfect as a grammatical category applies to one with this as its characteristic meaning. Completeness is closely related to pastness and hence perfect aspect is semantically similar to past tense: the difference is that with perfect aspect the emphasis is on the current or resultant state, while with past tense it is on the past situation itself. The meaning of the English *have* + past participle construction is not a prototypical instance of perfect aspectual meaning, but in case (a) – where *have* is in the present tense – we do find that the past situation is presented as crucially connected with the present: it is for this reason that we apply the term 'perfect' in English. It should also be added that perfect

have is among the two or three catenative verbs that come closest to qualifying as auxiliaries (in the sense explained in Ch. 4, fn. 7).

One final point we should make about perfect ***have*** is that it cannot head the complement of various other aspectual verbs, such as ***begin***, ***stop***, progressive ***be***, etc. Thus we cannot reverse the direction of dependency in *has begun/stopped/ been reading the report* to give **He began/stopped/was having read the report*.

3. Modality

3.1 The modal operators

What we are calling the 'modal' operators – ***can***, ***may***, ***must***, ***will***, etc. – are used to convey a considerable range and variety of meanings; in the space available here we can do no more than illustrate some of the main types, but this will suffice to provide a basis for our discussion in the next subsection of the general semantic category of modality and the associated grammatical category of mood. We will group the uses under three headings:

(a) Epistemic uses

(13) i   *He may be ill*
    ii   *He must be a friend of hers*
    iii *He will have finished by now*

The non-modal counterparts are respectively *He is ill, He is a friend of hers, He has finished by now*. If I use the modal versions rather than the latter, the reason would typically be that I do not have the (immediate) knowledge that would jus- tify my asserting the non-modal ones. 'Epistemic' derives from the Greek word meaning "knowledge": these uses are thus called epistemic because they involve implications concerning the speaker's knowledge of the situation in question. In (i) I don't know that he's ill but there is a possibility that he is; in (ii) his being a friend of hers is not something I have stored in my mind as a piece of knowledge but something I present as a necessary conclusion from what I do have more direct knowledge of; in (iii) I am not able to assert from direct observation that he has finished but I predict that when we are in a position to know one way or the other it will be confirmed that he has.

(b) Deontic uses

(14) i   *You can/may have another apple*
    ii   *He must be in bed before 8 o'clock*
    iii *You shall have your money back*

'Deontic' derives from the Greek for "binding": in these uses we are concerned with obligation, prohibition, permission and the like. Thus (i) would most typi- cally be used to give you permission to have another apple and (ii) to impose an obligation on him to be in bed before 8 o'clock (or on someone else to ensure that he is), while with (iii) I would in effect bind myself, put myself under an obligation, to see that you have your money back.

(c) Subject-oriented uses

(15) i   *Liz can run faster than her brother*
    ii *Liz wouldn't lend me the money [so I borrowed it from Ed]*

These are 'subject-oriented' in that they involve some property, disposition or the like on the part of whoever or whatever is referred to by the subject: in (i) we are concerned with Liz's physical capabilities, in (ii) with her willingness.

Lots of sentences, taken out of context, allow more than one interpretation. *He must be very tactful*, for instance, can be interpreted epistemically, "I conclude that he is very tactful", or deontically, "It is necessary that he be very tactful". The examples given in (13)–(15), moreover, are intended as prototypical illustrations of the three categories of use: not all examples fall so easily into one or other of the categories. They will nevertheless serve to give some idea of the meanings conveyed by the modal operators.

3.2 Modality and mood

Just as we distinguish between TENSE, a category of grammatical form, and TIME, a category of meaning, so it is important to distinguish grammatical MOOD from semantic MODALITY. The area of meaning termed modality contrasts with the meaning involved in an assured factual assertion. Of the uses outlined in the last subsection the epistemic and deontic are those that fall within this area – we accordingly speak of epistemic modality and deontic modality. To return to the earlier examples, the non-modal *He is ill, He is a friend of hers, He has finished by now* would characteristically be used to make assured factual assertions, whereas (13i–iii) all involve some qualification; the qualification is of course much greater in (i) than in the others, but (ii) and (iii) are still clearly less assured than their non-modal counterparts. Similarly we may compare (14i–iii) with *You have an apple there, He is in bed now, You have your money back now*: these again would characteristically be used for assured factual assertions, whereas (14i–iii) would typically be used for permitting, directing, undertaking rather than for asserting facts. Cutting across the dimension contrasting epistemic modality and deontic modality (and various other types too) is another dimension where we contrast the modality of possibility, as in (13i), (14i), the modality of necessity, (13ii), (14ii), and so on.

Modality is expressed by a variety of linguistic devices, lexical, grammatical and prosodic. There are a considerable number of lexical items with modal meanings. They include most of the operators: *may, must, can, will, shall, should, ought, need*, and also *be* and *have* in some of their uses, as in *You are to be back by six, If they were to try again [they would be in trouble], You'll have to work harder.* There are also non-operator catenatives with modal uses: *allow, permit, oblige*, etc. (cf. *You aren't allowed to do that*) – and *need* and *have* have modal meanings whether they behave as operators or not. In addition we find modal adjectives, such as *possible, likely, probable, certain, sure, necessary,* and modal adverbs, such as *perhaps, maybe, possibly* and other derivatives from the adjectives. Turning to grammar, the interrogative and imperative constructions have modal meanings – assured factual assertions are normally in declarative form. And the use of the past tense for factual remoteness, as in (5) above, clearly involves modal meaning. Prosodic expression of modality is illustrated, for example, in rising intonation overlaid on a declarative: with such intonation, *He is ill,* say, will be interpreted as a question rather than an assured factual assertion.

Mood involves the grammaticalisation of modality. More specifically, mood applies to a system of the verb, marked inflectionally or analytically (by auxiliaries, say), where just one term, the most elementary, is characteristically used in making assured factual assertions, while the other terms, by contrast, are characteristically used to express various kinds of modality. Again, then, English does not have mood as a grammatical category: the modal operators *may, can, must,* etc., are catenatives rather than auxiliaries, the contrast between declarative, interrogative and imperative is a system of the clause rather than the verb, and although the semantic difference between *if Ed came tomorrow* and *if Ed comes tomorrow* is a matter of modality this is not the primary or characteristic use of the verbal contrast between *came* and *comes* – on the basis of the primary use we have taken this contrast to be one of tense, not mood.[2]

3.3 Modality in relation to time and tense

There are just two tenses in English, past and present: unlike such languages as French and Latin, English has no future tense. That is to say that there is no verbal category in English whose primary use is to locate in future time the situation described in the clause.

Futurity is of course very often indicated by means of *will*[3] – compare

(16) i   *He saw her every Friday*
   ii   *He sees her every Friday*
   iii *He will see her every Friday*

The *will* construction, however, does not satisfy the conditions for analysis as a

---

[2] The account of verb inflection presented in this book is simplified in that it considers only the *was* variant in examples like *If her father was/were still alive, he would be over eighty.* Speakers who use *were* in this construction (and similarly after *wish*) make some formal distinction between past time and factual remoteness and can be regarded as having a residual mood distinction in the verb. Thus [*He*] *is* [*ill*] and [*He*] *was* [*ill*] will contrast in tense, [*if he*] *is* [*alive*] and [*if he*] *were* [*alive*] in mood. Traditional grammars of English have a fully fledged mood system interacting with tense to give: past indicative ([*He*] *took* [*it*]), present indicative ([*He*] *takes* [*it*]), past subjunctive ([*if he*] *took* [*it now,* . .]), present subjunctive ([*I insist that he*] *take* [*it*]), present imperative (*Take* [*it*]); such an analysis, however, involves a great deal more syncretism than can be justified for Modern English.

[3] Or, under much more restrictive conditions (e.g. with 1st person subjects), *shall:* I will discuss the issue in relation to the more general case of *will,* but the essence of the argument applies equally to *shall.* In traditional grammar, *shall take* and *will take* are analysed as future tense forms.

future tense. Grammatically *will* is a catenative, not an auxiliary – hence not the marker of a verbal category. And even if we reanalysed the catenative operators as auxiliaries, *will* would belong grammatically with *can*, *may* and *must*, which would be mood markers: like them it has no non-tensed forms and shows no person–number agreement with the subject. It enters into relations of contrast with *can*, *may* and *must*, so that we have, for example, *He may go* vs *He will go* vs *He must go*, etc., but not **He may will go*, **He will must go*, or the like. Conversely, it does not enter into such contrastive relations with the tense markers; on the contrary, the lexeme *will* always carries either the past tense inflection (*would*) or the present (*will*): the relation of *would* to *will* matches that of *could* to *can*.

From a semantic point of view *will* involves elements of both futurity and modality. In an example like *She will be in London now* the modal component is more salient: this is epistemically 'weaker' (less assured), clearly, than *She is in London now*. Nevertheless, there is also an element of futurity – relating not of course to the time of her being in London but to the time of verification: it is, as it were, a prediction. In *She will be in London next week* the futurity component is more salient, but even with future time situations there remains a modal component in *will*. As we have seen, *will* is not essential for future situations – we could also have *She is in London next week*. And the form with *will* is, at least latently, epistemically weaker than the form without it. Compare, for example, a pair like *Kim will win tomorrow's final* and *Kim wins tomorrow's final*. The former is perfectly normal but the latter is not: unless the match has been rigged, we do not have enough present knowledge to justify an epistemically unqualified assertion about the future in such cases. It is in the nature of things that the future should fall less within the domain of what is known than the present or the past, and hence there is a natural association between futurity and modality – an association reflected in the meaning of *will*. Thus *will* has semantic as well as grammatical affinities with the more obviously modal operators *may*, *can*, *must*, etc. Notice, moreover, that with the other modals too the time of the situation is very often interpreted as future – compare *It may rain* (*this afternoon*), *You can go* (*as soon as you've finished*), *You must try harder next time*, *It should be ready soon*.

There is also some association between pastness and modality inasmuch as the past is, in varying degrees, 'remote' from the present, thus not immediately accessible. This association is reflected in the use, already noted, of the past tense to indicate factual remoteness as well as past time. The modal use of the past tense is for the most part confined to subordinate clauses, but even in main clauses the past tense – provided, significantly, that it is carried by a modal operator – can have a meaning relating to modality rather than time: compare *You may/might be right* (where *might* suggests a slightly remoter possibility), *Can/Could you come earlier next time*(?) (with *could* considered more polite, again more tentative, than *can*), or our earlier *He'll be/He'd be about seventy now* (with *'d* more tentative than *'ll*). Indeed with the modal operators this modal use of the past tense is much more frequent than the past time use: the latter is quite restricted, occurring chiefly in combination with the subject-oriented uses (cf. (15ii), or *She could swim when she was six months old*, etc.).

EXERCISES

I. Future time use of the present tense

In (17)–(21) we have a future time situation but a verb in the present tense. All are grammatical but some are anomalous or unnatural in that to accept them we need to imagine some rather special context or revise our usual assumptions about the world or culture we live in: discuss the examples of this kind, suggesting contexts or assumptions that would make them acceptable.

(17) *Australia beats Sweden in the Davis Cup semi-final later this year*
(18) *Tom gives his lecture tomorrow*
(19) *The sun sets at 4.55 tomorrow*
(20) *He dies next week*
(21) *John is tall in two hours*

II. Backshifting in indirect reported speech

Imagine that Kim utters each of (22)–(27) on a certain Friday and Max reports this on the following Monday by means of a sentence beginning *Kim said that* ... Complete Max's utterance in each case by giving (α) the backshifted version and (β) the non-backshifted version. Version (α) will be perfectly acceptable in all cases, but (β) will not; which are those where version (β) would be anomalous and why?

(22) *No one will understand my theory*
(23) *I have already written three chapters of my book*
(24) *I have to slip out and get some milk*
(25) *Tom is arriving on Sunday*
(26) *I have a weak heart*
(27) *I have a headache*

III. Conditionals

The following are examples of the 'real' conditional construction: give the corresponding 'unreal' conditionals. (As there is a grammatical requirement in Modern English that the superordinate clause in the unreal conditional construction contain a modal operator, it will be necessary to add *will* in (31).)

(28) *If he finds out what you've said, he'll be furious*
(29) *If that is true, we may be able to claim compensation*
(30) *If he saw her last night, he will surely have told her the news*
(31) *If they appoint Kim, we're in for a lot of trouble*

IV. The progressive

Give the progressive counterpart of each of the following and comment on the difference in meaning between the progressive and non-progressive versions.

(32) *Kim reads 'The Times'*
(33) *Kim read 'The Times'*
(34) *[Kim has] read 'The Times'*

(35) *She always drinks tea*
(36) *I mark assignments this week-end*

V. The perfect

Give the perfect counterpart of (37) and the present perfect counterpart of (38) and in each case comment on the difference in meaning.

(37) i   *She works for IBM*
      ii   *He goes to bed early*
      iii *Kim left at six*
      iv   *[She must] write to her father*
(38) i   *She overslept this morning*
      ii   *She lived in Canberra all her life*
      iii *They found a serious mistake in the proposal*
      iv   *It was a pleasure meeting you*
      v   *The prime minister resigned*

VI. Deontic and epistemic modality

Discuss the modal interpretations of (39)–(44). Where both deontic and epistemic interpretations are possible, explain the difference in meaning between them; for those which allow only one, suggest why the other is excluded.

(39) *He must work faster than the other candidates*
(40) *She must have finished by now*
(41) *He may have told her about it when he saw her in Sydney*
(42) *You may not see her again*
(43) *It needn't have been John who did it*
(44) *You needn't answer if you don't want to*
(45) *He should get his hair cut*
(46) *It will have been destroyed before the new government took office last week*

6

Nouns and noun phrases

1. Nouns

The general term 'noun' is applied to a grammatically distinct word class in a language having the following properties:

(a) It contains amongst its most central members those words that denote persons or concrete objects.

(b) Its members head phrases – noun phrases – which characteristically function as subject or object in clause structure and refer to the participants in the situation described in the clause, to the actor, patient, recipient, and so on.

(c) It is the class to which the categories of number, gender and case have their primary application in languages which have these grammatical categories. The 'primary' application of these categories is to be distinguished from their 'secondary' application, as when they are attributable to a rule of agreement. Number in English, for example, applies both to nouns and (in combination with person) to verbs, so that we may contrast, say, *The dog bites* and *The dogs bite*. But it applies here primarily to *dog* and secondarily to *bite* because the verb takes its (person–) number property from the subject – and the reason we put it this way rather than the other way round is that the semantic distinction is a matter of how many dogs are involved, not how many acts of biting. This third property is less important than the first two as it is not necessary for a language to have number, gender or case as inflectionally or analytically marked categories in order for it to have a class of nouns; nevertheless, a great many languages do have one or more of them and we there find the categories applying primarily to the class which by properties (a) and (b) qualifies as the noun class. As far as English is concerned, number is evidently an important category for the characterisation of nouns, whereas gender and case are not: they apply to only a very few nouns of the pronoun subclass.

84

At the English-particular level, the three most important properties of nouns, it will be recalled, concern their function, their dependents and their inflection.

(a) Function. Nouns usually occupy the head position in the structure of NPs, and the main functions of NPs are: (α) subject, object or predicative in clause structure; (β) complement in PP structure; (γ) complement in PossP structure. In addition to functioning as head of an NP, most nouns can function as dependent – as modifier of the following noun head. Thus in the NPs *student grants, the Thatcher government, a university professor* we have nouns not only in head position (*grants, government, professor*) but also in modifier position (*student, Thatcher, university*).

(b) Dependents. Nouns take a different range of dependents than other words: the most distinctive are: (α) determinatives such as *the, a, my, which, some, this, that*, etc.; (β) adjectives as pre-head modifier; (γ) restrictive relative clauses. A more detailed account of NP structure will be given in the following sections.

(c) Inflection. Prototypical nouns enter into inflectional contrasts of number, singular vs plural. The singular form is the lexical stem, while the plural is formed by a variety of morphological processes. Regular plurals are formed by suffixing: (α) /ɪz/ or /əz/ (*horses*); (β) /s/ (*cats*); or (γ) /z/ (*dogs*) – the choice among these variants is determined in the same way as for the 3rd person singular present tense ending of verbs (see 3.3). The most frequent irregular plurals are formed by vowel change: *man→men, mouse→mice*, and so on. Some plurals are syncretised with the singular: *sheep, species*, etc.

Again we will not take space to describe the irregular forms in detail. We shall distinguish four main subclasses of noun – common nouns, proper nouns, pronouns, and cardinal numerals. Common nouns form the unmarked subclass, the one about which nothing special need be said, while proper nouns and pronouns will be surveyed in §§10 and 11; cardinal numerals lie at the periphery between the noun and determinative classes and it will therefore be more convenient to leave them for consideration in the next chapter.

2. Noun phrase structure

We turn now from nouns to NPs – to phrases with a noun as head. The next eight sections will be concerned with the structure of NPs, the types of dependent found therein, and the NP systems of number, count vs mass, and definiteness.

Leaving aside elliptical structures, an NP will consist of a noun as head, alone or accompanied by one or more dependents. Some dependents precede the head, others follow: we will distinguish them as pre-head and post-head dependents. The pre-head dependents are of two main types, determiners and modifiers, and for the post-head dependents we recognise the same three types as we distinguish in clause structure – complements, modifiers and peripheral dependents:

(1) i   *those fast cars*   Detnr   Mod   Head
     ii *her belief in God*   Detnr   Head   Comp
     iii *a man with one eye*   Detnr   Head   Mod
     iv *Higgins, whom they all feared*   Head   Periph-Dep

3. Determiners

Determiners have the form of: (α) determinatives – *the, some, which*, etc. (recall that 'determiner' is here used as the name of a function, 'determinative' of a class[1]); (β) PossPs – *the dog's, your father's, the King of Spain's*, etc.; (γ) cardinal numerals: *one, two, three*, etc.; (δ) embedded NPs expressing quantification: *a dozen, two dozen, a few*, etc.

An NP may contain up to three determiners, as in *all her many virtues*. The relative order is fixed (witness **many all her virtues*, etc.) and we will therefore distinguish three determiner positions, I, II, III. We take II as basic, and define I and III by reference to II. II is the position of the definite article *the*, the indefinite article *a*, the possessives *my, your*, etc. – and all other determiners which enter only into relations of contrast, not combination, with these. *Some*, for example, belongs here because we have *the book, some book*, but not **the some book, *my some book*, and so on. Positions I and III are then filled by the items which can respectively precede and follow position II determiners. The main forms, or types of forms, to be found in the three positions are shown in (2).

(2) I   *all, both; such, what* (exclamative); *half, one-third, three-quarters*, and other fractions; *double, twice, three times*, etc.

     II   *the; a/an*; the demonstratives *this, these, that, those; my, your, the boy's, the King of England's*, and other possessives; *we, us, you; some, any, no, either, neither, another; each, enough, much, more, most, less; a few, a little; which, what* (interrogative or relative)

     III *one, two, three*, and other cardinal numerals; *(a) dozen; many, several, few, little; every*.

There are, however, very severe limitations on how forms from the three positions may combine: a comprehensive grammar will need to give detailed rules that will allow, say, *both these books* but not **both some books, her every gesture* but not **this every gesture*, and so on.

What is assigned to position I in its exclamative use because here it can precede *a*: *What a marvellous idea it was!*. In its interrogative and relative uses, however, it cannot combine with *a* (or any other item from II) and thus belongs to position II: *What (*a) book would you recommend?* (interrogative), *What (*some) money I have [is in the bank]* (relative). *Few* and *little* belong under III because they can follow *the*, demonstratives, possessives, relative *what*, etc., as in *these few correc-*

---

[1] 'Determiner' is often used as a class term, and 'determinative', a much less common term, is occasionally applied to the function.

tions, what little money I have. A few and *a little* by contrast are each single determiners, not a sequence of II (*a*) + III (*few/little*): in *a few corrections*, for example, *a* does not enter into construction with *corrections*, for it requires a singular (*a correction*, not *a corrections), and similarly it is clear that in *Show a little gratitude* the *a* goes with *little*, not *gratitude*. Similarly we must distinguish *that many corrections* (with *that many* a single determiner) vs *these many corrections* (with *these* and *many* separate determiners). Note then that some words, such as *this* and *that*, and also *the, any* and *no*, belong both to the class of determinatives and to the class of adverbs of degree: as determinatives they enter into construction with nouns (*this decision, the many drawbacks*), while as adverbs of degree they enter into construction with adjectives, adverbs or determinatives ([*He's*] *this tall, The sooner* [*he leaves, the better*], [*I haven't got*] *that much* [*money*]).

Determiners play a major role in the NP contrasts singular vs plural, count vs mass and definite vs indefinite: we will accordingly take these up now before turning to modifiers and their relationship to determiners.

4. Number

Prototypical noun lexemes, we have seen, have two inflectional forms contrasting in number: in such cases the number is selected independently of the lexeme. Elsewhere, however, there is no contrast and the number, sometimes singular, sometimes plural, is an inherent property of the lexical item, as illustrated in

(3) i   *equipment, knowledge, muck, wetness*   } Singular
    ii *news, linguistics, mathematics*

(4) i   *clothes, dregs, remains, earnings, pyjamas, scissors*   } Plural
    ii *cattle, people* ("persons"), *police* ("policemen/women")

The items in (3ii) do not look like singulars in that they end in -*s*, but clearly they are singular (cf. *This news is excellent* vs **These news are excellent*) and the -*s* is not here to be analysed as the plural suffix. Similarly, those in (4ii) do not look like plurals, but very clearly are: they are syntactically plural (cf. *These cattle are in need of attention*) even though they cannot be said to carry the plural inflection.

The category of number applies to NPs as well as to nouns. Normally the number of an NP derives from that of the noun head, so that the NPs *a shortage of paper* and *a shortage of papers*, say, will both be singular by virtue of having singular *shortage* as head. One exception to this is illustrated in

(5) i   *A lot of paper was destroyed*
    ii *A lot of papers were destroyed*

As is evident from the verb form, *a lot of paper* is singular but *a lot of papers* is plural. Thus here the number of the NP derives not from the head *lot* but from the embedded NPs *paper* and *papers* within the *of* phrase complement. *A lot* might be described as 'number-transparent' – it allows the number of the NP embedded within the *of* phrase complement to flow through, as it were, and fix that of the whole NP. (The *of* phrase may be omitted in ellipsis, as in *A lot was/ were destroyed*, but then the number of the NP *a lot* depends on the understood complement.) Other examples of number-transparent expressions are *lots, plenty, the rest/remainder* and, for some speakers, *a number* (though the latter allows only a following plural, not a singular like that of (i)). Semantically *a lot of* in (ii) is equivalent to *many*, and this is reflected in the number assignment. Structurally, however, they are quite different: *many papers* is a simple NP with *many* determiner and *papers* head, while *a lot of papers* is a complex NP with *lot* head of the upper NP, *papers* head of the embedded one.[2]

Normally any person–number property in the verb is determined by agreement, or 'concord', with the NP subject – it is on this basis that we have argued that *the news* is singular, *the cattle* and *a lot of papers* plural. There are, however, certain places where semantic factors intervene to produce grammatical 'discord'. Thus we have 3rd person singular verbs with grammatically plural subjects in *'The Three Musketeers' is well written*, where the reference is to a single novel, or in *Eight cups isn't enough*, where one is talking about the quantity of cups, a semantically singular concept (though concordant *aren't* is equally possible). The opposite situation – non-(3rd person) singular verb with singular subject – is found with **collective** nouns, as in *The jury have not yet reached a decision*. (Again, concordant *has* is possible, and tends to be preferred in US English.) A collective noun denotes a set or collection of separate members. And it is of course the semantic plurality of the members that overrides the grammatical singularity of the collective noun when a discordant verb form is selected. Such discord is not always possible: we could not substitute a discordant form in, say, *The jury consists of twelve women* (where the predicate applies to the jury as a whole).

We noted at the end of §3 that determiners play a role in the number system: this is because some of them are normally restricted to NPs with a singular or with a plural head. Thus *a, another, either, neither, much, a little* (and for some speakers *less*), *every, little* and *one* require a singular head. And *both, we, us, a few, many, several, few*, the cardinal numerals, *a dozen*, and so on, require a plural. In addition the demonstratives **this** and **that** have contrasting number forms (*this/these, that/those*) selected in agreement with the head.

5. Count and mass uses of nouns

Consider now the interpretation of the noun *cake* in

(6) i *Kim offered me a cake*
     ii *Kim offered me some more cake*

In (i) *cake* has an 'individuated' or **count** interpretation; a typical contextualisation could be one where there is a plate with a number of separate small cakes on, with Kim inviting me to take one: *a cake* applies to an item from a larger set of discrete

---

[2] Some grammars match the syntax to the semantics by treating *papers* as head of *a lot of papers* as well as of *many papers*: *a lot of* is then some kind of 'complex' determinative.

units that could be counted. In (ii), on the other hand, *cake* has an 'unbounded' or **mass** interpretation: it is here conceived of as a substance rather than as a unit. Similarly *coffee* has a count interpretation in *I'll just get myself another coffee* but a mass interpretation in *I'd rather have coffee than tea*: the former involves individuation (in this particular case typically into servings – cups, say), while the latter is concerned simply with coffee the substance, liquid or solid. With a count interpretation it generally makes sense to ask 'How many?': *How many cakes/coffees did you have?*, whereas with a mass interpretation the corresponding question would ask 'How much?': *How much cake/coffee did you have?*.

Interpretation as count or mass depends primarily on the following factors:

(a) Number. A plural normally triggers a count interpretation: in *Kim offered me some more cakes*, for example, *cake* has the interpretation that it has in (6i), not (ii). Exceptional cases where a plural does not have a count interpretation involve nouns which are inherently, non-contrastively plural; thus *how many* does not combine with such plurals as *dregs, remains, earnings*, etc., from (4i).

(b) Determiners. With singular nouns, the determiners *one, a, another, each, every, either, neither* force a count interpretation, whereas *enough, much, most, little* and unstressed *some* or *any* induce a mass interpretation – compare *another/ every cake* with *enough/some* (= /səm/) *cake*. A singular common noun without any determiner – more precisely, without any determiner from positions II or III – will normally take a mass interpretation: *He drinks whisky, She had lost all interest in the project*.

(c) Inherent properties of the noun. Some nouns occur only with a mass interpretation. The clearest are those like *equipment* and *information* which not only have no plural counterparts but which also exclude the determiners requiring a count interpretation: *They have good equipment/*a good equipment*. Such plurals as *dregs, remains, earnings* mentioned under (a) above, also take only a mass interpretation even though they are plural. Conversely, there are nouns like *individual, entity, unit, thing*, which take only a count interpretation. It is then standard practice in grammars to talk of mass nouns (such as *equipment*) and count nouns (such as **individual**). But it should be borne in mind that the majority of nouns can be used with either kind of interpretation – although one will very often be significantly more normal, frequent, easy to contextualise than the other. *Knowledge*, for example, is used as a mass noun in straightforward cases like *They had little knowledge of the subject*, but although it has no plural it can combine with *a* (provided there is some modifier present), as in *They had a good knowledge of the subject*: the *a* indicates that the knowledge in question is treated as separable from other areas of knowledge, as bounded or delimited, so that we have here an individuated, count interpretation, albeit a non-prototypical one. *Book* is normally used as a count noun, but it is just possible to use it as a mass noun, as in *These creatures have been living on a diet of book*. A glance at a dictionary will show that words in general and nouns in particular typically exhibit **polysemy**, i.e.

have a range of meanings – and the lexical entry for a given noun will then often contain a mixture of basically mass meanings and basically count meanings. *Silver*, for example, is primarily used to denote a certain metal, and this is a basically mass meaning, but it can also have a sense incorporating "medal", as in *We won a silver in the women's marathon*, which is a count meaning. However, it is certainly not necessary to cater fully for the count/mass distinction in the lexicon: some of the variation can be handled by means of general rules. Given, for example, that *coffee* denotes a substance from which drinks are made and thus has a basic mass meaning, it is predictable that it can be used in a count sense incorporating either "serving" (*I'll get myself another coffee*) or "kind/variety" (*This isn't a very good coffee: it's too bitter*).

6. Definiteness

Two of the most important determiners are the definite article *the* and the indefinite article *a(n)*. The contrast is seen in an elementary pair of examples like

(7)   i   *The dog* [*was barking*]   Definite
      ii *A dog* [*was barking*]   Indefinite

As the name implies, *the* indicates that the description contained in the rest of the NP – in this case *dog* – is presented as sufficient, in the context, to 'define' the referent, to distinguish it from everything else. The simplest case is where the description is unique, as in *the Prime Minister of Australia from 1972 to 1975*: there is only one person (Gough Whitlam) satisfying that description, and hence *the* is in order. More often, however, the speaker or writer relies on the context to supplement the information given in the description. There are, for example, millions of dogs, so that it would be appropriate for me to use (i) only if the context was such as to make clear which I was referring to. One common case is where the referent has been mentioned before: *A dog and a couple of cats had been locked up in the shed; the dog was barking* – here indefinite *a dog* introduces a dog into the context of discourse and we can then go on to refer to that same dog by means of definite *the dog*. But (i) does not of course require previous mention of the dog: the question of which dog I am referring to may be contextually resolved by virtue of my owning a single dog, of there being a single dog in the house I was in, and so on.

Indefinite *a* then simply indicates that the following description is not presented as defining. If the description clearly ɪs defining, *a* will be out of place (cf. *The/*An oldest boy in the class was just over 15*), but *a* certainly does not require that the description be non-unique: *He was reading a book on acoustic phonetics by Martin Joos* in no way commits the speaker to there being more than one such book. *A* is used only with singular count nouns, while *the* can also occur with plurals and mass nouns (*The dogs were barking, The equipment is faulty*).

The category of definiteness applies to NPs in general, not just those containing the definite or indefinite article. Other determiners that mark an NP as definite are the demonstratives **this** and **that**, *we/us* and *you*, possessives and *both* – *this* *cup, we Australians, your nose, both parties*. The NP is again presented as providing defining information, but this time part of that information is given by the determiner itself: *your nose* refers to something defined by the two properties of being a nose and of being yours. A definite NP may also be marked as such by the head alone, when this position is filled by a proper name, a definite personal pronoun (*I, you, he*, etc.) or a demonstrative pronoun (*this, that*). Thus the referent of *I* is defined by the property of being the speaker or writer, that of *John* by the property of bearing that name – and since there are in fact lots of people (and indeed animals) named *John*, successful reference will depend on the question of which John is intended being contextually resolved, just as with the *the dog* in (i).

The contrast between definite and indefinite is not to be confused with that between **specific** and **non-specific**. The latter contrast is illustrated in

(8) i *Kim was talking to a doctor*
    ii *Kim was looking for a doctor*

It follows from (i) that there was some specific doctor – Dr Richards, for example – that Kim was talking to, but it does not similarly follow from (ii) that there was a particular doctor that Kim was looking for: we will say, then, that in (i) *a doctor* is specific, while in (ii) – or at least in the more natural interpretation of (ii) – it is non-specific. Non-specific NPs are usually indefinite, but they do not have to be: *Kim was looking for the best place to park*, for example, does not imply that there was some specific place that she was looking for. Whether an NP is interpreted as specific or non-specific depends in general on the larger construction in which it appears: in (8), for example, the difference is attributable to the semantic properties of **talk** and **look for**, with the NP itself, *a doctor*, being the same in either case. There are, however, two determiners, *any* and *either*, which occur exclusively in non-specific NPs. This is why we could not replace *a* by *any* or *either* in an example like *When I arrived Kim was talking to a doctor*, for the context requires a specific reading for the final NP.

Also cutting across the definite/indefinite division is that between **generic** and **non-generic**:

(9) i *The whale [is an endangered species]*   Generic, definite
    ii *The whale [had beached itself]*   Non-generic, definite
(10) i *A wallet [is for keeping paper money in]* Generic, indefinite
    ii *A wallet [was lying on the desk]*   Non-generic, indefinite

The whale in (9i) has a generic interpretation in that it applies to the class of whales as a whole, and *a wallet* in (10i) is generic in that the sentence expresses a generalisation applying to members of the class of wallets. Generic NPs are necessarily non-specific, but not all non-specific NPs, of course, are generic: (8ii), for example, does not express a generalisation about doctors. Generic NPs usually have one of the following forms: *the* + singular count noun, *a* + singular count noun, plural count noun (*Wallets are for . . .*), singular mass noun (*Mercury is used in thermometers*). The semantic contrast between *the* and *a* is not the same as in non-generic NPs and in some cases they are interchangeable: *The/A leopard has a dark-spotted yellowish-fawn coat.*

7. Pre-head modifiers

The pre-head modifier position can be filled by expressions from a variety of classes – notably, but not exclusively: (α) adjectives: [*a*] *big* [*mistake*], *young* [*children*]; (β) nouns: [*a*] *Yorkshire* [*accent*], *steel* [*girders*]; (γ) participial forms of verbs: *falling* [*prices*], [*the*] *predicted* [*result*]; (δ) PossPs: [*an*] *old people's* [*home*], [*a*] *ladies'* [*toilet*]. Strictly speaking, the modifiers in (α)–(δ) should be analysed in the first instance as phrases rather than words, for they may themselves have a modifier–head structure: *a very big mistake, a North Yorkshire accent, rapidly falling prices*. In the first of these, for example, *very* modifies *big* and *very big* in turn modifies *mistake*.

There is no grammatical limit to the number of pre-head modifiers a noun head may take. *A strong Yorkshire accent* has two, *a big black Holden sedan* has three, and so on. Considerable restrictions apply to the relative order of modifiers: for example, nouns follow most kinds of adjective (cf. **a Yorkshire strong accent*), and adjectives of colour normally follow adjectives of size (*a big black cat* is much more natural than *a black big cat*). But it is difficult to decide to what extent the restrictions are to be handled by rules of grammar; *a black big cat* is hardly UNGRAMMATICAL – its status is surely different from that of *many her virtues, where the requirement that *her* precede *many* is very clearly a matter of grammar.

Let us turn now to the distinction between the determiner and modifier functions. At the language-particular level they are distinguished primarily by linear order: determiners normally precede modifiers. (The order modifier + determiner is restricted to cases where the modifier begins with *how, so, too* and the determiner is *a*: *how big a mistake, too serious a crime*.) The prototypical determiners are *the, a* and items which behave grammatically like them, while the prototypical modifiers are gradable adjectives like **big, strong, good**, etc. (more properly the phrases headed by them). Gradable adjectives are those that inflect for grade and/or take degree modifiers as in *bigger, very big*, etc. Such adjectives can normally be used predicatively as well as attributively – compare *The dog was big* (predicative) and *the big dog* (attributive); the central determiners, by contrast, are not used predicatively: *Dog was the. The distinction between the two kinds of dependent is far from clear-cut: such position III determiners as *many* and *few* are gradable and are occasionally used predicatively (*Her virtues were many/few*) while such modifiers as *mere* and *utter* are non-gradable and restricted to attributive use. Nevertheless the differences between *the* and **big**, say, are significant enough to justify our recognising different functions here even if the boundary between them is somewhat fuzzy.

At the general level, the determiner position is one characteristically filled by members of a closed class and involved in the marking of such NP systems as definiteness, number, quantification, countability. The modifier position within the NP is, by contrast, one that characteristically is filled by members of the open class of adjective phrases, is optional and serves semantically to restrict the 'denotation' of the head. Take an elementary example like *the black dog*. The denotation of **dog** is the set of all entities to which the term **dog** can be properly applied, i.e. of which it would be true to say 'This is a dog'. The modifier *black* restricts the denotation: *black* **dog** applies to a smaller set than **dog** alone. But the determiner *the* does not similarly narrow down the denotation – to entities that are not only dogs and black but also 'the': it signals rather, as we have said, that the description *black dog* is sufficient in the context to pick out the intended referent. The modifier function is of course not confined to the structure of NPs: it occurs also in the structure of VPs, AdjPs, AdvPs, and so on. A broader general definition is then that modifiers characteristically add further truth conditions to those given in the head: if we compare *This is a dog* with *This is a black dog*, *He is tall* with *He is very tall*, *She danced* with *She danced gracefully*, the conditions under which the second member of each pair could be truly asserted are more restricted than those under which the first could be, and this is clearly due to the modifiers *black*, *very* and *gracefully*.

8. Post-head dependents

Post-head dependents in NP structure are of three kinds, complements, modifiers and peripheral dependents:

			Class	Function
(11)	i	[*the author*] *of this novel*	PP	
	ii	[*the fact*] *that he was unmarried*	Content cl	Comp
	iii	[*the need*] (*for us*) *to help her*	Infinitival cl	
(12)	i	[*a man*] *of honour*	PP	
	ii	[*the letter*] *which Kim had written*	Relative cl	
	iii	[*the man*] *to do it*	Infinitival cl	
	iv	[*people*] *living in Chelsea*	Participial cl	Mod
	v	[*a man*] *eager for recognition*	AdjP	
	vi	[*the opera*] *'Carmen'*	NP	
(13)	i	[*the letter,*] *which Kim had written*	Relative cl	
	ii	[*this idea,*] *that it was a fake,*	Content cl	Periph-Dep
	iii	[*Derek Smith,*] *the new Treasurer,*	NP	

Peripheral dependents are distinguished prosodically from modifiers and complements: they are spoken with a separate intonation group (in writing they are normally marked off by commas or stronger punctuation marks). They are always freely omissible and have something of the character of a parenthesis. They are always semantically non-restrictive. The distinction between complements and modifiers matches that which we drew in our analysis of clause structure, but is a good deal less clearly defined, for whereas some complements in clause structure are seen to be such by virtue of being obligatory, there are no clear cases of nouns that require a complement. The distinguishing criterion is thus that complements depend for their occurrence on the presence of a noun head of the appropriate class. This is most easily seen with finite subordinate clauses: any common or proper noun can take a relative clause as dependent (hence modifier) but only a comparatively small subclass of common nouns can take a content clause as dependent (hence complement): *the fact/idea/suggestion/ *car/*man/*arrival that he was unmarried*. With infinitival clauses, modifiers are comparable to relative clauses (*the man to do it*, for example, is comparable to *the man who should do it*), whereas complements are comparable to those dependent on a verb or adjective (the NP *Kim's desire to escape* corresponds to *Kim desires to escape*, where *to escape* is very clearly a complement of the verb *desires*, and similarly the NP *Kim's eagerness to escape* corresponds to *Kim is eager to escape*, where *to escape* is complement of the adjective *eager*). With PPs the preposition in a complement is selected by the noun head, whereas in a modifier it is potentially semantically contrastive. This distinction is evident in the pair: *her reliance on the premier* (complement) vs *the book on the table* (modifier); that *reliance* takes a PP with *on* is something that has to be specifically recorded in its lexical entry, whereas the *on* in the modifier could be replaced by any other preposition of place. Again, the clearest cases of complements have analogues in VP or AdjP structure: compare *her reliance on the premier* with *She relies on the premier*, *her eagerness for recognition* with *She is eager for recognition*. Note, however, that whereas one of the most central types of complement in VP structure, the object, is prototypically realised by an NP, an NP cannot function as complement within a larger NP – we generally have instead a PP, usually (though not invariably) with *of* as head: compare *He wrote the novel* with *the writer of the novel*, *He married the princess* with *his marriage to the princess*.

Cutting across the distinction between the various types of dependents is the relation of **apposition**. The prototypical appositional construction is exemplified in (13iii). Here we have two NPs placed alongside ('apposed to') each other in a relation of equivalence – Derek Smith and the new Treasurer are one and the same. The order is reversible – and since either could occupy head position, either can stand alone, so that we have the four possibilities: [*He interviewed*] *Derek Smith, the new Treasurer*; [*He interviewed*] *Derek Smith*; [*He interviewed*] *the new Treasurer, Derek Smith*; [*He interviewed*] *the new Treasurer*. This central type of apposition is non-restrictive; restrictive apposition is found in *the opera 'Carmen'* and *your friend the bank-manager*. Again there is a relation of equivalence (the opera is 'Carmen') and the second term could stand alone (*We're going to see the opera 'Carmen'*; *We're going to see 'Carmen'*), but although the dependent term is grammatically omissible its presence is semantically required to justify the selection of a definite NP (what defines the referent is *opera 'Carmen'*, not *opera* alone). Further removed still from the central type is that where the second term is a content clause, as in peripheral dependent (13ii), and complement (11ii). The equivalence between the two terms brings this within the definition of apposition (this idea was that it was a fake), but although the second term could often stand alone it by no means always can: we can, for example, omit *the fact* in *The fact that he was unmarried surprised us* but not *the rumour* in *The rumour that he was unmarried was quite unfounded*.

9. Constituent structure

In our discussion so far of noun-headed constructions we have tacitly assumed just two levels of constituent structure – that of the noun (word) itself and that of the noun phrase of which it is head. These are certainly the major levels, and we will continue in the following chapters to confine our attention to these two. We should note in passing, however, that this is undoubtedly a simplification: a more detailed grammar will need to recognise a richer hierarchical structure. Consider first such an example as

(14) *a federal government inquiry*

where the head *inquiry* is modified by *federal government*. The latter consists of adjective + noun in a modifier + head relation, but it differs from the constructions we have been calling NPs in that the absence of a determiner makes it unable to occupy such prototypical NP positions as subject and object: **Federal government has instituted an inquiry*, **She criticised federal government*. There is evidence, then, that we should recognise a noun-headed construction intermediate between the noun and the full NP. And if we assign *federal government* to this intermediate construction in (14), we shall also do so in [*She criticised*] *the federal government*, where it will be head rather than modifier: thus determiners will enter the constituent structure at a higher level than modifiers (just as the subject does in clause structure). And in *Federal governments encounter special problems*, say, the expression *federal governments* will be a constituent at two levels in the hierarchical structure: it will still belong to the intermediate category but, as there is no determiner this time, it will also constitute an NP. It is arguable, furthermore, that peripheral dependents should enter the structure at a higher level than determiners (again analogously to the way in clause structure they enter at a higher level than the subject – see 4.9). The modifier in (12ii) is part of the description *letter which Kim had written* which defines the referent, but the peripheral dependent in (13i) is not – the context will be such that *letter* itself defines the referent. The immediate constituents of (12ii), on the proposed analysis, will be *the* + *letter which Kim had written*, while those of (13i) will be *the letter* (an NP, head of the larger NP) + *which Kim had written* – a bracketing reflected prosodically.

Consider, finally, NPs containing 'focusing dependents':

(15) *Even/Only your father was taken aback*

Even and *only* focus on *your father*, implying a contrast between your father and others in the context of discourse. They do not fit into either of the categories of pre-head dependent that we introduced in §2, determiners and modifiers, and they should probably be regarded as entering the constituent structure at a higher level than determiners (but lower than peripheral dependents). They are somewhat loosely integrated into the structure – and with NPs following the verb they more often appear as dependents in clause structure than within the NP (compare *They even surprised your father* and *They surprised even your father*).

10. Proper nouns

The general definition of a **proper noun** is that it belongs to a grammatically distinct class of nouns which characteristically function as the head of NPs serving as proper names. A prototypical proper name is the institutionalised name of some specific person, place, organisation, etc. – institutionalised by some formal act of naming and/or registration. It is necessary to distinguish between proper NOUNS and proper NAMES for two reasons:

(a) Although a proper name may have the form of a proper noun, as in the case of *John* or *London*, it need not have. Thus *The Open University* is a proper name but not a proper noun: what distinguishes it from, say, *the older university* is precisely that it is the official name of a particular institution.

(b) Proper nouns do not always function as the head of NPs serving as proper names. Thus in *They weren't talking about the same Jones* the proper noun *Jones* is head of the NP *the same Jones* but this is clearly not a proper name. Similarly in *He likes to think of himself as another Einstein, The Smiths are coming round tonight*, etc.

At the language-particular level, the property distinguishing central proper nouns from common nouns in English is that they can form a definite singular count NP on their own, without a determiner. In *John was falling*, for example, *John* has the same kind of interpretation as an NP of the form *the* + common noun (e.g. *the boy*). Central proper nouns do not enter into construction with *the* unless it carries nuclear stress (*Are you referring to "the Attlee?*) or is accompanied by another dependent (*He's not the John I meant*).
More peripheral to the proper noun class are examples such as *Rhine, Hague, Himalayas, father*. Names of rivers and mountain ranges do take *the*, as in *the Rhine, the Himalayas*: the heads here differ from common nouns in that the definite article is more or less obligatory and non-contrastive – any other use (as perhaps in *This river is hardly another Rhine*) will be very clearly derivative from their use as the head of a proper name. Kinship terms like *father* resemble central proper nouns in being able to stand alone as a definite singular count NP (*Father is in the garden*) but differ in combining freely with *the* (*The father was much smaller than the son*): their somewhat marginal status reflects the fact that they do not serve as proper names in the sense given above.

11. Pronouns

There are several distinguishable subclasses of pronoun: I will review them in turn before outlining the properties which apply to the class of pronouns as a whole.

11.1 *Personal pronouns*

The central personal pronouns are shown in (16):

(16)

	1st person		2nd person		3rd person			
	Sg	Pl	Sg	Pl	Sg			Pl
					Masc	Fem	Neut	
Nominative	*I*	*we*	*you*		*he*	*she*	*it*	*they*
Accusative	*me*	*us*			*him*	*her*		*them*

We should also include two more marginal members: generic *one* (as in *One should always read the small print*) and existential *there* (as in *There is a fly in my beer*).

The general definition of **personal pronoun** is that it is the most basic class of pronoun to which the category of person applies. (The qualification 'most basic' serves to exclude reflexives and possessives.) **Person** is then the category where the terms are distinguished by the role of the referent in the utterance-act. 1st person forms are characteristically used to refer to the speaker/writer, or to a group including the speaker/writer, 2nd person forms are characteristically used to refer to the addressee(s) or to a group including the addressee(s), and 3rd person forms are characteristically used to refer to non-participants in the utterance-act. The 'characteristically' is needed because *we* can be used to refer to the addressee (as with a doctor addressing a patient: *How are we today?*), *you* can be used non-specifically for people in general (as in *You could buy these for less than a shilling before the War*, which might be addressed to someone who wasn't born before the War), and 3rd person forms can be used in reference to the speaker/writer or addressee(s) (as when, in reply to *Max is going to show us how to do it*, Max says: *Max/He is going to do no such thing*). At the language-particular level, we will define 1st person simply as a form of *I* or *we* (or corresponding reflexives, possessives), 2nd person as *you* (or *yourself*, etc.) and 3rd person as any other pronoun or indeed noun. The ordering '1st', '2nd', '3rd' reflects the priority that is given to speaker/writer over addressee and to addressee over non-participant: a group consisting of speaker/writer + addressee(s) and/or one or more non-participants will be referred to by 1st person *we* and a group consisting of addressee(s) + non-participant(s) by 2nd person *you*.

At the language-particular level, the personal pronouns are distinguished by their ability to occur (in nominative form) as the subject of an 'interrogative tag' [*The Queen wasn't amused,*] *was she?*, [*There had been a misunderstanding,*] *hadn't there?*, [*One shouldn't do that,*] *should one?*. A further point is that except for the marginal *there*, they have reflexive counterparts – *myself, ourselves, oneself*, etc.

We should also note that except for *who*, all lexemes which inflect for case belong to the class of personal pronouns, English having less case inflection than many languages. The general term **case** applies to an inflectionally or analytically marked system of the noun or pronoun where some of the contrasting categories are distinguished by being associated with different functions in clause structure. Thus **nominative** and **accusative** are definable at the general level as distinct cases associated respectively with the subject of a finite clause and with the direct object: if the NPs in subject and direct object function characteristically have, for all or some subclasses of noun as head, distinct case inflections or analytic case markers we will call these cases nominative and accusative respectively. The English *I* and *me* series of forms clearly satisfy these definitions, though they of course have other uses than those of subject of a finite clause and direct object. Nominatives are found in formal style in predicative function (*It was I*) and as subject of a present-participial clause functioning as peripheral dependent in a superordinate clause ([*They decided to appoint Kim*,] *she being the only one with any relevant experience*). Many speakers use nominatives for coordinated pronouns, irrespective of the function of the whole coordinative expression – thus not only *Kim and I* [*went with them*] (subject), but also, contrary to the prescriptivist's rule, [*They invited*] *Kim and I* (object). The accusative has a wide range of uses: direct object, indirect object, complement of a preposition, subject of an infinitival clause (*For him to do it* [*would be a mistake*]) and, except in formal style, predicative (*It was me*), subject of a participial clause ([*He insisted on*] *us being kept informed*) and subject of a clause where there is ellipsis of the predicate or predicator ([*He was faster than*] *me*). Its range of use is so extensive that the simplest way of giving rules for case selection is to specify the conditions under which a nominative occurs, and then say that an accusative occurs anywhere else.[3]

The three definite singular personal pronouns are distinguished as respectively **masculine, feminine** and **neuter**, terms in a system of **gender**. They satisfy the general definitions of the three gender categories in that they characteristically refer to males, females and inanimates respectively. The familiar 'characteristically' is needed because the correlation between form and meaning is again imperfect: *he* is used for a non-specific member of a set including females as well as males (as in *If any student wishes to take part in the seminar, he should consult his tutor*, where many speakers would have *they*, which is less formal and which avoids what is increasingly perceived as a 'sexist' bias in *he*); *she* is commonly used of ships and (typically by males) such other inanimates as a car or the like (especially when the speaker is personally involved with it, e.g. as owner or driver of the car); *it* can be used of male or female animals, and of babies.

The personal pronouns are generally used either deictically or anaphorically. The concepts of deixis and anaphora are relevant to a considerable variety of forms, but it will be convenient to introduce them in the present context: as we shall see, they both figure in the general definition of pronoun.

An expression is used **deictically** when its interpretation is determined in relation to certain features of the utterance-act: the identity of those participating as speaker/writer and addressee, together with the time and place at which it occurs.

---

[3] 'Nominative' and 'accusative' are the traditional general terms but modern grammars of English quite often use 'subjective' and 'objective' respectively.

The reference of *I*, for example, is to whoever fills the participant role of speaker/ writer for the utterance containing it. *The Prime Minister of Australia from 1972 to 1975*, by contrast, is non-deictic: the reference does not depend on who is speaking when, where and to whom. *The Prime Minister of Australia* on its own, however, will often have a deictic component in its interpretation: other things being equal, it will refer to the person who is Prime Minister of Australia at the time of utterance. The difference between *The Prime Minister of Australia* and *I* is, firstly, that the former also contains a large non-deictic component of meaning whereas the meaning of *I* is purely deictic and, secondly, that the former can readily be used non-deictically (*In 1975 the Prime Minister of Australia was sacked by the Governor-General*), whereas *I* is always used deictically. Other kinds of expression which are characteristically used deictically are the locatives *here* and *there*, the demonstratives **this** and **that**, and temporals like *now, then, today, yesterday, tomorrow, last/next Tuesday/March*, etc. – and the inflectional category of tense, which is primarily used, as we have seen, to relate the time of the action, process, state, expressed in the clause to the time of the utterance.

An expression is used **anaphorically** when its interpretation derives from that of an antecedent in the same text. For example, in the natural interpretation of *I asked John to help me but he wouldn't* the pronoun *he* refers to John: it is interpreted thus by virtue of its anaphoric relation to the antecedent *John*. Prototypically, the antecedent precedes the anaphoric expression (or 'anaphor'). However, under certain conditions – roughly, when the anaphor is in a clause subordinate to that containing the antecedent – the reverse order may be found, as in one interpretation of *When he got home John went straight to bed*. (Another interpretation would have *he* anaphoric to a preceding NP.) Again, it is not just pronouns that may be interpreted anaphorically: other examples are the adverbs *there* and *then*, *so*, the demonstratives **this** and **that**, and definite NPs with *the*. Compare *He moved to Sydney in 1960 and has lived there ever since* (*there* = "in Sydney"), *I don't know if he's read it but I hope so* (*so* = "(that) he's read it"), *A man and a woman got on the bus; the man was wearing a military overcoat* (*the man* refers to the one introduced into the context by the antecedent *a man*). The most straightforward cases of ellipsis are likewise interpreted anaphorically: in *He tried to mend it but he couldn't* the elliptical second clause is understood by virtue of its relation to the first as "He couldn't mend it".

11.2 Reflexive and reciprocal pronouns

The **reflexive pronouns** are compounds in -*self/*-*selves*: *myself, ourselves; yourself, yourselves; himself, herself, itself, themselves; oneself.*

Two uses may be distinguished:

(17) i *Tom himself signed the letter*   Emphatic use
     ii *Tom hurt himself*   Basic use

In (i), *himself* is in apposition to *Tom*, serving to emphasise that it was Tom as opposed to someone else who signed the letter; commonly, the pronoun is moved to the right, yielding the non-kernel construction *Tom signed the letter himself*. We regard (ii) as the 'basic' use in that it is the one which brings these pronouns within the application of the general term 'reflexive': where a language has distinct sets of pronouns for the constructions illustrated in (17) it is those figuring in (ii) that will be called 'reflexive' (with those figuring in (i) being called 'emphatic'). In the reflexive use the pronoun usually functions as complement in VP or PP structure. The idea behind the term 'reflexive' is that the pronoun 'reflects' some other NP in the clause (*Tom* in our example). A few verbs or idioms require a reflexive (cf. *Tom perjured himself/*him, Tom took it upon himself/*him to repay the debt*), but for the most part reflexive pronouns, in their basic use, contrast with personal pronouns. Thus (ii) contrasts with *Tom hurt him/her/me/* ... The difference is that in (ii) the pronoun is anaphoric to *Tom*, whereas in *Tom hurt him* it cannot be – it will have its antecedent in an earlier sentence or be interpreted deictically. In the most straightforward cases (and they are the only ones we have space to consider here), a reflexive is selected instead of a personal pronoun if the antecedent and the pronoun are in the same clause. A general definition of reflexive pronouns, then, is that they are pronouns with the following properties: (α) they enter into a close structural relation with their antecedent – the antecedent is characteristically subject of the clause containing the pronoun; (β) they are distinct from the personal pronouns, and often contrast with reciprocal pronouns.

The **reciprocal pronouns** in English are *each other* and *one another*. (Both are written as sequences of two words but grammatically they are best analysed as single pronouns functioning as head in NP structure.) They occur under the same structural conditions as reflexive pronouns in their basic use – i.e., in the straightforward cases, in the same clause as their antecedent. The semantic contrast between reciprocals and reflexives may be explained by reference to (18):

(18) i   *They had defended one another*   Reciprocal
      ii   *They had defended themselves*   Reflexive

Suppose that 'x' stands for any member of the set referred to by *they*, and 'y' for any other member. Then the meaning of (i) is that for each pair x, y in the set, x had defended y, while that of (ii) is that for each member x in the set, x had defended x, or that the set as a whole had defended itself.

11.3 Possessive pronouns

There are three sets of possessive expressions: an open class of PossPs (2.6) and the closed classes of pronouns and determinatives shown in (19):

(19) i   *mine, ours; yours; his, hers, its; theirs*   Pronouns
      ii   *my, our; your; his, her, its; their*   Determinatives

The determinatives appear only in determiner function, as in *my novel*. This position can be also filled by a PossP (*Kim's novel*), but whereas a PossP can occur in an elliptical NP just before the site of the missing head, a possessive determinative cannot: *Pat's novel was a success but Kim's/*my was a disaster* (= "Kim's/my novel"). One major use of the possessive pronouns is to fill the gap created by this restriction on the determinatives: *Pat's novel was a success but mine was a disaster*. *Mine* is here interpreted anaphorically as "my novel": instead of an elliptical NP we have one with a pronoun as head.

Besides this anaphoric use, the possessive pronouns have two uses which they share with PossPs. One is the predicative use, as in *This is mine/Kim's*. The other is as complement to *of* in a PP that itself is post-modifier in a larger NP: *a friend of mine/Kim's*. Since the possessive determiners are mutually exclusive with the other position II determiners, we cannot have **a my/Kim's friend*: the construction *a friend of mine/Kim's* fills that gap. The larger NP cannot normally have *the* as determiner: **the friend of mine/Kim's*; as the possessive determiners are definite the gap left by the ungrammaticality of **the my/Kim's friend* is simply filled by *my/Kim's friend*.

The general term **possessive pronoun** applies to a distinct subclass of pronouns belonging to the set of possessive expressions. The latter express a variety of relations, several of the most obvious and frequent of which can be subsumed under the concept of possession, so that 'possessive' is an appropriate term for them. (Compare the range of interpretations of *Ed's bicycle, Ed's nose, Ed's job, Ed's wife, Ed's ideas, Ed's death*.)

11.4 Other classes of pronoun

(a) The **demonstrative pronouns** *this* and *that* (lexemes which also belong to the class of determinatives). Their most basic use is deictic, as in *This is better than that*. The referents of *this* and *that* here will normally differ in respect of their location: relatively close to the speaker in the case of *this*, relatively distant for *that*. In their deictic use they are characteristically accompanied by some pointing gesture or the like: this is what makes the general term 'demonstrative' applicable. They can also be used anaphorically, most often with a clause as antecedent, as in *No one understood him, but this/that wasn't at all unusual* (*this/that* = "for no one to understand him").

(b) **Interrogative** and **relative pronouns**. The pronouns *who, whom, whose, what* and *which* (together with their compounds in *-ever: whoever*, etc.) occur in interrogative and relative clauses: see 9.4 and 11.3 respectively.

(c) **Indefinite pronouns**. The most central members of the class of indefinite pronouns are those that are morphological compounds of *every, some, any* or *no* with *thing, one* or *body: everything, everyone, everybody*, etc. These have the distinctive property of taking simple adjectival modifiers as post-head dependents: *everything valuable, somebody clever*.

After these, the clearest member is *none*, as in *I'd like an apple but there are none left* (where it is interpreted anaphorically as "no apples"). For the rest, there are a fair number of indefinite words, such as *some, any, either, many, much,*

several, etc., which can occur with a following noun head, alone, or with an *of*
phrase

(20) i   *He gave me some apples*
    ii   *[I'm taking a few apples;] would you like some too?*
    iii   *Some of the apples were bad*

In (i) *some* is clearly a determinative; in (ii)–(iii) it is commonly analysed as a pronoun, but it is not easy to choose between this analysis and one where it is still a
determinative, functioning as determiner in an elliptical headless NP.

11.5 Pronouns as a class

The general definition of pronoun is that it is a grammatically distinct class of
noun-like words (typically a subclass of noun) whose most central members are
characteristically used either anaphorically or deictically.

At the language-particular level English pronouns are distinguished by their
inability to combine with position II or III determiners.[4] (A few of them do allow
certain position I determiners: *All you in this group [remain seated]*, *Both these
[are broken]*.) Pronouns are in fact very much more limited than common nouns
with respect to the kinds of dependents they take; usually they constitute a complete NP by themselves and some of them, such as the reflexives, wholly exclude
dependents. The dependents that are found with pronouns, however – mainly
PPs, and relative clauses – are such as also occur with common nouns. Note, for
example, the restrictive relative clauses in *you who know his work, that which
impressed me most* (a use of *that* not covered above), *nothing that can't be cured*:
such clauses modify only nouns.

As will be clear from what has been said above, most pronouns in English have
anaphoric or deictic uses (the main exceptions are the interrogatives and compound indefinites): the class thus falls very clearly within the application of the
general term 'pronoun'. The property of having anaphoric or deictic uses does
not, however, figure in the language-particular definition; note, then, that *one*, as
in *That apple is bad but this one is OK*, which is characteristically interpreted anaphorically or deictically, is a common noun, not a pronoun: it takes the same
range of dependents as common count nouns.[5]

---

[4] Some words belong to both pronoun and common noun classes, and in the latter use they can,
of course, combine with determiners. In *Is it a he or a she?* or *Tom's a nobody*, for example, *he*,
she and *nobody* are common nouns – with a clear difference in meaning from their use as pronouns.

[5] In its anaphoric use *one* differs from pronouns in that its antecedent is characteristically less
than a full NP. Thus in *Ed bought a new car; it was smaller than the old one* the pronoun *it* has
the NP *a new car* as antecedent whereas *one* has just *car*. I should add, however, that many
grammars do analyse this *one* as a pronoun.

12. Nominalisation

The term **nominalisation** applies to a variety of grammatical processes that yield nouns or expressions bearing significant resemblances to nouns or NPs.

(a) Affixation and compounding. One type of nominalisation yields nouns that are overtly marked by the morphological processes of affixation or compounding. A number of suffixes form deverbal and de-adjectival nouns. Thus *-er, -ee, -ation, -ion, -ment, -ing*, etc. are added to the lexical stems of verbs to form nouns like *worker, payee, consideration, contemplation, management, shooting*. Similarly *-ity, -ty*, and, especially, *-ness* form nouns from adjectives, as in *rapidity, loyalty, decisiveness*. Suffixes like *-ship, -ess* and prefixes like *ex-, counter-, super-* yield nouns from more elementary nouns: *friendship, countess, counter-espionage, ex-mayor, supertax*.

There are vast numbers of compound nouns: the majority of compounds belong to the noun class. We cannot here go into the description of the various types of compound noun distinguished according to the nature of, and relation between, the compounds (compare *blackbird*, Adj + N; *bottleneck*, N + N; *hang-man*, V + N, with N understood as subject of V, "a man who hangs [people]"; *pushbutton*, V + N, with N understood as object of V, "a button which one pushes"; and so on). Compounds are single words and as such are to be distinguished from two-word phrasal expressions with the structure modifier + head; compare, for example, compound *greenhouse* and phrasal *green house*, with *green* an adjective modifier (a pair which illustrates how the meaning of a compound may not be predictable from the meanings of the parts), or compound *goldsmith* and phrasal *gold watch*, with *gold* a noun modifier. Compounding is not always reflected in the orthography: many compounds are written as two words (*birth control, income tax*, etc.) and there is indeed often a certain amount of vacillation in the orthography (cf. *starting point, starting-point, startingpoint*). A better guide, though one not without its problems, is stress: normally in the compound there will be a single word stress, on the first element, whereas in the phrasal construction there will be two, one on each element (though one – prototypically the second – may be stronger than the other by virtue of being the nuclear stress in the intonation group) – compare *He bought a greenhouse* and *He bought a green house*.

(b) Conversion, and NPs without noun heads. The majority of nouns resulting from conversion derive from verbs or adjectives. Deverbal conversion, as in *attempt, cut, go, leap, move*, etc., is straightforward: the *attempt* of *They attempt too much* is a prototypical verb, while that of *They made another attempt* is a prototypical noun, so that there can be no doubt that we have conversion from one class to another. De-adjectival conversion presents more of a problem, for here we need to distinguish between the phenomena illustrated in

(21) i *She's an intellectual*
    ii *There are many items on the agenda: the most important of them concerns the rule changes*

(i) does involve conversion: *intellectual* is a noun (contrasting with plural *intellectuals*) deriving from the adjective of, say, *She's highly intellectual – intellectual* must be entered in the lexicon as both adjective and noun. The same does not hold for *important*, however. It is, of course, a prototypical adjective in *This is most important*, but it is also an adjective in (21ii). Any gradable adjective can occur in this kind of construction, and we can have inflectional as well as analytic superlatives (e.g. *the funniest of them*): postulating conversion, transfer from the adjective class to the noun class, would accordingly be inappropriate here. *The most important of them* thus does not have a noun as head. In other respects, however, it is like an NP: it occurs in the same functional positions as NPs (subject, object, etc.), and its actual and potential dependents are of the type we find in NPs (note the determiner *the*, the possibility of adding a relative clause modifier, as in *the most important of them that affects us*, and so on). It is best analysed as a peripheral type of NP construction, one without an overt noun head: we take *most important* to be an AdjP functioning as modifier to a 'zero' head (compare *the most important one of them*, a central type of NP with *one* as head). Examples like *The strong should help the very weak* should be handled in the same way: note the absence of number inflection and the fact that *very* (in the sense "to a high degree") characteristically modifies adjectives, not nouns. But it is not always easy to distinguish between the two types of nominalisation shown in (21).

(c) Subordination of clauses. A further type of nominalisation arises when clauses are embedded to function in positions characteristically filled by NPs, such as subject:

(22) i   *That he is indeed guilty* [*is now evident to everyone*]
     ii   (*For John*) *to give up now* [*would be disastrous*]
     iii   (*Her*) *being a solicitor* [*matters very much*]

The subordinate clauses here are finite, infinitival and present-participial respectively. *That he is indeed guilty* in (i) is nominalised in the sense that it is like an NP in its function, but that is as far as the nominalisation goes: it clearly remains clausal in its internal structure and thus though it is functionally LIKE an NP we shall not say that it actually IS an NP. The same goes for the infinitival construction; it differs more from the pattern of a kernel clause than does (i), but not in ways that make it more nominal. The degree of nominalisation is considerably greater in (iii) and although we are classifying it too as a clause it is very peripheral to that category, falling in the borderline area between clause and NP.

There are several respects in which a present-participial clause is more like an NP than is a finite or infinitival clause. Like an NP subject, a present-participial clause can follow the tensed verb, e.g. in interrogatives, but cannot normally be extraposed; contrast the behaviour of finite and infinitival clauses:

(23) i   **Is that he is indeed guilty now evident to everyone?*
     ii   **Would for John to give up now be disastrous?*
     iii   *Does her being a solicitor matter very much?*

(24) i   *It is now evident to everyone that he is indeed guilty*
    ii   *It would be disastrous for John to give up now*
    iii **It matters very much her being a solicitor*[6]*

Furthermore, the subject of a nominalised present-participial clause can be a PossP or possessive determinative – and the most characteristic function of these is, of course, determiner in NP structure. Thus *his being an atheist* [*is irrelevant*] is much more like the NP *his atheism* in its structure than is the kernel clause *He is an atheist*. For the most part there is a choice between a possessive and an NP (in accusative case if it is a case-variable pronoun): *him being an atheist* is a variant of the above, belonging to a more informal style. This latter construction represents a lesser degree of nominalisation than the one with the possessive.

The nominalised present-participial construction is to be distinguished from that containing a deverbal noun with the suffix *-ing*. Compare, for example:

(25) i   *Sacking the secretary*
    ii   *The sacking of the secretary* } [*was a mistake*]

In (i) *sacking* is a verb with *the secretary* as its direct object: the whole expression, *sacking the secretary*, is a VP constituting a (subjectless) clause. In (ii) *sacking* is a noun and the phrase it heads, *the sacking of the secretary*, is an NP, not a clause. In 1.1 we outlined the grammatical criteria for distinguishing *destroy* as a verb and *destruction* as a noun, and precisely the same criteria apply here. In (i) *sacking* is like *destroy* in that it excludes *the*, has an object and would take a modifier with the form of an AdvP (*sacking the secretary peremptorily*). Conversely, in (ii) *sacking* is like *destruction* in that it combines with *the*, has a PP complement rather than an object, and would take a modifier with the form of an AdjP (*the peremptory sacking of the secretary*). The degree of nominalisation is clearly much greater in (ii) than in (i).

EXERCISES

1. Noun phrase identification

Identify all the NPs in the following examples, bearing in mind that one NP may have another as a constituent (usually a non-immediate constituent). For each NP, pick out the noun head.

(26) *I didn't much like the suggestion that the candidates should be listed on the ballot-paper in order of seniority*
(27) *Everyone in the house had been asleep at the time*
(28) *One very good reason for giving her a second chance is that she didn't receive adequate notice of the interview last time*

[6] Some speakers judge this acceptable. Increasing the length and complexity of the present-participial clause, however, reduces the acceptability (cf. *her father's having been a solicitor at the time*), so that present-participial clauses undoubtedly behave more like an NP with respect to extraposition than do the other two types.

(29) *All those arrested at the demonstration had their fingerprints taken*
(30) *She took several expensive-looking silk shirts out of the drawer and placed them in a small suit-case she had brought with her*
(31) *He sent me a book on Buddhism which his wife had written*

II. Combinations of determiners

Examine the sets of determiners given in (2) above and construct six NPs with an acceptable combination, and six with an unacceptable combination, of: (α) I + II; (β) II + III; (γ) I + II + III.

III. Count vs mass interpretations

Do the following NPs have a count or mass interpretation?

(32) *[This is] an excellent Riesling*
(33) *[Would you like] tea [or] coffee [?]*
(34) *I [can't afford to have] my teeth [filled with] gold*
(35) *[We stand] a fair chance [of winning] a gold [in the women's 3000 metres]*
(36) *[Can I have] some more ice-cream [?]*
(37) *Neither candidate [performed very well]*
(38) *[I'm going to get myself] another coffee; [would you like] one [too?]*
(39) *[We had] lamb [for lunch four times last week]*
(40) *[They live on] the outskirts of Sydney*
(41) *John [doesn't like] Riesling*

IV. Definite vs indefinite

Classify the following NPs as definite or indefinite.

(42) *I [am meeting] my wife's boss [on] Tuesday*
(43) *[Have] you [got] enough money [?]*
(44) *Several windows [were broken]*
(45) *This proposal [looks more promising than] that one*
(46) *The parents of one of the victims [are suing the bus company]*
(47) *Over three hundred people [died in the crash;] they [were all French]*
(48) *Both candidates [performed well]*

V. Structural analysis

Analyse the following NPs, and those embedded within them, in terms of the functions head, determiner, modifier, complement, peripheral dependent.

(49) *the Prime Minister's statement in Parliament on these matters*
(50) *unreasonable expectations of an improvement in conditions*
(51) *some interesting books on astronomy that he had found*
(52) *several remarkably good student essays on the theory of evolution*
(53) *magnificent Renaissance paintings*
(54) *a visit to the house where she had been born*
(55) *my sister, who worked for the Government*

VI. Structural synthesis

Construct NPs with the structures shown below (where both the function and the class of the elements are specified – 'Detnr:PossP' means a determiner with the form of a PossP).

(56) Detnr:PossP + Mod:AdjP + Head:N + Mod:clause
(57) Detnr(I):Detve + Detnr(II):Detve + Mod:N + Head:N
(58) Detnr:Detve + Mod:AdjP + Head:N + Comp:clause
(59) Detnr:Detve + Head:N + Comp:PP + Mod:clause
(60) Head:N + Mod:PP + Mod:clause

VII. Pronouns and their antecedents

Can the pronoun *he* have *John* as its antecedent in the following examples? Which are not covered by the simplified rules given in the text (§§11.1–2)?

(61) *He didn't realise it but John was about to make a major discovery*
(62) *Unwell though he was, John agreed to go with them*
(63) *John underestimated him*
(64) *John talked to him*
(65) *John had no money on him*
(66) *No one dared tell John how funny he looked*

VIII. Nouns and verbs

Are the words containing the suffix *-ing* in the following examples nouns or verbs – or ambiguously either?

(67) *I much regret telling them about it*
(68) *Ed's writing is atrocious*
(69) *I saw Kim running away*
(70) *The riding of bicycles in this park is strictly prohibited*
(71) *Swimming is fun*
(72) *She likes singing*

7

Adjectives, determinatives and numerals

1. Adjectives

At the general level, 'adjective' is applied to a grammatically distinct word class in a language having the following properties:

(a) It contains among its most central members the morphologically simplest words denoting properties or states; among the most frequent and salient are those relating to size, shape, colour, age, evaluation ("good", "bad", etc.) and the like.

(b) Its members are characteristically used either predicatively (very often as complement to the verb "be") or attributively, as modifier within NP structure.

(c) It is the class, or one of the classes, to which the inflectional category of grade applies most characteristically in languages having this category. (Adjectives often carry such other inflections as case, gender, number, but secondarily, by agreement, rather than being the primary locus for them.)

Whereas it is generally accepted that all languages distinguish grammatically between nouns and verbs, not all languages have a distinct adjective class. In languages which do, there is a tendency for verbs to be dynamic (denoting actions, events, etc.), adjectives static; note in this connection that in English adjectives generally occur very much more readily in the non-progressive construction than in the progressive, whereas this is not so with the majority of verbs (so that while *Ed moved* and *Ed was moving* are equally natural, *Ed was tall* and *Ed was being tall* are not). Nouns often share with adjectives the ability to be used predicatively (again often with the verb "be"), but a more distinctive function of nouns is to head phrases used referentially, and this is usually not characteristic of adjectives – compare *That animal is an elephant/big* (predicative use) vs *He shot the elephant/*the big* (referential use). The properties denoted by adjectives are often scalar, gradable, and it is then a further characteristic of the adjective class

108

to contain numerous pairs of gradable opposites (or 'antonyms': *big ~ small, old ~ young, hot ~ cold, good ~ bad*); the relation of oppositeness plays an important role in the structure of vocabularies and the adjective class is the main repository for the morphologically simplest pairs of gradable opposites.

At the language-particular level, the main distinctive properties involve function and degree modification/inflection.

(a) Function. Adjectives function as head in AdjP structure, with the two main functions of AdjPs in turn being: (α) predicative, complement in copulative and complex-transitive constructions (the predicative use of adjectives); (β) pre-head modifier in NP structure (the attributive use). A third, much less frequent, function is (γ) post-head modifier in NP structure (the postpositive use). Compare

(1) i   [*She became*] *anxious*   Predicative
    ii [*an*] *anxious* [*parent*]   Attributive
    iii [*anyone*] *anxious* [*to leave immediately*] Postpositive

In general the postpositive use is restricted to constructions where the head of the NP is a compound indefinite pronoun (such as *anyone*), and/or the adjective itself has a post-head dependent (such as *to leave immediately*) – exceptions mainly involve expressions like *the bishop designate, the heir presumptive*, etc. The prototypical adjective occurs, like *anxious* in (1), in all three uses, but certain more peripheral members are found in just one or two. A few are excluded from attributive function: *afraid, asleep, awake, content, loath*, etc. (cf. **an afraid child*). Some, by contrast, are used only attributively: *main, principal, mere, utter* (*the main disadvantage*, but not **That disadvantage was main*). One or two – *designate, elect*, etc. – occur only postpositively.

(b) Degree modification and inflection for grade. The prototypical adjective is gradable, and as such takes degree expressions as modifier: *almost, as, how, much, pretty, quite, rather, so, this, that, too, very* and such *-ly* adverbs as *exceedingly, extremely, sufficiently*, etc. The most distinctive are *too* and *very*, since in the relevant senses ("to an excessive degree", "to a great degree") these do not modify nouns or verbs. A special case of degree specification is comparison, and this may be expressed either inflectionally, as in *taller* and *tallest*, the comparative and superlative forms of *tall*, or analytically, by means of the degree adverbs *more* and *most*, as in *more reasonable, most reasonable*. For the most part only stems of one or two syllables inflect – and indeed not all of these permit inflectional comparison.

In regular adjectives the comparative and superlative inflectional forms result respectively from adding to the lexical stem the suffix /ər/[1] and either /ɪst/ or /əst/ (these being regional/social variants). In some cases suffixation is accompanied

---

[1] In many varieties of English, the /r/ is dropped under the same conditions as apply to the dropping of word-final /r/ in general, namely unless it is followed without an intonational break by a vowel (in some styles by a vowel within the same word – which there will never be in the case of comparative /ər/).

by phonological modification of the stem: for example, stems spelled with final *-ng* are in most varieties pronounced with final /ŋ/ when word-final but with /ŋg/ when followed by an inflectional suffix – /lɒŋ/~/lɒŋgər/. The most frequent irregular forms are *better* and *best*, forms of either **good** or **well** (as either adjective, *He was well/better*, or adverb, *He sang well/better*), *worse* and *worst*, forms of **bad**, **ill** or the adverb **badly**. Comparative *other* has no absolute or superlative counterpart.

Not all adjectives permit degree modification: there are a significant number of non-gradables like *anthropological, linguistic, parliamentary*, etc. These generally denote categorial as opposed to scalar properties. It should be borne in mind, however, that very often an adjective that is non-gradable in its central, most basic sense can be used in an extended sense as gradable. Nationality adjectives like *British*, for example, are primarily categorial: someone or something either belongs to the category British or not; but they can be used in a secondary sense denoting a gradable property, as in *He's very British* ("very much like the British stereotype"). Similarly *wooden* is categorial in its primary sense ("made of wood"), but gradable in a metaphorical sense ("clumsy, stiff, inexpressive").

2. Dependents in AdjP structure

An AdjP consists of an adjective as head, alone or accompanied by one or more dependents. The dependents, a good deal less varied and complex than in VP or NP structure, can again be divided into complements and modifiers.

(a) Complements. These generally take the form of PPs, content clauses or infinitivals:

(2) i   *[Kim is] fond of animals*
     ii   *[I was] sure that it was mine*
     iii *[They were] eager to meet her*

The PP *of animals* in (i) qualifies as a complement by virtue of being obligatory. There are, however, only a handful of adjectives that take obligatory complementation (**fond**, **loath**, **tantamount**, . . .): for the rest we will use the subclassification criterion. Thus in *afraid of the dark, eager for recognition, keen on sport, similar to her mother*, and so on, the PP complements depend on adjectives of the appropriate class: *afraid* selects *of*, *eager* selects *for*, **keen** *on*, and so on. Similarly the subordinate clauses in (ii) and (iii) require the right kind of adjective as head: we could not replace *sure* by *tall*, say, nor *eager* by *paraplegic*. Complements are normally found only with adjectives in predicative or postpositive function – compare predicative (i), postpositive *someone fond of animals*, and attributive **a fond person of animals*.[2]

---

[2] The main exception involves a special case of the infinitival construction, as in *an easy person to get on with*, where *to get on with* is complement to *easy* (compare predicative *She is easy to get on with*).

(b) Modifiers. These involve the expression of degree. They generally take the form of degree adverbs (more strictly, AdvPs), PPs (especially with comparative *as/than*), content clauses (usually in construction with *so*), or infinitivals:

(3) i   [*It was*] *remarkably/so/too/very big*
     ii [*He is*] *thinner/more helpful than he used to be*
     iii [*I was*] *so tired that I fell asleep*
     iv [*They are*] (*too*) *young to go on their own*

The adverbial modifiers precede the head – except for *enough* ([*He wasn't*] *old enough*). Modifiers occur with adjectives in all three of their uses, but with attributive adjectives PPs and clauses are placed after the noun head, resulting in a discontinuous AdjP: compare [*The bucket was*] *bigger than we needed*, predicative (continuous), with [*a*] *bigger* [*bucket*] *than we needed*, attributive (discontinuous).

3. Adjectivalisation

We use the term **adjectivalisation** for a variety of grammatical processes that create adjectives or expressions that bear significant resemblances to adjectives or AdjPs:

(a) Affixation and compounding. The most straightforward type of adjectivalisation results in the creation of an adjective by the morphological processes of affixation or compounding. Suffixes forming denominal adjectives include *-ful*, *-less*, *-ly*, *-ish*, etc., while the most productive suffix forming deverbal adjectives is *-able*: see 2.4.3 for examples. Special mention should be made of the suffix *-ed*: this can be added to nouns, as in [*a*] *walled* [*garden*], but more often is added to an adjective + noun phrasal expression: *long-haired, loud mouthed, simple-minded, blue-eyed*.[3] A number of affixes create adjectives from more elementary adjective stems: these are predominantly prefixes – *un-* (*unkind*), *non-* (*non-negotiable*), *in-* (*inattentive*), *dis-* (*dishonest*), *super-* (*superhuman*), *over-* (*overconfident*) – but also include one or two suffixes, such as *-ish* (*greenish*). The most productive type of compound adjective has a participial form of a verb as the second stem: [*a*] *record-breaking* [*swim*]; [*a*] *good-looking* [*fellow*], *home-made* [*bread*], *self-addressed* [*envelopes*]. We also find compounds made up of noun + adjective: *tax-free, blood-red*, etc.

(b) The use of nouns as modifier. The prototypical modifier of a noun is an adjective, and we can therefore speak of adjectivalisation when a word of another class is used in this function. Adjectivalisation of this type is especially common with nouns (or larger noun-headed expressions, as discussed in 6.9): *a boy actor, student grants, the Reagan administration, the New Zealand government, a government inquiry*. Note, however, that the degree of adjectivalisation here is not suffi-

---

[3] Note that the noun is always singular: *blue-eyed*, not **blue-eyesed*. This, together with the fact that the noun can have only a single modifier, makes it quite different from the possessive construction of *the King of Spain's daughter* (2.6): *-ed* is clearly an affix, not a clitic.

cient for us to want to say that the modifiers ARE adjectives: they are, rather, nouns (or noun-headed expressions) used in a characteristically adjectival function, i.e. as modifiers of other nouns. In spite of the functional similarity between [a] *boy* [*actor*] and [a] *great* [*actor*] there are significant differences between *boy*, a noun, and *great*, an adjective. Firstly, *a great actor* can be related to *The actor is great*, but *a boy actor* cannot be similarly paired with *The actor is boy*. Rather, we have *The actor is a boy* contrasting with *The actors are boys*, where the status of **boy** as a noun is clear from the number inflection and the article. Secondly, *great*, being a prototypical adjective, is gradable, but *boy* is not: *a very great actor*, but not *a very boy actor*. Thirdly, *great* could be followed by another adjective modifier, as in *a great new actor*, but the *new* would precede *boy*, as in *a new boy actor*: adjectives normally precede nouns. Note, moreover, that while *great* can be coordinated with another adjective, *boy* cannot: *a great but modest actor* vs *a boy but mature actor*.

Just about any common or proper noun can function as modifier (given an appropriate head), so that we shall not want to assign each such item to two parts of speech in our lexical entries: instead we simply allow that the modifier function, although most characteristically filled by an adjective, can also be filled by a noun.

(c) Participles and de-participial adjectives. The general definition of participle, it will be recalled, is that it applies to a word class sharing properties of verbs and adjectives. Dictionaries tend to define a participle as a verbal adjective, which is to give priority to the adjectival properties: 'verbal adjective' implies a type of adjective. This is not an analysis we shall wish to follow, however, for the forms in question certainly have uses that are considerably more verbal than adjectival. The boundary between the peripheries of the verb and adjective class is not sharply defined, but we can nevertheless distinguish in a well-motivated way between, say, *Those wounded by the gunman included three cabinet ministers*, where *wounded* is a verb, and *He assumed a very wounded expression*, where it is an adjective. We will employ the term 'participle' in a more limited sense than in traditional grammar, restricting it to word-uses that fall within the verb class, so that *wounded* is a participle in the first example, but not the second. And rather than call it a 'verbal adjective' in the second use we will say, in keeping with our usual terminology, that it is a 'deverbal adjective' or, more specifically, a 'de-participial adjective' – an adjective derived (by conversion) from the participial form of a verb.

Our concern here will be to clarify this distinction between participles (participial verbs) and de-participial adjectives. We will discuss the issue initially with respect to past participles and adjectives derived therefrom, considering the following range of examples:

(4) i   [*The lawyer had*] *considered* [*the contract invalid*]
    ii   [*The contract was*] *considered* [*invalid by the lawyer*]
(5)   [*The contract*] *considered* [*invalid by the lawyer was revised*]
(6)   [*The concert began with a rarely*] *heard* [*work by Purcell*]

} V

(7) i [*On top of the cupboard was a badly*] *broken* [*vase*] ⎫
     ii [*The vase was already*] *broken*   ⎬ Adj
(8) i [*You see before you a very*] *worried* [*man*]   ⎭
     ii [*He seems very*] *worried*

The most straightforward cases are (4), (5) and (8): *considered* is very clearly a participial form of a verb and *worried* is equally clearly a de-participial adjective. We will look first at these and then at the intermediate cases (6) and (7).

(4i) illustrates the perfect use of the past participle, while (ii) illustrates its passive use. In (i) *considered the contract invalid* is complement to the perfect catenative **have**; this construction is very easily seen to be verbal in that the participle has exactly the same range of potential dependents as tensed forms of the verb – *considered*, for example, here has an object + objective predicative just as in *The lawyer considers the contract invalid*. A past participle in its passive use differs in its complementation from corresponding tensed verbs in that the latter will normally have an extra object while the participle allows the *by* phrase 'agent' (see 12.2). Thus past participle *considered* in (ii) has *by the lawyer* as agent, whereas corresponding past tense *considered* in *The lawyer considered the contracts invalid* has *the contracts* as object. Apart from this one systematic difference, attributable to the process of passivisation, the complementation is just the same as for tensed forms. I have chosen *considered* as my example because *consider* is a complex-transitive verb: the verbal character of *considered* is thus particularly easy to see from the fact that it has as dependent a predicative (*invalid*), a type of complement not found with adjectives.

In (4) *considered* heads a clause functioning as complement to a catenative, which is not a position where adjectives are found: there is thus no occasion to speak of adjectivalisation here. In (5), however, *considered invalid by the lawyer* is modifier in NP structure: as the most elementary type of modifier in NP structure is adjectival, we can apply the concept of adjectivalisation to (5). But the argument just given for analysing *considered* as a verb in (4ii) applies equally to (5), and we again take *considered* as head (predicator) of a participial clause. It is thus important to see that the adjectivalisation is a matter of the subordinate clause as a whole (*considered invalid by the lawyer*) being functionally comparable to an adjective phrase, not of the participle itself functioning like an adjective word.

In (8), by contrast, *worried* is a prototypical adjective. In the first place, it occurs both attributively and predicatively, as in (i) and (ii) respectively. And secondly it is gradable, taking, moreover, such degree modifiers as *very* which do not occur with verbs.

The *broken* of (7) differs from *worried* with respect to this second property: it is non-gradable. But it is like *worried* in being able to occur both attributively, (i), and predicatively, (ii). The latter is to be distinguished from the superficially similar passive construction of (4ii). Compare, then

(9) i *The vase was broken by Kim*   Passive clause
     ii *The vase was already broken* (= 7ii)   Copulative clause

These are distinguishable both grammatically and semantically. Grammatically the *be* of (ii) is replaceable by such verbs as *seem, look*, etc., whereas the *be* of (i) is replaceable by *get*. Thus in (ii) *be* belongs with the copulative verbs, and *broken* has the function of predicative, whereas in (i) *be* is the passive catenative and the clause is the passive counterpart of active *Kim broke the vase*. Semantically, (i) describes an event, whereas (ii) describes a state (resulting from an earlier event) – note the event/state ambiguity of *The vase was broken*, which is analysable as an 'agentless' passive (cf. 12.2) or a copulative clause like (ii) without the *already*.[4] We will thus analyse *broken* in (7) as an adjective, though its non-gradability makes it a less central member of that class than *worried*, less fully adjectivalised. As an adjective, it is derived by conversion from the past participle, and there is a further factor supporting the recognition of such a lexical-morphological process even when the resultant adjective is non-gradable. This is that the process displays the incomplete productivity and partial semantic irregularity that are characteristic of lexical morphology (cf. 1.5). For example, we do not have adjectives deriving from such participles as *blamed, killed, noticed* (cf. **They seemed blamed*), and such adjectives as *bound, supposed* (*He's bound/supposed to tell her*), *engaged, related* (*He's engaged/related to Kim*) have senses not found in the corresponding verbs.

The most problematic case is (6). Not only is *heard* non-gradable: it differs significantly from the *broken* type in that it cannot be used predicatively. Thus *This work is rarely heard* belongs to the passive construction of (9i), not the copulative (ii). The degree of adjectivalisation is appreciably greater than in (5): the modifier is in the more characteristically adjectival pre-head position and *heard* cannot be followed by any dependents of its own (cf. **a rarely heard by concert-goers work*). On the basis of its inability to appear in predicative function, I have taken (6) to be a verb rather than an adjective, but it lies very much in the fuzzy borderline area between the two categories.

Present participles and adjectives derived from them can be dealt with fairly summarily, for much of the above discussion applies to them too. They differ from past participles in that they are involved in processes of nominalisation as well as adjectivalisation – but nominalisation (as in *Sacking the secretary was a mistake*) has already been dealt with in 6.12. They also differ from past participles in that they cannot normally be construed as passives, and we have no analogue of *broken* in (7). For present purposes, then, we can confine ourselves to the following range of examples:

(10)   [*Anyone*] *considering* [*such behaviour acceptable must be mad*] } V
(11)   [*He was concerned about the rapidly*] *falling* [*share prices*] }
(12) i   [*It was a very*] *entertaining* [*evening*] } Adj
     ii [*The evening was very*] *entertaining* }

(10) is the analogue of (5): there is adjectivalisation in that the subordinate clause *considering such behaviour acceptable* is modifying the noun head *anyone*, but

---

[4] This semantic contrast is effectively lost when dynamic *break* is replaced by a static verb. Compare, for example, passive *He was well liked by his colleagues* and copulative *He seemed well-liked*.

considering itself is clearly seen to be a verb because its complementation is the same as that of tensed forms of **consider**. (12) is similarly the analogue of (8): *entertaining* is a prototypical adjective, gradable and able to occur both attributively and predicatively. And finally (11) is the analogue of (6), lying towards the boundary between the verb and adjective classes. *Falling* differs from *entertaining* in that it is non-gradable and cannot occur in predicative function (PC): *The share prices were falling rapidly* is not a copulative clause but has **be** as the progressive catenative with a present-participial clause as complement (note that we cannot replace **be** by copulative **seem**, etc.). The construction illustrated in (11) is, moreover, highly productive: the present participles of verbs that occur freely without complements are found here – compare *The baby was sleeping* ~ *the sleeping baby, The sun was setting* ~ *the setting sun*, with *The man was using a stick* ~ **The using man, The minister was relying on her staff* ~ **The relying minister*. It is, therefore, better to handle the construction by means of a syntactic rule governing the occurrence of verbs than by entering items like *falling, sleeping, setting* in the lexicon as adjectives.

(d) PPs and subordinate clauses. The concept of adjectivalisation is also applicable to certain kinds of PP. In

(13) i *a man of honour*
     ii *an honourable man*

the PP modifier *of honour* in (i) is functionally and semantically similar to the AdjP modifier *honourable* in (ii); compare also *a boy with blue eyes* with *a blue-eyed boy*, and so on. However, the adjectivalisation involved in (i) is again very different in kind and degree from that in (ii). *Honourable* is clearly an adjective – a prototypical one; *-able* is a class-changing suffix deriving an adjective from the noun *honour*. *Of honour*, on the other hand, is not an adjective – merely functionally similar to one. It is not a word but a phrase, and by virtue of its structure the phrase belongs to the PP class.[5] (Note that the same PP *of honour* is not always functionally similar to an AdjP – compare *They talked of honour*, where it is complement of the verb, not modifier of a noun.) The PP, being a syntactic construction rather than a morphological formation, is more versatile than the denominal adjective: there is, for example, no morphological way of adjectivalising NPs like *a criminal record, relatives in China, an embarrassing situation*, and so on (cf. **a criminal-recorded man*), but they can readily be made complement in a PP with modifying function: *a man with a criminal record/with relatives in China/in an embarrassing situation*.

The same points hold for subordinate clauses. A clause such as *The man got the other job* can be subordinated to function as modifier to a noun: [*The man*] *who got the other job* [*had no qualifications at all*]. *Who got the other job* is adjective-like in function by virtue of modifying the noun *man*, and to this extent the sub-

---

[5] The term 'adjectival phrase' is, however, quite commonly applied to such expressions in traditional grammar, where the concept of phrase, as we have noted before, is quite different from that adopted in this book.

ordination process represents a kind of adjectivalisation; but *who got the other job* is not of course an adjective, nor an adjective-headed phrase – it is a clause.[6] And again the syntactic clausal construction allows for the expression of much more complex and varied meanings than can be expressed in a single adjective (there is, for example, no adjective meaning "who got the other job"). The example just given is a finite clause (of the relative class); but we also have non-finites modifying nouns – infinitival, as in [*the first person*] *to arrive*, or participial, as in (5) and (10) above.

4. Determinatives

At both the general and language-particular levels, the term **determinative**, the name of a class, will be defined by reference to the functional category of determiner. Determinatives are thus words belonging to a syntactically distinct class whose characteristic function is that of determiner in NP structure.

In English, as we have seen (6.3), the determiner position can also be filled by phrases which, by virtue of their own internal structure, belong to the class of PossPs (e.g. *the boss's* [*mistake*]) or NPs (e.g. *a dozen* [*eggs*]). The remaining determiners are then determinatives (or, in some cases, determinative phrases): *the*, *a*, *this*, *these*, *that*, *those*, *my*, *your*, . . ., *some*, *any*, etc.

Prototypical determinatives such as *the* are syntactically very different from prototypical adjectives such as **happy**. In the first place, *the*, unlike **happy**, cannot be used predicatively (*People are happy*/*the) or postpositively (*somebody happy*/ *the) – and as pre-head dependent in NP structure it has a different function from an adjective, determiner as opposed to modifier (cf. 6.7). Secondly, *the* is ungradable and cannot take any dependents of its own (contrast [*She is*] *happier*/*very happy with the result*). At its periphery, however, the determinative class has strong affinities with the adjective class, and it is debatable just where the boundary should be drawn.[7] The most adjective-like of the determinatives are *few* and *many*: both are gradable, with *few* inflecting for grade (*few*, *fewer*, *fewest*) and both taking such degree adverbs as *very*, and both are occasionally found in predicative function (*Its virtues are few*/*many*). The most determinative-like of the adjectives are those that are restricted to attributive use and disallow dependents – words such as *utter*, *mere*, *principal*, and so on.

5. Numerals

There are a number of distinguishable series of numerals, most notably:

(a) Cardinal numerals (more specifically integers – whole numbers): *one*, *two*, *three*, . . ., *ten*, *eleven*, . . ., *twenty*, *twenty-one*, . . ., *a*/*one hundred*, *a*/*one hundred and one*, . . .

---

[6] Traditional grammars commonly apply the term 'adjectival clause' in such cases.
[7] Traditional grammars usually subsume determinatives under the adjective category; some then distinguish at the level of subclassification, between 'limiting adjectives' (our determinatives) and 'descriptive adjectives'.

(b) Ordinal numerals: *first, second, third, ..., tenth, eleventh, ..., twentieth, twenty-first, ..., (one) hundredth, (one) hundred and first, ...*

(c) Fractions, *a/one half, a/one third, two thirds, a/one quarter, a/one fifth, ...*

To some extent they form a system sui generis, one that is not readily describable in terms of the categories that we use elsewhere in the language. For example, it is not easy to decide whether the cardinal numbers larger than a hundred are to be analysed grammatically as single words or as multi-word expressions. Thus *two hundred and four*, say, is formed by coordination, which is normally a syntactic process (only exceptionally do we find coordination between morphological units, units smaller than a word, as in *pre-and-postwar*), yet it enters as a whole into further processes that are clearly morphological – both lexical, as in the formation of the ordinal *two hundred and fourth*, and inflectional, as in the formation of the plural *two-hundred-and-fours* (cf. *Three two hundred and fours are six hundred and twelve*). We might then regard them as very peripheral members of the word category. Yet these morphological processes, certainly the lexical one, do not apply to numerals beginning with the article *a*, though they do to the corresponding versions with *one*: [*the*] *one*/**a hundred and fourth* [*person in the list*], so that *a hundred and four* and the like is yet further removed from a prototypical word.

There are also problems concerning their part of speech classification. The cardinal integers certainly have uses in which they are nouns, notably those where they carry the plural inflection: [*They went out in*] *threes*, [*Two*] *twos* [*are four*]. One major use is as determiner in NP structure: *one* [*mistake*], *thirty-five* [*apples*]; here they have affinities with the determinatives, but rather than assign them to both noun and determinative classes, it is simpler to regard them as forming a subclass of (non-prototypical) nouns, able to function in both head and determiner positions. Even in determiner function they retain the noun-like property of being able to take as their own dependents an article + adjective: *a good fifty copies*, *a measly three replies* (where *a* and *good/measly* are dependents of *fifty/three*, not of *copies/replies*). *Hundred, thousand, million*, etc., are closer to the prototypical noun in that they occur in the plural in a wider range of structures than the others: *hundreds* [*of books*], [*many*] *thousands* [*of people*].

The ordinal numerals are basically adjectives, having both attributive and predicative uses: *He was the third person in the queue, He was third in the queue*. There are also nouns derived by conversion from the lower ordinals and with a meaning that incorporates some understood head: e.g. *They both got firsts* ("first-class degrees"). Fractions are NPs with the structure determinative + head; note the inflectional number contrast in the head: *one third* vs *two thirds*.

EXERCISES

I. Grading

Consider the following adjectives: *annual, atomic, awkward, certain, experimental, feline, female, feminine, medical, perfect, pneumatic, serious, sulphuric, true.* Which have uses where they are gradable, and which have uses where they are non-gradable? Give illustrative examples, and comment on the difference of meaning in cases where both uses are found.

II. Inflection for grade

(a) Pick out from the following list those which have inflectional comparative forms corresponding to them: *aged, angry, attractive, bored, common, dogged, humble, intelligent, long, mature, obstinate, pure, quiet, rare, right, shallow, tired, unfriendly, unhappy, wicked.* How much of the data can be accounted for by general rules?

(b) Formation of the comparative. The addition of the comparative suffix may be accompanied by a phonological modification to the stem. The main such modifications are illustrated in the comparative counterparts of (α) *feeble, humble, noble*; (β) *strong, young.* What are the phonological modifications involved here? (There is variation in the pronunciation of the words in (β) such that the modification does not hold for all speakers.)

III. Complements and modifiers

Are the post-head dependents in (14)–(18) complements or modifiers?

(14) [*He was*] *very articulate for a seven-year-old*
(15) [*I'm not*] *very sanguine about it*
(16) [*I was*] *glad you could join us*
(17) [*They are*] *rather young to be reading a book like that*
(18) [*He wasn't*] *able to solve the problem*

IV. Adjectives vs nouns

Which of the following are adjectives and which are nouns? Give syntactic reasons for your answers.

(19) [*He became*] *king* [*at the age of 18*]
(20) [*He looked*] *foolish*
(21) [*He looked an utter*] *fool*
(22) [*That is*] *nonsense*
(23) *French* [*has more complex verb inflection than English*]
(24) [*He has a*] *French* [*wife*]
(25) [*The*] *French* [*are usually good at this sort of thing*]
(26) [*They were discussing some recent federal*] *government* [*legislation*]
(27) [*He shows little concern for the plight of the*] *unemployed*
(28) [*She bought him a*] *silk* [*shirt*]

V. Adjectives and participles

Which of the following are verbs (participle forms) and which are adjectives (de-participial adjectives) – and which are ambiguous between the two?

(29) [*The kettle was*] *boiling*
(30) [*the*] *rising* [*sun*]
(31) *Sleeping* [*dogs don't bark*]
(32) [*a*] *humiliating* [*experience*]
(33) [*They keep*] *humiliating* [*him*]
(34) [*I want it*] *destroyed*
(35) [*It should be completely*] *ignored*
(36) [*She looks*] *bored*
(37) [*the recently*] *recaptured* [*prisoner*]
(38) [*Most of the documents*] *removed* [*were of little significance*]
(39) [*The bill was*] *paid*
(40) [*I don't like being*] *blamed* [*for things I haven't done*]

8

Adverbs and prepositions

1. Adverbs

At the general level the adverb is definable as a grammatically distinct word class with the following properties:

(a) Its central members characteristically modify (or head phrases which modify) verbs, adjectives and other adverbs. In languages which distinguish between adjectives and adverbs the primary difference is that adjectives modify nouns (or stand in a predicative relation to noun phrases) while adverbs modify verbs; the modifiers of verbs can, to a very large degree, also modify adjectives and adverbs, so that we then extend the definition of adverb to cover modifiers of all three open classes other than nouns.

(b) Central members commonly express manner or degree; other frequent meanings (often associated with grammatically less central members) include time and place.

(c) It is commonly the case that many members, especially those belonging to the manner subclass, are morphologically derived from adjectives.

Consider now, at the language-particular level, the properties of adverbs in English.

(a) Function. Adverbs, or the phrases they head, occur in a rather wide range of functions, notably (though not exhaustively): (α) modifier in VP structure ([*She spoke*] *clearly*); (β) modifier in AdjP structure ([*She's*] *extraordinarily* [*bright*]); (γ) modifier in AdvP structure ([*She did it*] *rather* [*well*]); (δ) peripheral dependent in clause structure (*Frankly,* [*he's a dead loss*]); (ϵ) complement in VP structure ([*They put us*] *ashore*).

120

However, the sets of words occurring in these five functions are far from wholly the same: the differences are greater than the comparable ones for the other major parts of speech, so that the adverb, as we have noted, is the most heterogeneous of them. The most central function is (α): a prototypical adverb always has the potential to modify the verb. Many words occurring in this function are also found in both (β) and (γ), especially adverbs of degree: [*I*] *quite* [*liked it*] (α), [*It was*] *quite* [*good*] (β), [*We drove*] *quite'*[*slowly*] (γ); [*She sang*] *magnificently* (α), [*a*] *magnificently* [*accurate account*] (β), [*They performed*] *magnificently* [*well*] (γ). Others occur in (α) and (β) but not (γ): [*He took it*] *philosophically* (α), [*a*] *philosophically* [*absurd thesis*] (β), *[*He argued*] *philosophically* [*absurdly*] (γ). The great majority of words found in functions (β) and (γ) are allowed also in (α); the main exceptions are *this, that, very, too* ("excessively"): [*It was*] *that/very* [*long*] (β), [*He hadn't done it*] *that/very* [*carefully*] (γ), *[*We liked it*] *that/very* (α). These may accordingly be regarded as slightly marginal members of the adverb class.

Function (δ), peripheral dependent, covers a number of distinguishable subtypes. For example, words like *however* (as in *However, it was mine* – not the interrogative *however* of *I'll do it however long it takes*), *nevertheless, therefore* serve as connectives between the clause and what precedes, whereas *frankly, surprisingly, inevitably*, as in *Frankly/Surprisingly/Inevitably it was a failure*, express some kind of comment on the rest of the clause – they might be analysed as modifiers of the clause rather than of the verb. Items from this second category generally occur also in functions (α) or (β) (*They spoke frankly* (α), *a surprisingly/inevitably long delay* (β)) and can be regarded as quite central to the adverb class. The first category – the connectives – do not, and may thus be regarded as nonprototypical members of the class.

Complement, (ε), is not a prototypical adverbial function: the elements most tightly related to the verb are typically NPs, with AdvPs having the looser modifying relationship. Among the main adverbial complements are locatives, like *ashore* in our example. We have noted (4.8) that there are both locative complements and locative modifiers: *downstairs*, for example, is a complement in *They were going downstairs*, a modifier in *They were talking downstairs*. Some adverbs – like *ashore* and *downstairs* – occur in either function, and this provides the primary basis for including (ε) within the set of adverbial functions. But there are others, most notably what we have called the 'particles' (*in, on, off*, etc.) which occur only in complement function – compare *They were going in* vs *They were talking in*. Such words thus lie very much at the periphery of the adverb class – there is a very considerable difference in the grammatical behaviour of, say, prototypical *magnificently* on the one hand, and peripheral *in* on the other.

(b) Dependents. The structure of AdvPs is similar to that of AdjPs, but somewhat simpler: adverbs take a more limited range of dependents than do adjectives. Very few adverbs take complements, and the complements are always PPs: *independently/regardless of her efforts*. Thus whereas the adjective *eager*, say, takes an infinitival complement (*eager to please us*), the adverb *eagerly* does not (**eagerly* *to please us*).[1] We also noted above that adjectives take a greater variety of modifiers than adverbs (recall the contrast between [*a*] *philosophically absurd* [*thesis*] and *[He argued] philosophically absurdly*). Nevertheless prototypical adverbs are like prototypical adjectives in taking degree adverbs as modifiers (*very eagerly* ~ *very eager*): the major difference between adverbs and adjectives is in function. It is worth adding, however, that some subclasses of adverb – for example, the connectives *however, nevertheless*, etc. – do not allow any dependents at all.

(c) Morphology. A handful of adverbs – *soon, well*, etc. – inflect for grade (like prototypical adjectives): *soon, sooner, soonest; well, better, best*. For the most part, however, the comparative and superlative categories are marked analytically rather than inflectionally: *frankly, more frankly, most frankly*. Much more important for the characterisation of adverbs in English, then, is lexical morphology: specifically, a high proportion of adverbs are derived from adjectives by suffixation of *-ly*. As we noted in 2.4.4, the *-ly* suffix is neither a necessary nor a sufficient condition for adverb status: *often, soon, yet*, etc., have no *-ly* but are nevertheless adverbs, *cowardly, princely* and the like have the *-ly* suffix but are adjectives. The lexical-morphological criterion is thus clearly secondary to the functional criterion (a) above. It remains important, however, not simply because of the high proportion of *-ly* adverbs, but also because other adverbs are for the most part syntactically replaceable by *-ly* ones. In *They often disagree*, for example, *often* is replaceable by *usually*, as *just* or *yet* are by *recently* in *I've just seen it* and *I haven't seen it yet*. It is worth noting in connection with what was said above concerning the peripheral nature of the complement function (ε), that *-ly* adverbs rarely occur in this function: we could not substitute *-ly* adverbs for, say, the *ashore* of our *They put us ashore*, the *in* of *She brought it in*, etc.

2. Adverbialisation

Adverbialisation, a concept analogous to nominalisation and adjectivalisation, presents no new problems and can be discussed quite briefly. Again we distinguish between morphological processes yielding words actually belonging to the adverb class and syntactic processes yielding expressions which are merely functionally similar to adverbs.

(a) Morphological adverbialisation. There are far fewer affixes forming adverbs than there are forming nouns or adjectives. The most important is the *-ly* suffix already considered. Three others worth mentioning are: (α) the suffix *-wise*, forming manner adverbs, such as *clockwise*, or adverbs in peripheral dependent function, such as *healthwise*; (β) *-ward(s)*, added to a few adverbs/prepositions, as in *backward(s), outward(s)*, etc; (γ) the prefix *a-*, as in *ashore, aboard*, which also,

---

[1] In *He spoke eagerly to please us* the *to please us* is not a dependent of *eagerly* but of *spoke* – as is evident from the fact that it could occur without *eagerly* or be separated from it (*He spoke eagerly to the boss to please us*); the meaning is 'In order to please us, he spoke eagerly'.

however, forms adjectives (*asleep, ablaze*). In formal style we find compound adverbs formed from *where/there* + preposition: *wherein, therefrom*, etc.

(b) Syntactic adverbialisation. The major kind of expression which can function like an adverb is the PP. Adverbs can typically be matched with PPs that have not only the same function but also essentially the same meaning – compare *carefully* with *with care/in a careful way, soon* with *in a short while, usually* with *on most occasions, spectroscopically* with *with a spectroscope, there* with *to/at that place*, and so on. Notice, however, that PPs can also function like adjectives: the sharp distinction in form between adjectives and adverbs is not retained in the process of adjectivalisation/adverbialisation by means of prepositions. Compare, for example, [*a*] *patient* [*woman*] with [*a woman*] *with a lot of patience*, on the one hand, [*She listened to him*] *patiently* with [*She listened to him*] *with a lot of patience*, on the other. This is not to say that all PPs function equally readily like an adjective and like an adverb: for example, PPs with temporal prepositions such as *before* and *after*, or those with a clause as complement (*because/since it was raining, if/unless it's too expensive*) can function as modifier to a verb but hardly, if at all, to a noun.

Another kind of syntactic adverbialisation involves clause subordination. Thus the infinitival clause [*He left at nine*] *to catch the last bus*, for example, is functioning as modifier in VP structure, while the finite content clause [*I was so broke*] *that I couldn't join them* is modifier in AdjP structure. The degree of adverbialisation is significantly less than with PPs in that although such subordinate clauses have broadly the same function as adverbs, we do not normally find anything like the close semantic equivalence to adverbs illustrated above for PPs.

3. Prepositions

At the general level the preposition is one type of **adposition**, the other type being the postposition. Prepositions normally precede their complements, while postpositions follow. The adposition may then be defined as a grammatically distinct closed class of words with the following properties:

(a) They include, among the most central members of the class, words expressing such spatial relations as "at", "in", "on", "under", "over", "to", "from", "through", etc. Very often they also include words serving to show the semantic role and/or grammatical function in the clause of their NP complement; for example, in English *by* marks the agent phrase in passive clauses (*He was interrogated by the police*), *to* marks the recipient role with such verbs as *give, send*, etc. (*He gave the money to Kim*).

(b) They usually show no inflectional contrasts.

(c) They head phrases functioning as dependents of verbs, nouns and adjectives; where the dependents of the verb can be either NPs or PPs, the NPs will tend to occupy the more nuclear functions of subject and object, the PPs the less nuclear one of adjunct. In *Kim read the report in the morning*, for example, the NPs *Kim* and *the report* are respectively subject and object, while the PP *in the morning* is adjunct.

(d) They prototypically take an NP complement.

In English, adpositions are obviously prepositions: the normal order is adposition + complement, not the reverse (*with an axe*, not **an axe with*).[2] Departures from this order arise in those non-kernel constructions, such as relative or interrogative clauses, where the complement of a preposition is moved to clause-initial position leaving the preposition 'stranded' on its own: *Which class shall we put him in?*. This is characteristic of relatively informal style; in the more formal variant, the preposition is fronted too: *In which class shall we put him?*.

At the language-particular level, clear members of the closed preposition class in English have the following properties:

(a) Inflection. They do not enter into inflectional contrasts. Although this is a negative property, it helps differentiate prepositions from verbs, adjectives and nouns, which prototypically do inflect.

(b) Complementation. They can take as complement an NP [*He will resign*] *before/towards the end of the year* or a tensed declarative clause, 'TDC', [*He will resign*] *before/unless a vote is taken*. The following lists give the commonest prepositions classified according to their compatibility with these two kinds of complement.[3]

(1)   Prepositions taking NP or TCD complements

NP	TDC	
+	−	*about, above, across, against, around, at, behind, below, beneath, beside(s), between, beyond, but, by, despite, down, during, from, inside, minus, of, off, on, opposite, out* (mainly US dialects), *outside, over, past, plus, round, through, throughout, to, toward(s), under, underneath, up, upon, via, with, within, without*
+	+	*after, as, before, except, for,*[4] *in, since, than, till, until*
−	+	*although, because, given, if, provided, so, supposing, though, unless, whereas, while*[5]

[2] It is arguable, however, that *ago* and possessive *'s* should be included in the category of adpositions, in which case they would be postpositions.

[3] Traditional grammar has a different analysis here. Words introducing tensed declarative clauses are classified not as prepositions but as conjunctions, a class that also covers coordinators and subordinators.

[4] The *for* that takes a TDC (*He was sorry to hear this, for he had been very fond of her*) is semantically different from the one taking an NP.

[5] Several of those with a minus in the NP column may appear to take an NP complement, as in [*She developed an interest in politics*] *while an undergraduate*. The complement here, however, is best analysed as an elliptical clause in which the NP is functioning as predicative – compare the non-elliptical *while she was an undergraduate* (see 11.7).

In most cases tensed declarative clause complements do not contain the subordinator *that*; *that* is, however, required with *in* and is optional with *except*, *given*, *provided*, *supposing*, *so*.

Most of the above words also belong to other classes. *Provided*, for example, is a preposition in *I'll go provided it's not raining*, a participial verb form in *She had provided the inspiration* – analogously for *given* and *supposing*. More importantly, many of them also belong to the adverb class: *down* is a preposition in *I fell down the stairs* but an adverb in *I fell down*, where there is no complement; similarly for *about*, *above*, *across*, *around*, *behind*, etc.[6]

With prepositions, therefore, a complement is obligatory. More precisely, it is obligatory in kernel clauses: in non-kernel [*The knife*] *he cut it with* [*was blunt*] the complement of *with* has been lost, and in *Such behaviour will not be put up with* it has been reassigned to subject function by passivisation.

NPs and tensed declarative clauses are not, however, the only kinds of complement allowed by prepositions. The complement may also be: (α) an interrogative clause ([*It depends*] *on whether we can afford it*); (β) a present-participial clause ([*He resigned*] *after reading the report*); (γ) a verbless clause ([*She stood*] *with her back to the door*); (δ) an AdjP ([*We regarded her*] *as very competent*); (ε) a PP ([*He emerged*] *from behind the bush*). A fair number of prepositions take a present-participial clause – but note that they are distributed over all three subclasses given in (1): *about*, *above*, *against*, *at*, etc., from the first, *after*, *as*, *before*, etc., from the second, *while* from the third. Only a few take any of the other four kinds of complement.

(c) Modification. Prepositions allow only a modest amount of modification – significantly less, in general, than is found with the open classes. Some, such as *but*, *although*, *whereas*, allow none. The most widespread kind of modification is by expressions of temporal or spatial extent: *three hours after the start*, *far below the surface*. Degree modification with *very much* (not *very* alone) tends to occur with metaphorical rather than literal meanings of prepositions: [*I'm*] *very much against the idea* but hardly [*It was leaning*] *very much against the wall*.

(d) Function. Prepositions function as head in PP structure; PPs in turn have a variety of functions, within the structure of a VP, clause, NP, AdjP, AdvP or a larger PP, as illustrated in (2), where the PP is underlined:

(2)

		Function	Construction
i	[*I*] *did it in the morning*	Modifier	VP
ii	[*He*] *put it in the box*	Complement	
iii	*In my view it was a mistake*	Periph-Dep	Clause
iv	*In the box would be the best place*	Subject	

---

[6] As observed in §1 above, these are somewhat peripheral to the adverb class. An alternative analysis would exclude them altogether and treat them as belonging to the same class when they do not have a complement as when they do; this has a good deal to commend it, but it is arguable whether the general term 'preposition' would then be an appropriate one.

v	*her belief in God*	Complement	} NP
vi	*a man in the front row*	Modifier	
vii	*eager for recognition*	Complement	} AdjP
viii	*big for a three-year-old*	Modifier	
ix	*independently of such considerations*	Complement	} AdvP
x	*too quickly for comfort*	Modifier	
xi	*from behind the bush*	Complement	PP

This is not to say that all prepositions are found in all of these functions – far from it. Virtually all can occur as head in phrases functioning as adjunct (modifier in VP or peripheral dependent in clause). In this respect they are like adverbs; they differ most sharply from adverbs in their complementation and in the fact that many of them do also occur in other constructions, especially (vi). Two prepositions not found in the adjunct construction are *than* and *but*, while *of*, although overall the most frequent preposition, is here more or less restricted to idiomatic expressions like *of course*, *of his* (etc.) *own free will*, and so on.

The more nuclear dependents of the verb, subject in clause structure and complement in VP structure, are prototypically filled by NPs. PP complements (cf. 4.7) are mainly either (α) of place, direction or time, or else (β) complements to prepositional verbs, where the verb selects from a handful of short prepositions, *of*, *as*, *in*, *on*, *for*, *to*, etc. PP subjects are rare, almost restricted to the non-kernel reversed version of the identifying *be* construction, as in (iv) (cf. 12.3): the prepositions will be mainly those of place or time. PP complements in NP structure show essentially the same range as those in VP structure. Modifier in NP structure permits the widest range, but those from the third set in (1) above – *although*, *because*, etc. – are largely excluded. Very few prepositions are found in the constructions of (vii–x); (xi) mainly involves prepositions of place or time – but also *of*, as in *because of the rain*, etc.

The complement in a PP, we have seen, can be an NP; this NP may in turn contain a smaller PP as post-head dependent: *with the producer of the show, for people with red hair*. PPs of this kind contain the sequence Prep (Detve) ... N ... Prep ..., and a number of such sequences exhibit varying degrees of 'lexicalisation', as in *by dint of*, *by means of*, *by virtue of*, *for the sake of*, *in front of*, *in spite of*, *on behalf of*, *on the strength of*, *with the exception of*, and so on. **Lexicalisation** is the process of forming lexical items (single units of vocabulary). Most lexical items are words or lexemes but they can also be larger: these are idioms, and with idioms there may be conflict instead of the usual congruence between what counts as a unit from a lexical point of view and what counts as a unit from a grammatical point of view. In *They're pulling John's leg*, for example, the lexical unit is ***pull*** + the possessive component + *leg*, but this is clearly not a grammatical constituent. Such a mismatch between lexicon and grammar is found in the above Prep (Detve) N Prep sequences. In *for the sake of the premier*, for example, *for the sake of* belongs together lexically, but grammatically the immediate constituents are not *for the sake of* + *the premier* but *for* + *the sake of the premier* (compare *for the premier's sake*).[7] Lexicalisation leads to large-scale reduction in the range of permitted grammatical contrasts – contrasts in inflectional number for the noun (**by virtues of*), in choice of determiner (**for this sake of the premier*), in presence or absence of modifiers (**in immediate front of*), and so on.

EXERCISES

I. Adverbs

Identify the adverbs in (3)–(8). Replace those morphologically formed by suffixation of *-ly* by adverbs not so formed, and – where possible – replace those without this suffix by *-ly* adverbs; the replacements should leave the syntactic structure of the sentence unchanged – but may of course change the meaning.

(3)   *He was therefore forced to resign*
(4)   *They had performed quite creditably*
(5)   *She lives locally*
(6)   *We left separately*
(7)   *Don't make up your mind too precipitously*
(8)   *I usually go with them at week-ends*

II. Adverbs vs adjectives

Are the following adverbs or adjectives? Give syntactic reasons for your answers.

(9)   *[Don't work too] hard [!]*
(10)   *[He pressed it] harder [than he needed to]*
(11)   *[The first problem seemed] harder [than the second]*
(12)   *[It was a] hard [act to follow]*
(13)   *[Don't be too] hard [on him]*
(14)   *[She seemed] well [enough to go to school]*
(15)   *[She did remarkably] well*
(16)   *[Can't you do] better [than that?]*
(17)   *[We had] better [tell her mother]*
(18)   *[I fell] asleep*
(19)   *[She went] ashore*

III. Complementation of prepositions

For each of the prepositions *as, because, before, except, for, from, in, of, on, since, while, with*, say whether it can take as complement: (α) an NP; (β) a PP; (γ) a present-participial clause; (δ) an interrogative clause introduced by the subordinator *whether*; (ε) a tensed declarative clause. Where the answer is 'yes', give an illustrative example.

---

[7] Many grammars, however, make the grammar match the lexicon, treating *for the sake of* and the like as grammatical units – so-called 'complex prepositions'.

IV. AdvPs and PPs

Identify the AdvPs and PPs in (20)–(25). Where possible, replace the AdvPs by PPs and the PPs by AdvPs without changing the syntactic functions.

(20) *Quite obviously we need to get it replaced*
(21) *He still relies rather heavily on his parents*
(22) *Who is the guy with the funny hat on?*
(23) *They rarely go out in the evening*
(24) *They were playing too fast for us beginners*
(25) *I had nevertheless brought in most of the washing*

V. Prepositions and participles

Are the following words prepositions or participial forms of verbs? Give syntactic reasons for your answers.

(26) *[They were] provided [with plenty of food and water]*
(27) *[I'll come along,] provided [your parents agree]*
(28) *[Anyone is welcome,] including [you]*
(29) *[Anyone] wanting [more information should consult their tutor]*
(30) *[It's not too bad], considering [the price]*
(31) *[He has been suspended on full pay] pending [a full investigation into the matter]*

9

Clause type

1. Categories of grammatical form and categories of meaning

The main terms in the system of clause type were illustrated in 1.4 as follows:

(1) i   *You are careful*   Declarative
     ii   *Be careful*   Imperative
     iii *Are you careful?*   Interrogative
     iv   *How careful you are!*   Exclamative

Declarative is the unmarked term: all kernel clauses are declarative and at the language-particular level the other terms will be defined by reference to the syntactic properties distinguishing them from this basic type of clause.

General definitions for the four syntactic classes can conveniently be given together. Declarative, imperative, interrogative and exclamative are general terms applying to syntactically distinct clause classes whose members are characteristically used, respectively, to make statements, issue directives, put questions and make exclamatory statements.[1] 'Directive' covers commands, requests, instructions, prohibitions and the like.

Declarative, imperative, interrogative, exclamative are categories of grammatical form; statement, directive, question and exclamatory statement are categories of meaning. More specifically, the particular dimension of meaning along which statement, directive and question are distinguished is called **illocutionary force**, so that they are different illocutionary categories. The general definition of the technical term 'clause type' is, then, that it applies to a system of clause classes whose members are characteristically used with different kinds of illocutionary force.

The correlation between the grammatical and illocutionary categories is by no means one-to-one. We illustrated this point in our discussion of notional definitions in 1.1, observing that declarative *Passengers are requested to remain seated* and interrogative *Would you mind speaking a little more slowly?* would most naturally be used to issue directives (requests), while imperative *Get well soon*

---

[1] Some of the terms apply also to verb forms: for example, many languages, unlike English, have a distinct imperative verb inflection.

129

would not normally be used to issue a directive but rather to express a wish (for statement, directive and question are not the only illocutionary categories). Many other such examples could be given. It is thus important to keep in mind that the correlation between the two sets of categories provides a basis for the general definitions of the clause types rather than for the language-particular definitions.

In examining the relation between clause type and illocutionary force we should note the following points:

(a) Contrasts of clause type apply to subordinate clauses as well as to main clauses, whereas only utterances of main clauses will have illocutionary force. Thus declarative *I know who did it* has interrogative *who did it* embedded within it, but a normal utterance of it would simply be a statement: there would be no illocutionary force attaching to subordinate *who did it*. This is not to deny that there is a significant relation between subordinate interrogatives and questions, but it is a good deal less direct than with main clause interrogatives.

(b) In main clauses, clause type is not the only factor determining illocutionary force: intonation, the selection of verbs like **request** that actually denote an illocutionary act (cf. the *Passengers are requested* ... example), and various other grammatical, lexical or prosodic factors – and also contextual ones – may be relevant too. Clause type does nevertheless have a special status among the various determining factors: it represents the basic grammaticalisation of illocutionary force. It thus provides the starting point for our description: we will say that a normal utterance of a declarative main clause will have the force of a statement unless there are special factors which override clause type in the determination of illocutionary force.

(c) It is perfectly possible for an utterance to belong to more than one illocutionary category at the same time. Given the appropriate context, an utterance of *It gives me great pleasure to declare this Exhibition open* would serve not only to make a statement (about my feelings) but also – and more importantly, we may assume – to open the Exhibition. Opening an exhibition belongs to the category of 'declarations' (an illocutionary term not to be confused, of course, with syntactic 'declarative'); other examples include placing someone under arrest (cf. the policeman's *You are under arrest*), naming a ship, a baby or whatever (cf. the dignitary's *I name this ship 'Prince Hal'*), and so on – cases where the very act of utterance brings about the state of affairs specified therein (the Exhibition's being open, your being under arrest, the ship having the name 'Prince Hal'). We will invoke the concept of overriding the clause type in the determination of illocutionary force both when the expected force is supplanted by another and when it is supplemented by another. Thus it will apply both to a case like *Sleep well* (normally used as a wish in contrast to the expected directive) and to one like *It gives me great pleasure to declare this Exhibition open* (used as a declaration in addition to the expected statement).

The following sections will take up the four clause types in turn. We will examine the language-particular grammatical properties and the correlation with illocutionary force. For the most part we will confine our attention to main clauses, leaving subordinate clause type to the next chapter.

2. Declaratives

Declarative is, we have said, the unmarked clause type. It will accordingly be defined negatively at the language-particular level as simply lacking the special grammatical properties that distinguish the marked types.

In the absence of overriding factors, the normal use of a declarative main clause will be to make a statement. The prototypical statement is true or false. Thus the statement made by uttering *Tim has left* in a given context will be true if the person referred to by means of the NP *Tim* has indeed left at the time of utterance, false if he has not. It remains, then, only to consider various overriding factors that may interfere with this simple correlation between declaratives and statements. The three main overriding factors are as follows:

(a) Intonation. Rising intonation (represented by '↑' in contrast to falling '↓') can make what would otherwise be a statement into a question: compare *You've finished* ↓ (statement) and *You've finished* ↑ (question). The same effect can be achieved in writing by means of a question-mark: *You've finished?* – but the range of illocutionary effects obtainable by varying the intonation is greater than with punctuation. To take just one example, high rising intonation is commonly used in certain varieties of English (such as Australian English) not to turn a statement into a question but to superimpose on a statement an implicit question as to whether the addressee is following/understanding, often suggesting some diffidence on the speaker's part. Thus *You put it in this box* ↑ might mean not "Do you put it in this box?", but "You put it in this box – do you follow me?".

(b) Performative use of illocutionary verbs. Verbs like **request, command, promise, ask, congratulate** and many more are 'illocutionary verbs' in that they denote illocutionary acts: one can request, command, promise, ask, congratulate, etc. by making appropriate utterances. Under certain conditions they are used **performatively**, i.e. to bring about the performance of the very act they denote. For example, an utterance of *I promise to finish tonight* would typically count as a promise rather than (or as well as) a statement. *I promised to finish tonight*, by contrast, would normally be used simply to make a statement, as *promise* (being in the past tense) is not here used performatively. The statement force is thus overridden only when the illocutionary verb is used performatively. Usually such verbs can be used performatively only when they are in the present tense and the clause they head is positive, declarative, non-subordinate and has a 1st person subject (or else is passive with no *by* phrase, as in the *Passengers are requested . . .* example).

(c) Markers of directive force. There are various ways (apart from that covered in (b)) whereby a declarative can be invested with directive force. Among them we may mention: (α) selection of a modal operator used deontically (cf. 5.3), especially with a 2nd person subject – *You must come in immediately* would normally be construed as a directive to come in; (β) *please* – as in *I'll have that hammer please*; (γ) expression of what the speaker wants or would like – *I want you to meet me at six, I'd like some more coffee if I may*.

3. Imperatives and other jussives

The most central kinds of imperative construction are illustrated in (2):

(2)   Positive   Negative

    i   *Be good*   iv   *Don't/Do not touch it*
    ii   *You be umpire*   v   *Don't you worry*
    iii *Somebody open the door*   vi   *Don't anybody move*

They have the following distinctive set of grammatical properties:

(a) The verb is in the base form. Thus imperative (ii) contrasts with declarative (and kernel) *You are umpire*. Because verbs other than *be* have the base form syncretised with the general present tense form, there may be ambiguity (in the verbal component): *You sit at the head of the table*, for example, could be an imperative (with typical use as a directive, telling you where to sit) or a declarative (with typical use as a statement – most saliently, about your habitual place at table).

(b) A 2nd person subject is omissible. The construction of (i), with *you* absent but 'understood', is much more frequent than that of (ii).

(c) The negative is formed with *don't* (or *do not*) – even where the first verb of the positive is *be* (*Be ruthless* ~ *Don't be ruthless*). An overt subject follows *don't*, as in (v) and (vi); (v) is then ambiguous in the verbal component between imperative and interrogative ("Is it the case that you don't worry?"), while (vi) is unambiguously imperative as 3rd person singular *anybody* would require *doesn't* in the interrogative.

As is evident from (iii) and (vi) the subject of an imperative can be grammatically 3rd person (though in such cases the addressees will normally be implicitly involved: (iii), for example, will be understood as "Somebody among you open the door"). It can, however, hardly be 1st person: *We open the window* will be construed only as a declarative. The corresponding imperative is *Let's open the window*. Here *let* serves as the marker of what may be called a 1st person plural imperative; this special use of *let* is to be distinguished from that found in such ordinary 2nd person imperatives as *Let me have a look, Let us go with you* (where *let us* cannot be reduced to *let's*).

3 Imperatives and other jussives

Imperatives constitute a subclass of a somewhat larger class of **jussive** clauses. (I introduced the subclass into the discussion before the primary class because 'imperative' is a very much more widely used term than 'jussive'.) Non-imperative jussives include main clauses like *The devil take the hindmost, God save the Queen, So be it*, and subordinate clauses like [*It is essential*] *that he accompany her*, [*I insist*] *that they not be told*. The construction exemplified here is productive only in subordinate clauses: the main clauses are virtually restricted to fixed expressions or formulae. Like imperatives, they have a base form as first verb, but they do not have properties (b) and (c) above – and there are also clear differences of meaning between them and imperatives. A number of other relatively minor main clause constructions might be included in the jussive category: *May you be forgiven!, If that is what the premier intends, let him say so*, and so on.

Imperatives, we have seen, are characteristically used to issue directives. Unlike a statement, a directive cannot be either true or false; rather, it is something that can be 'complied' with. Prototypically the aim of issuing a directive is to secure complying action or behaviour on the part of the addressee, as when I say *Open the door* (*please*) with the intention of getting you to open the door. The central kinds of directive are commands (orders), requests, instructions (cf. instructions/directions for use accompanying household appliances, cooking recipes, etc.); less central are advice and permission, though imperatives can certainly be used for these too (e.g. [⟨A⟩ *What do you advise?* ⟨B⟩] *Tell him you're too busy* or [⟨A⟩ *May I have one of these?* ⟨B⟩] *Yes, help yourself*).

One case where imperative clause type is overridden in the determination of illocutionary force has already been illustrated in the *Get well soon* type. This would not normally be construed as a directive because getting well soon is not standardly regarded as being under our control: it is a matter of expressing the wish that something may happen rather than trying to get the addressee to do something. Such examples tend to be very restricted with respect to the content of the wish: getting well, sleeping well, enjoying oneself, and so on.

A second case involves coordination, as in *Come round here again and I'll set the dog on you*. Literally, the first part of the utterance is a positive directive (to come round here again), but the utterance as a whole would typically have the force of a warning, a threat, thus a negative directive (not to come round again). An *and* coordination of imperative + declarative very often implies a conditional relation, so that in this example we derive the interpretation "If you come round here again I'll set the dog on you". The threat comes from the fact that having a dog set on you is something you'd normally want to avoid. This, of course, is a fact of life, not of grammar: the threat is not directly encoded in the grammatical structure – compare the grammatically equivalent *Come round on Tuesday and we'll finalise the agreement*, where the second part would not normally override the literal directive force of the first. In other cases, the relationship with a conditional may allow an imperative that would not readily stand on its own as a directive: *Own a big house and people think you're rich*. By itself, *Own a big house*, which involves a static situation, is much less natural than dynamic *Buy a big house*, say, but in the coordination the implied conditional "If you own a big house people think you're rich" enables it to be used without the unnatural directive force, and the illocutionary force of the whole would most likely be simply that of a statement.

4. Interrogatives

There are two main subclasses of interrogative clauses:

(3) i   *Which version would you prefer?*   Open interrogative
     ii *Would you prefer it?*   Closed interrogative

Open interrogatives contain one of the interrogative words *who, whom, which, whose, what, where, when, why* or *how*; the **closed interrogative** subclass is the unmarked term in the system, lacking this distinctive property. The crucial difference is not, however, the presence or absence of an interrogative word as such, for it is not uncommon in languages for the closed type to be distinguished from the declarative by the inclusion of an interrogative particle rather than by the repositioning of the subject, as in English. The difference is, rather, that in the open type the interrogative word constitutes, or belongs within, an element functioning as subject in clause structure or complement/modifier in VP structure. In (i), for example, *which* is not a mere interrogative marker: it is also determiner within the phrase (*which version*) that is functioning as object of *prefer*.

The class of interrogative words occurring in the open type includes members from several different parts of speech. *Who* and *whom* are nouns – more specifically, pronouns; *which, whose, what* can be either pronouns (*Which/Whose/What is it?*) or determinatives (*Which/Whose/What book shall we use?*); *when* and *where* are usually adverbs (*When/Where did you see him?* – cf. the PPs *at which time/place*) but can also be pronouns (*When/Where would suit you?* – cf. the NPs *what time/place*); *how* can be an adverb (of degree: *How big is it?*, or manner: *How did you do it?*) or an adjective (*How are you?*); *why* is an adverb. *Who* and *whom* are respectively nominative and accusative forms of *who*, but in clause-initial position *who* is commonly used with the function of object or complement of a preposition as an informal variant of *whom* (*Who/Whom did you see?*). *Who* and *what* differ as "human" vs "non-human" – except that in predicative function either can apply to humans, the difference here being that *who* is concerned with the subject referent's identity (*Who is he?* – *The boss's father*), *what* with his or her properties – profession, religion, nationality or the like (*What is he?* – *A phonetician*). *Which* is neutral with respect to the human/non-human contrast, but is always understood 'partitively' – i.e. it is a matter of selecting from some definite set, so that there is always an explicit or implicit *of* phrase (*Which of these books would you recommend?*).

As the above examples show, the interrogative word usually appears at the beginning of the interrogative clause. The formation of an open interrogative from a corresponding declarative thus typically involves the movement of the interrogative phrase to initial position: *She has gone somewhere* ~ *Where has she gone?*, *You are putting something in my tea* ~ *What are you putting in my tea?*. This movement accounts for the somewhat equivocal status of the interrogative phrase with respect to the constituent structure. In *Who will she say is right?*, for example, the *who* belongs from one point of view in the subordinate *be* clause, as subject (compare declarative *She thinks someone is right*), but from another point of view it belongs in the main *will* clause, as marker of the open interrogative clause type: the first corresponds to its position before movement, the second to its final position.[2] As noted in 8.3, a preposition with an interrogative phrase as complement may either accompany it in its movement to the front of the clause, as in formal style *To what are you referring?*, or else remain 'stranded' in its basic position, as in informal *What are you referring to?*.

There are two cases where the rule of interrogative phrase fronting does not apply. One is where the phrase is already initial by virtue of being subject of the interrogative clause: *Something is hurting her ~ What is hurting her?*. The second involves an uncommon construction where the interrogative phrase remains in its basic position: *You left at some time ~ You left at what time?*; this construction characteristically occurs in contexts of sustained questioning, such as interrogations or quizzes.

In main clauses, fronting of the interrogative phrase is accompanied by movement of the subject to post-operator position – 'subject–operator' inversion, as we shall call it. In subordinate clauses, by contrast, the subject normally retains its basic position: compare (3i) for example, with its subordinate counterpart [*I know*] *which version you would prefer*. As we noted in 3.7, if the declarative contains no operator, dummy *do* must be inserted before subject–operator inversion can apply: *You think someone broke it ~ Who do you think broke it?*. The latter thus involves interrogative phrase fronting, *do* insertion, and subject–operator inversion; it illustrates well the way in which non-kernel constructions can be structurally more complex, less straightforward than kernel ones.

Interrogatives of the closed type likewise undergo (in main clauses) subject–operator inversion and, where needed, *do* insertion. Thus the position of the subject in *Is he here?* or *Did she win?* may be contrasted with that in declarative *He is here*, *She won* or subordinate interrogative [*I wonder*] *whether he is here*, [*She didn't say*] *whether she won*.

Let us turn now to the semantics. Interrogative main clauses are characteristically used to put questions. While a statement is prototypically assessable as true or false and a directive specifies action or behaviour that would constitute compliance, a question has the distinctive property of defining a set of logically possible answers. For example, the set of answers to the question "Where is the carving-knife?" includes "The carving-knife is in the kitchen" (expressible as *The carving-knife is in the kitchen*, *It's in the kitchen* or simply *In the kitchen*), "The carving-knife is on the table", and so on – but not "My uncle is ill", "I don't

---

[2] When, as here, the interrogative word has a function within a subordinate clause embedded within the interrogative clause, there are restrictions on what kind of subordinate clause it may be. For example, it cannot be a relative clause – compare **What had she watched the boy who was writing?* with the well-formed declarative *She had watched the boy who was writing something*.

know", "Why do you ask?", and so on. Note, then, that we make a theoretical distinction between an **answer** and a **response**. If you say to me *Where is the carving-knife?*, I might say in response *In the kitchen* – in which case I would have given an answer; but I might equally well say *I don't know* – this would still be a response, but it would not be an answer. Or if you ask *Is Kim here?* the response *Yes, in the kitchen* gives an answer ("Yes") but additional information as well.

Answers to questions are usually statements. There is, however, a special type of question whose answers are directives. Such questions are called 'deliberative questions'; they are usually expressed by means of the modal operator *shall* or *will* (depending on the dialect): *Where shall/will I put the carving-knife?*. Answers here include the directives "Put the carving-knife in the drawer", "Put the carving-knife on the table", and so on.

We have said that a question defines a set of answers. It may do so in either of two ways. In the first place, it may be analysable as containing a 'variable' with each answer supplying a value for this variable. For example, the question "Who wrote the letter?" may be analysed as "What person$_x$ wrote the letter?", with the answers all specifying a value for the variable 'person$_x$': "Tom wrote the letter", "Your father wrote the letter", and so on. The set of possible values for the variable is in principle open, and we accordingly speak of such questions as open questions. In the second place, the question may explicitly or implicitly specify a set of alternatives, each of which constitutes a possible answer. Thus the answers to "Is he alive or dead?" are "He is alive" and "He is dead", the alternatives given in the question itself. Here then the set of answers is closed, limited to the alternatives, and we speak of them therefore as closed questions. One special case of the closed question is that where the alternatives differ as positive or negative: "Has he finished or has he not finished?". But here one of the alternatives is usually left implicit: "Has he finished?", "Has he not finished?"; the answers to such questions can be expressed as *yes* or *no*, hence the name **yes/no question**. Yes/no questions constitute the most frequent type of closed question.

The general terms open and closed interrogative are then defined as grammatically distinct clause classes characteristically associated with open and closed questions respectively. The relationship is, however, less straightforward for the closed type than for the open. The expression of an explicit closed question includes an *or* coordination – but sometimes this coordination falls within a single clause (*Is he alive or dead?*) and sometimes it involves separate clauses linked by the *or* (*Is he alive or is he dead?*): in this latter case we thus have two (or more) closed interrogative clauses but just one closed question. Note then that the clause *is he alive* can be used either as one element within a coordination expressing an explicit closed question (*Is he alive [or is he dead?]*) or on its own as the expression of an implicit closed question, a yes/no question (*Is he alive?*).[3]

---

[3] There is considerable variation in the terminology used in the literature for different kinds of interrogative and different kinds of question. Many writers fail to distinguish between 'interrogative' and 'question', using the latter term for both; this is particularly frequent at the level of subclassification. Where 'interrogative' is used, the commonest terms for the open and closed subtypes are probably '*wh*' and 'non-*wh*' interrogative: these reflect the fact that the

It should also be observed that an *or* in a closed question does not necessarily coordinate elements from which the alternative answers derive. Thus such a sentence as *Would you like some tea or coffee?* is ambiguous between the two kinds of closed question, yes/no (implicitly equivalent therefore to *Would you like some tea or coffee, or not?*) and non-yes/no (equivalent to *Would you like some tea or would you like some coffee?*). In speech the ambiguity would be resolved by intonation, with a rise on *coffee* in the yes/no interpretation, a rise on *tea* together with a fall on *coffee* in the other.

Usually one puts a question with the aim of eliciting an answer (the 'right' answer) from the addressee(s): in this case one ASKS a question. But it is not always so: I might just be wondering aloud, or I might use the question as a means of introducing the topic that I myself intend to go on to talk or write about (*How can this problem be solved? I believe the best approach would be ...*), or it might be a 'rhetorical' question – one whose answer is so obvious that there is no need to state it. It should also be borne in mind that the grammatical form of a question may encode information concerning the questioner's assumptions or expectations about the answer. For example, although *Has he finished?* and *Hasn't he finished?* are alike with respect to the answers they define ("Yes, he has finished" and "No, he hasn't finished"), they differ in that the first (in the absence of marked prosodic features) is neutral, whereas the second indicates that my previous expectation was that he has finished but that present evidence suggests that he may well not have.

Let us turn now to the main cases where interrogative clause type is overridden in the determination of illocutionary force. We will mention three:

(a) Closed interrogatives used as directives. In many contexts an imperative is regarded as too brusque, too direct for use as a socially appropriate request: more polite is to use an interrogative introduced by *Can you, Could you, Will you, Would you, Would you like to/care to/mind . . .ing, Would you be so kind as to*, and so on. Literally, *Can you open the door for me?* expresses a question about your ability to open the door for me, but in actual use it would be most likely intended and understood as a request to do so; the request force may be explicitly indicated by means of *please*: *Can you please open the door for me.*

(b) Open interrogatives used as directives. Interrogatives with *why* are commonly used as directives: *Why don't you see a doctor?* would often have the force of a suggestion that you should. The directive force may be reflected in the form of the clause – in the infinitival construction of *Why not see a doctor?*, or in the use of *do* in construction with *be* in *Why don't you be more careful?*, etc.

interrogative words in English (except for *how*) begin with *wh*, but this English orientation makes them unsatisfactory as general terms; another pair of terms is 'special' and 'general' interrogative. For 'open question' one will find (beside '*wh* question' and 'special question') 'x question' and 'information question'. Yes/no questions are sometimes called 'nexus questions' or 'polar questions', and 'alternative question' is often used for the other type of closed question.

(c) Closed interrogatives used as exclamatory statements. Given appropriate punctuation or prosodic modulation, clauses like *Was I glad to see her!*, *Haven't you grown!* and so on, can be used with the force of exclamatory statements, "How glad I was to see her!", "How you have grown!".

5. Exclamatives

Exclamative clauses are marked by one or other of the exclamative words *how* and *what*:

(4) i   *How tall Ed is!*
     ii *What a tall lad Ed is!*

How is more characteristic of formal or careful style than *what*. Exclamative *what* differs syntactically from interrogative *what* in that it belongs exclusively to the determinative class (it cannot be a pronoun) – and it occupies determiner position I (not II). There is also a difference in meaning: exclamative *what* is concerned with degree (e.g. the degree to which Ed is a tall lad in (4ii)), interrogative *what* with identity (e.g. the identity of the course Ed is taking in *What course is Ed taking?*). Exclamative *how* differs from interrogative *how* in that it belongs exclusively to the adverb class (it cannot be an adjective). It usually functions as degree modifier to an adjective, to an adverb or to *many, much, few, little* – but it can also occur as head of an AdvP on its own; in the latter case it differs semantically from the interrogative in again being concerned with degree, as opposed to manner – compare exclamative *How we hated it!* and interrogative *How did we manage it?*.

If the phrase containing the exclamative word is not subject, it is moved to the non-kernel position before the subject – compare (4i) with declarative *Ed is tall*. Usually the subject remains in its basic position before the predicator but it is occasionally inverted with the operator (*How often have I regretted that decision!*) or placed after copulative *be* (*How great would have been her disappointment if you had refused!*); such inversion is normally found only in formal literary style and applies only under heavily restricted grammatical conditions. Thus for the most part the order of subject and predicator distinguishes exclamatives from *how* and *what* interrogatives: the main case where ambiguity does arise in the verbal component is where *how* or *what* falls within the subject. *How much work remains to be done*, for example, could be exclamative ("What a lot of work remains to be done!") or interrogative ("What is the amount of work that remains to be done?"). Similarly *What strange people lived there* has either an exclamative interpretation ("How strange the people were who lived there!") or an interrogative ("Who were the strange people who lived there?"). But with *what* such ambiguities are rarer because of the different properties of exclamative and interrogative *what*: *What a lot of work remains to be done*, for example, is unambiguously exclamative because interrogative *what* cannot combine with *a*.

Exclamative clauses are standardly used to make exclamatory statements. An exclamatory statement is a statement with an overlay, as it were, of emotive or attitudinal meaning. When I use (4i), for example, to make a statement, I convey my feeling that the degree to which Ed is tall is in some way out of the ordinary, remarkable. Such an exclamatory component of meaning can be expressed by other means (e.g. by items like *so, such, remarkably* . . ., or by appropriate prosodic modulation), but it is only in exclamatives that it is grammaticalised, i.e. expressed by the marker of a grammatically distinct construction.

There are no features comparable to those given above for declaratives, imperatives and interrogatives which override exclamative clause type in the determination of illocutionary force.

6. Interrogative tags and echoes

One special kind of closed interrogative is the interrogative tag, which may be attached to a clause of any of the three non-interrogative types: declarative, imperative, exclamative. With declaratives the most frequent kind of tag is the 'reversed polarity tag', as in

(5) i   *He left alone, didn't he?*
    ii   *He didn't leave alone, did he?*

Thus the tag has the opposite polarity to that of the declarative: positive *He left alone* takes a negative tag, while negative *He didn't leave alone* takes a positive. The form of the tag is largely predictable from that of the declarative. It may be derived from the latter by reversing the polarity, converting to a closed interrogative, replacing the subject where necessary by a personal pronoun (6.11.1), and deleting everything except the operator, subject and *not* in the case of an analytic negative. Thus *Ed has left→Ed hasn't left→Hasn't Ed left?→Hasn't he left?→hasn't he?* – or, with the much less frequent analytic negative, *Ed has left→Ed has not left→Has Ed not left?→Has he not left?→has he not?*.

Contrasting with reversed polarity tags are 'constant polarity tags'. Here the polarity is the same as that of the declarative: *He left alone, did he?, He didn't leave alone, didn't he?* – though perhaps only a minority of speakers allow this with a negative. There is a clear difference in meaning between the two types of tag. The reversed polarity tag is used to ask whether, or seek confirmation that, what is said in the declarative is in fact so. The constant polarity tag, on the other hand, does not express doubt about what is said in the declarative, but has an emotive meaning, indicating disapproval or the like. We may thus distinguish the two types of tag as 'emotively-neutral' (reversed polarity) versus 'emotively-charged' (constant polarity).

Exclamatives take only reversed polarity tags: *What a fine voice she has, hasn't she?*. The exclamative is usually positive and the tag thus negative.

Imperatives allow a slightly wider range of tags: to *Open the door*, for example, we could add *can you?, can't you?, could you?, will you?, won't you?, would you?*. We saw above that certain kinds of interrogatives can be used to issue directives: the tags attachable to imperatives are elliptical versions of the simplest such interrogatives available for use as directives. Thus *can you?* would be elliptical for *Can you open the door?*, which could be used for a directive to open the door, just like the imperative itself – and similarly for *can't you?*, etc., though there are of course differences in politeness and emotive meaning among the various options. Negative imperatives allow fewer possibilities because fewer kinds of interrogative can be used for negative directives: *Will you not open the door?*, but not *Won't you open the door?*, can be used as a directive not to open the door, and thus *will you?*, but not *won't you?*, can be tagged to *Don't open the door*. Tags for 1st person imperatives are *shall we?* or *will we?*, depending on the dialect: *Let's open the door, shall/will we?*. Again they are elliptical versions of *Shall/Will we open the door?*, which would typically be used with directive force.

Finally we should mention the category of **echo questions**. Suppose you say to me *Give them to Max* and I reply (incredulously, perhaps) *Give them to Max?*. The two utterances are alike in the verbal component, and both have the form of an imperative – but yours would have the force of a directive (to give them to Max) while mine would have the force of a question ("Are you (really) telling me to give them to Max?"). More specifically, it would be what is called an echo question: it echoes what has gone before. There are two kinds of echo question: 'yes/no echoes', as in the example just given, and 'open echoes', as in *Give them to who?*, or *Give what to Max?*. The former seek confirmation of what was said, while the latter ask particularly for repetition of the word or phrase replaced by *who*, *what*, etc. Yes/no echoes are normally marked as such simply in the non-verbal component – 'normally', because there may also be changes in the category of person, as when you say *Give yourself a treat* and I echo *Give myself a treat?*. Open echoes substitute an appropriate interrogative word for some word or phrase. The echo marking is superimposed on the original utterance and constitutes a further factor overriding clause type in the determination of illocutionary force.

EXERCISES

I. Clause type and illocutionary force

Classify the following with respect to the system of clause type and suggest what illocutionary force an utterance of them would typically have.

(6) i   *Turn off that radio*
     ii *I order you to turn off that radio*
(7) i   *Have a safe journey*
     ii *I wish you a safe journey*
(8) i   *Please pass the scissors*
     ii *Would you be kind enough to pass the scissors?*
(9) i   *Would you like another sherry?*
     ii *Let me pour you another sherry*
(10) i   *What a fool I've been!*
     ii *Haven't I been a fool?*

II. Performative use of illocutionary verbs

Identify the verbs from the following list that can be used performatively: *anger, arrest, bet, command, demand, excite, forgive, frighten, like, move, object, offer, persuade, sentence, suggest, swear, telephone, tell, tempt.*

III. Declaratives with directive force

The following illustrate further kinds of declarative clauses that would readily be used with some sort of directive force; discuss the reasons which facilitate a directive interpretation.

(11) *It isn't polite to speak with food in your mouth*
(12) *If I were you, I'd try and get him to improve the offer*
(13) *It would be better to put it here*
(14) *You sit next to Father*

IV. Open interrogatives

(a) Where possible, form open interrogatives from the following declaratives, replacing the indefinite *some* phrase with the corresponding interrogative phrase. (It is not possible in all cases because of the grammatical restrictions on whereabouts the *some* phrase can occur.)

(15) *She saw someone*
(16) *They had been reading some book*
(17) *He said that he was going somewhere*
(18) *They arrested the guy who had injured someone*
(19) *Ed is in a bad temper because something has gone wrong at work*
(20) *He wonders whether they will appoint someone*
(21) *He thinks that they will appoint someone*

(b) Not all interrogative phrases have such a straightforward relation to a non-interrogative *some* phrase; comment on the following with respect to this issue.

(22) *How big is it?*
(23) *Which way shall we go?*
(24) *How is it you let him get the better of you?*
(25) *Why didn't you tell me?*

V. Interrogatives and exclamatives

Which of (26)–(31) are ambiguous between an open interrogative and an exclamative interpretation? For those that allow only one analysis, say what grammatical factors exclude the other. (Assume that all examples are complete sentences; they are presented here without final punctuation.)

(26) *How many times have I told you not to do that*
(27) *How much money was wasted*
(28) *What is left*
(29) *What excellent courses are available now*
(30) *How they laughed*
(31) *How did you persuade him*

VI. Interrogative tags

(a) Add reversed polarity tags and, where possible, constant polarity tags to the following.

(32) *She wrote it herself*
(33) *Tom likes playing the fool*
(34) *He didn't answer*
(35) *There wasn't enough food left*
(36) *Everybody had finished*
(37) *She used to live in Brighton*

(b) Why is it that either *will you?* or *won't you?* can be tagged to *Tell her where you're going*, but only the former to *Don't tell her where you're going?*

10

Negation

1. Clausal and subclausal negation

The clause system of polarity was introduced in 1.4 with the contrast between positive *They were helpful* and negative *They weren't helpful*. Positive and negative clauses are distinguishable syntactically in English by the following properties:

(a) Cohesive adjuncts. Positive clauses can be related by cohesive *so* or *too*, whereas negatives take *neither/nor* or *either*:

(1) i   *They were helpful and* $\left\{ \begin{array}{l} \textit{so/*neither/*nor was Kim} \\ \textit{Kim was too/*either} \end{array} \right.$

     ii   *They weren't helpful and* $\left\{ \begin{array}{l} \textit{neither/nor/*so was Kim} \\ \textit{Kim wasn't either/*too} \end{array} \right.$

(b) Emotively-neutral tags. As we noted in 9.6, emotively-neutral tags – as opposed to emotively-charged ones – reverse the polarity of the clause to which they are attached. Thus a positive clause takes a negative tag, and vice versa:

(2) i   *They were helpful, weren't they?*
     ii   *They weren't helpful, were they?*

These properties provide criteria for distinguishing between positive and negative clauses at the language-particular level for English. The criteria apply directly to declarative main clauses, but others can be classified derivatively [*I wonder*] *whether they were helpful*, say, is positive by virtue of its relation to *They were helpful*. At the general level the term 'negative clause' may be defined as applying to a grammatically distinct class of clause whose members are characteristically used to express logical negation. Logically negating a proposition reverses its truth value: thus if "They were helpful", for example, is true then "They weren't helpful" will be false, and vice versa.

    The most straightforward kind of negative clause in English has what we will call 'verb negation' – either inflectional (e.g. *weren't*) or analytic (*were not*). As we noted in 3.7, such clauses must contain an operator: if the corresponding positive has no operator, dummy ***do*** is added. Thus the negative of *They helped us* is *They didn't/did not help us*, and so on.

Where *not* follows a catenative verb we must distinguish according as it belongs with the catenative itself or with its complement:

(3)   i   *He ought not to tell her*   Superordinate clause negative
    ii   *He proposes not to tell her*   Subordinate clause negative

In (i) the *not* belongs in the ***ought*** clause, which is therefore negative, whereas in (ii) it belongs in the ***tell*** clause, so that the ***propose*** clause is positive (cf. *He proposes not to tell her and so do I*). *Not* comes to occupy the same linear position in the two constructions because it follows the verb it modifies when the latter is tensed but precedes it when it is non-tensed, and with *to*-infinitivals it usually precedes the *to* as well. Non-operator catenatives follow the pattern of (ii); operators usually follow that of (i), but some allow (ii) as well, if the *not* is prosodically linked to the following verb. Thus *We could not answer* may have *not* in the superordinate clause ("We were not/would not be able to answer") or, much less usually, in the subordinate clause ("We could refrain from answering"); the subordinate clause negation is more readily obtained by inserting an adjunct between the operator and *not*: *We could always not answer, [couldn't we?]*. When the negation is inflectional rather than analytic, only the superordinate type is possible: *We couldn't answer* excludes the second interpretation.

There are other ways of marking a clause negative than by verb negation; the principal such markers are given in (4) and illustrated in (5):

(4)   i   *nothing, nobody, no one, nowhere, none, no* (determiner in NP structure, as in *no respite*, modifier in comparative AdjPs or AdvPs, as in *no faster*); *never; neither* (determiner or head in NP structure, as in *neither (candidate)*, or cohesive adjunct, as in (1ii)), *nor* (cohesive adjunct), *neither . . . nor* (correlative coordinators marking a single negation);
    ii   *not*, when in construction with *even, only, much, many, enough, one*, etc.;
    iii   *few, little* (determiner or head in NP structure, as in *little (patience)*, and – marginally – modifier in comparative AdjPs or AdvPs, as in *little better*); *rarely, seldom; barely, hardly, scarcely*

(5)   i   *There was nothing to worry about, [was there?]*
    ii   *Not even John offered to help, [did he?]*
    iii   *Kim hardly spoke [and nor did Tom]*

The items in (4i) are analysable into a negative component together with a corresponding positive element, so that the non-verb negation (5i), for example, is equivalent to the verb negation *There wasn't anything to worry about, [was there?]*. The correspondences between negative and positive items are shown in (6) and (7):

(6)   i   *nothing, nobody, no one, nowhere; none/no*   Negative
    ii   *anything, anybody, anyone, anywhere, any*   Positive
(7)   i   *never; neither/nor; neither . . . nor*   Negative
    ii   *ever; either; either . . . or*   Positive

Cohesive *nor* corresponds to *either*, as in (1ii) above, coordinator *nor* to *or*, as seen in the equivalence between *She knew neither the address nor the phone number* and *She didn't know either the address or the phone number*. Such equivalences are found only when the verb negation construction has the item from (ii) in post-verbal position: we have, for example, *Nobody saw it*, but not **Anybody didn't see it*.

Unlike the markers of verb negation, the items of (4) may appear in a non-finite clause embedded as complement within the larger clause that they mark as negative: *Kim is telling no one about it [and neither is Ed]*. Here *no one* belongs in the subordinate **tell** clause, but it is the superordinate **be** clause that is negative – compare the verb negation counterpart *Kim isn't telling anyone about it*. This situation usually involves operators, such as the progressive **be** here, but it is found with certain other catenatives too, as in *You certainly saw them do nothing wrong, [did you?]*.

Consider now the contrast illustrated in

(8) i   *He at no time consulted his colleagues on the matter*
     ii *He in no time completely revitalised the company*

(i) is a negative clause with non-verb negation, just like (5). But clause (ii) is positive: note that the tag is *did he?* for (i) but *didn't he?* for (ii). We will therefore distinguish between **clausal negation** and **subclausal negation** according as the syntactic domain of the negative element is the whole clause, as in (i), or merely part of the clause, as in (ii). Compare, similarly, *Not a single mistake was found* (clausal) and *One not very important mistake was found* (subclausal). More obvious cases of subclausal negation involve negative affixes added to a stem by a process of lexical morphology: *un-* (*unhelpful*), *in-* (*inattentive*), *non-* (*non-refundable*), *dis-* (*disloyal*), *a-* (*amoral*), etc.; *They were unhelpful*, for example, is clearly a positive clause by the criteria we have given.

The two kinds of negation can combine, as in *No one has absolutely no redeeming feature*. Semantically the two negatives here cancel each other out, for the meaning is "Everyone has some redeeming feature", but grammatically they do not: the clause is negative, not positive, as is evident from the polarity of the tag (*do they?*). Thus the first negative is clausal, the second subclausal. One special case of the double negative involves the denial of a previous negative assertion, as in *I "didn't consult no one [– I consulted Kim and Pat]*.[1]

The distinction between clausal and subclausal negation is relevant to the rule of subject–operator inversion. We observed in 3.7 that the rule applies in various constructions besides interrogatives, including that where a negative has been moved to pre-subject position. The negative triggering inversion, however, has to be a marker of clausal negation. Thus if we front the negative in (8i) we need **do** insertion and inversion: *At no time did he consult his colleagues on the matter*; but

---

[1] In non-standard English *I didn't consult no one* will be interpreted as 'I didn't consult anyone'; in this case it is not semantically a double negative but simply involves double marking of a single clausal negation.

this is not so with the subclausal negative in (ii): *In no time he completely revitalised the company.*

2. Non-affirmatives

Although we labelled the items in (6ii) and (7ii) 'positive' in contrast to the negatives in (i), they tend to occur more freely in negative clauses than in positives – compare

(9)   i   *She isn't feeling any better*
      ii **She is feeling any better*

This section investigates the restrictions whose violation is illustrated in (ii). There are two issues to consider: which items are subject to the restrictions and which constructions permit the items concerned. We will introduce the term **non-affirmative** to facilitate discussion of both issues: we will say that *any*, as used in (9), is a non-affirmative item and that it is restricted to non-affirmative contexts such as the negative.[2]

The main non-affirmative items are: (α) *any* and its compounds (*anything*, etc.); (β) *ever*; (γ) *either*; (δ) *at all* (*She didn't like/*liked them at all*); (ε) *yet* (*She doesn't know/*knows the result yet*); (ζ) **dare** and **need** (*He needn't/*need go*); (η) **can** *help/ stand* + present-participial complement (*I can't/*can help/stand forgetting things*); (θ) **give** *a damn*, **lift** *a finger* and similar idioms (*He didn't give/*gave a damn who heard it*).

The restrictions do not always, however, apply to all uses of the items – so that we should in general talk of non-affirmative uses rather than simply non-affirmative items. Stressed *any*, for example, meaning roughly "no matter which/what" and hence often, by implication, "every", can occur in affirmative contexts, as in *Any doctor will tell you it's bad for you*. So too can *ever* with the sense "all time", as in *I'll love you for ever*. *Either* is non-affirmative only in its cohesive use (*I didn't like/*liked it either*). *Yet* is non-affirmative only in the sense "so far, by this/ that time", as in *I haven't read it yet*: contrast the less usual "still" sense of *There is yet time*. Finally **dare** and **need** are non-affirmative only in their use as operators (where they have only tensed forms and no person–number distinctions): contrast *She had dared to contradict him, He needs a haircut*.

The range of non-affirmative contexts is illustrated in:

(10)   i   *He will never do any better*   Negative
       ii   *Do you want any more to eat?*   Interrogative
       iii *If it gets any worse* [*call the doctor*] ·   Conditional
       iv   *Liz worked harder than any of the others*   Comparative
       v   *Ed is too tired to do any more*   *Too*
       vi   *Only John knows anything about it*   *Only*
       vii *Max forgot to tell anyone*   **Forget**, etc.

The negative in (i) is normally clausal (compare subclausal **He will in no time do*

---

[2] An alternative term is 'non-assertive'.

any better). And the negative marker, like *too* and *only* in (v) and (vi), must pre-cede the non-affirmative (thus *Nobody did anything*, but not **Anybody did nothing*). **Forget** in (vii) is just one of a number of verbs and adjectives creating non-affirmative contexts: others are **deny, dissuade,** *loath, reluctant,* etc.

There are clearly semantic resemblances among these constructions: all of (ii)–(vii) can be related by implication to a negative. (ii) implies that you may not want any more and (iii) that it may not get any worse. (iv) implies that the others didn't work as hard as Liz and (v) that Ed won't do any more. And similarly (vi) implies that no one other than John knows anything about it, (vii) that Max didn't tell anyone.[3]

3. Semantic scope and marked focus in clausal negation

Let us now look a little further at the interpretation of clausal negation. Consider first the following examples:

(11) i *Ed hadn't read the report, obviously*
 ii *Ed hadn't read the report carefully*

These differ with respect to what is called the semantic **scope** of the negation – i.e. with respect to how much of the semantic content the negative applies to. Thus in (i) "obviously" falls 'outside' the scope of the negative, is not part of what is negated, whereas in (ii) "carefully" falls 'inside' the scope of the negative. In (i) the negative applies to "Ed had read the report" and then "obviously" applies in turn to "Ed had not read the report"; in (ii), by contrast, the negative applies to "Ed had read the report carefully". This (together with the semantics of *obviously*) is why (i) entails *Ed hadn't read the report*, whereas (ii) does not – on the contrary it implies that he had read it.

Syntactically, *obviously* in (i) is a peripheral dependent, while *carefully* in (ii) is a modifier; there is thus a difference in syntactic constituent structure to match the difference in semantic scope. The correlation between form and meaning is not always as straightforward as it is here, however. Peripheral dependents always fall outside the scope of clausal negation – but modifiers do not invariably fall inside. Whether or not they do depends on a variety of factors: the kind of adjunct, its linear position and prosodic properties of the utterance. Modifiers preceding the negative marker are typically outside its scope: contrast, for example, *Kim deliberately didn't reveal his whereabouts* (where the negation applies just to "Kim revealed his whereabouts") and *Kim didn't reveal his whereabouts deliberately* (where, in the absence of special prosodic indications to the contrary, it applies to "Kim revealed his whereabouts deliberately"). Post-verbal modifiers of manner are inside the scope, as in (11ii), whereas for those of reason or purpose the unmarked case is that they fall outside the scope, as in *Ed hadn't read the report because he was too busy*. However, such reason or purpose modi-

---

[3] Cohesive *either* requires a stronger and more direct negative implication than the others, being restricted to constructions (i), (v) and (vii): *Ed was too tired to notice anything, either*; *She for-got to tell anyone, either*.

fiers can be brought within the scope of the negative by prosodic means. Such a sentence as *He didn't marry her because she was a millionaire*, for example, allows for the reason to fall outside or inside the scope of negation, according to how it is said. In the former case, which corresponds to the prosodically more neutral utterance, it entails *He didn't marry her*, with the modifier giving the reason why he didn't. In the latter case, corresponding to an utterance with an intonational fall–rise on *millionaire*, the negative applies to the whole of "He married her because she was a millionaire": there is here an implication that he married her, but for some other reason than that she was a millionaire.

So far we have been assuming that subjects and complements all fall within the scope of clausal negation, but in fact here too things are more complicated. The major complication arises from the interaction between negation and quantification. Consider, for example:

(12) i *Not all the candidates can go*
    ii *All the candidates can't go*

In (i) the negative marker is located within the subject and has the "all" quantification within its scope – "It is not the case that all the candidates can go". (ii), on the other hand, allows for different scopes. In one interpretation it is equivalent to (i): this corresponds to a prosodically marked utterance with fall–rise intonation on *all*. In a second interpretation "all" is outside the negative scope, and we need an analysis along the lines of "For all candidates x, x can't go", where x is a variable ranging over the set of candidates; in this interpretation (ii) is logically equivalent to *No candidate can go*.[4]

One final complication we should mention is that very exceptionally even the verb itself may fall outside the scope of the negative. This mismatch between grammatical form and meaning is found only with a subset of the modal operators, such as **must**, **ought** and (in its epistemic use) **may**. Thus *He mustn't do that again* is grammatically a negative clause (witness the tag *must he?*, and so on), but semantically the deontic modality is outside the scope of the negation. The meaning is "There is an obligation on him not to do that again", not "There is no obligation on him to do that again" – this latter meaning is expressed by *He needn't do that again*.

Prototypically the meaning of clause negation is that the conditions for the truth of what falls within its scope are not satisfied. If, for example, I say,

(13) *The technician didn't mend the typewriter*

---

[4] In some cases there may be three interpretations available. *He hadn't read many of her novels*, for example, can be understood in any of the following ways (given in order of likelihood): (α) 'There weren't many of her novels that he had read' – the implication is that he had read few of them; (β) 'There were many of her novels that he hadn't read': this requires a prosodic break between *he hadn't read* and *many of her novels*; (γ) 'He hadn't read just many of her novels – he had read them all, or most': this requires contrastive fall–rise stress on *many* (though such a contrastive fall–rise on *many* is not inconsistent with interpretation (α), if the speaker is contradicting or correcting what has just been said). (α) and (γ) differ from (β) in having 'many' inside the scope of the negative, and (α) differs from (γ) in having the negation of a quantifier mean 'less than' (as usual), rather than 'more than' (highly marked).

I am saying that the conditions for the truth of "The technician mended the typewriter" are not satisfied. These positive truth conditions include the following: someone did something; the technician did something; someone did something to the typewriter; the technician did something to the typewriter; just prior to the time in question, the typewriter was not in sound condition; someone did something to the typewriter which caused it to be in sound condition; the technician did something to the typewriter which caused it to be in sound condition; – and so on: the list can easily be filled out. The statement expressed by (13) will be true if any one or more of these conditions fails to be satisfied. Such failure could arise in a variety of ways: it might be that someone other than the technician mended the typewriter, that the technician mended something other than the typewriter, that the technician worked on the typewriter but didn't succeed in restoring it to sound condition, and so on. We will speak of these as different 'contextualisations' of (13): they are not different 'meanings', for the sentence is not ambiguous – it simply does not specify the source of failure of the positive truth conditions.

Different contextualisations of a negative will often differ in likelihood. For example, I am more likely to use (11ii) above, *Ed hadn't read the report carefully*, in a context where Ed had read the report but not carefully than in one where he hadn't read it at all: if I knew he hadn't read it at all, why should I confine myself to saying only that he hadn't read it carefully? But it is important to bear in mind that we are dealing here with the likelihood of contextualisations, not with entailments: in saying (11ii) I will imply, other things being equal, that Ed had read the report, but (11ii) certainly does not ENTAIL *Ed had read the report*. For clearly there is nothing logically inconsistent about saying *Ed evidently hadn't read the report carefully: indeed, I'm inclined to doubt whether he had read it at all*.

One important source of such implications is marked information focus. An information focus is signalled prosodically, by means of phonological prominence (involving stress and intonation), and it may be marked, as opposed to unmarked, by virtue of its position and/or by virtue of the contrastive nature of the stress/intonation. For example, an utterance of (13) will have marked information focus if the main phonological prominence is given to *technician* or *mend* rather than *typewriter* or if *typewriter* is given contrastive prominence (e.g. by a fall in pitch from high to low, followed by a rise). Selection of a marked information focus in a negative clause typically serves to restrict the range of natural contextualisations for it. Thus if I utter (13) with *the technician* as marked information focus I emphasise that the non-satisfaction of the truth conditions for the positive involves the technician (in the role of mender of the typewriter): such an utterance of (13) will thus commonly imply that someone other than the technician mended the typewriter. But again the implication does not have the strength of an entailment. My reason for selecting *the technician* as marked information focus need not be to contrast the technician with someone else who did mend the typewriter: it could be that the technician is the only one that I have the relevant knowledge about – cf. *The "technician didn't mend the typewriter, though I don't know whether anyone else did*. The same applies to utterances of (13) with *mend* or *the typewriter* as marked information focus: these will respectively tend to imply, but not entail, that the technician did something to the typewriter other than mend it and that the technician mended something other than the typewriter.

EXERCISES

I. Clausal and subclausal negation

Is the negation in the following examples clausal or subclausal, or ambiguous between the two? Give syntactic evidence in support of your answers.

(14) *I know nothing about it*
(15) *The culprit was certainly nobody we knew*
(16) *Nobody could have argued the case more persuasively*
(17) *He rarely sees her these days*
(18) *She suddenly appeared from nowhere*
(19) *He loses his cool over nothing*
(20) *There's little to be gained by staying on*
(21) *Only rarely does she lose her temper*

II. Superordinate and subordinate clause negation

Does the *not* in the following examples belong syntactically in the superordinate clause or the subordinate one, or ambiguously in either? Again, give supporting evidence.

(22) *It is not working properly*
(23) *He pretended not to understand*
(24) *He is not to go with them*
(25) *You must not talk to them about it*
(26) *She had better not encourage him*
(27) *He would rather not see her again*
(28) *He will sometimes not eat a thing all day*
(29) *You may not reply*

III. Non-affirmatives

(a) Do you judge the following to be acceptable or not?

(30) *He used to buy anything*
(31) *She has yet read it*
(32) *He was unhappy either*
(33) *Either of them could do it*
(34) *Either of them is here*
(35) *She disliked him at all*

(b) Does the *it* in the following examples fall in a non-affirmative context?

(36) *I dissuaded her from buying it*
(37) *I had enough time to study it carefully*
(38) *Too many people had seen it*

(39) *He was too lazy to finish it*
(40) *Only half of them had read it*
(41) *She went without it*

IV. Semantic scope of the negative

Does the unbracketed expression in the following examples fall inside or outside the scope of the negative – or can it be construed either way?

(42) *[He didn't speak] very clearly*
(43) *[You] must[n't tell her]*
(44) *Should[n't you sign both copies?]*
(45) *[She didn't feel] well*
(46) *Many [of them didn't like it]*
(47) *[They hadn't read it] all*
(48) *Everyone [can't go]*
(49) *[He] may [not like it]*
(50) *[We must do better next time,] must[n't we?]*
(51) *[I'm not going] because she asked me to*

11

The subordination of clauses

1. Classification and marking of subordinate clauses

A **subordinate** clause is one functioning as dependent within a larger construction that is itself a clause or a constituent of one. A **main** clause is one that is not subordinate. A **complex sentence** is then definable as one containing a subordinate clause. A **compound sentence** is one containing two or more main clauses: see Ch. 13. And, finally, a sentence which is neither complex nor compound is said to be a **simple sentence**:

(1) i *I know that she works very hard*   Complex sentence
     ii *He's rather lazy but she works very hard*   Compound sentence
     iii *She works very hard*   Simple sentence

The above definitions derive directly from the grammatical structure, and apply at both general and language-particular levels. The next higher clause above a subordinate clause in the constituent hierarchy is said to be **superordinate** to it, but we do not need a class of superordinate clauses. For classification purposes the significant distinction is between subordinate and main clauses – and a superordinate clause can belong to either of these classes: [*I didn't agree with the guy*] *who said that it was easy* is subordinate, whereas *The guy said that it was easy* is a main clause, though both are superordinate to *that it was easy*.

Prototypically, a main clause can stand alone as a sentence and a subordinate clause cannot. This is because the process of subordination prototypically affects the structure of the clause, so that subordinate clauses are differentiated structurally from main clauses. The principal distinguishing markers are as follows:

(a) Subordinators – members of a closed class of words defined precisely by their role in marking clause subordination, e.g. *that* in (1i).

(b) Relative words – *who, whom, which*, etc.; thus in [*The man*] *who came to dinner* [*stole the silver*] the *who* is a marker of the relative subordinate clause, contrasting with non-relative *the man* in the comparable main clause *The man came to dinner*.

152

(c) Non-finiteness – whereas virtually all main clauses are finite, subordinate clauses are very often non-finite; as such they will have a non-tensed verb and may also differ in the form of the subject: compare [*I didn't approve of*] *his/him doing it that way* with main clause *He does/did it that way*.

(d) Ellipsis – subordinate clauses very often lack elements that would be present in a comparable main clause: compare subjectless [*John likes*] *driving fast cars* with main *John drives fast cars*.

(e) Order – relative phrases are shifted to front position, so that the order of elements in subordinate [*The book*] *which she recommended* [*was unobtainable*] differs from that in the main clause *She recommended the book*. For the rest, the order of elements in subordinate clauses tends to remain closer to the kernel order than does that in non-kernel main clauses; note, for example, that the subordinate counterpart of the interrogative main clause *Where is he?* is *where he is* (as in *I wonder where he is*): the latter has the subject and predicator in their basic order, whereas the former has them inverted.

Not all subordinate clauses contain one or more such markers: subordination is not always reflected in the internal structure. The subordinate status of [*I know*] *he is here*, for example, derives from its function as complement of **know**, but it is not differentiated internally from main *He is here*. This is why it is only prototypically the case that a subordinate clause cannot stand alone as a sentence: *he is here* obviously can. (Conversely, the process of putting two main clauses together in a compound sentence may affect the structure, as in *Kim wrote the first two chapters and Pat the other three*, where the second clause is reduced by ellipsis. This is why a main clause can only prototypically stand alone as a sentence: *and Pat the other three* certainly can't.)

Of the above five markers of subordination, we will briefly examine the first, the subordinators, in §2 below, and consider the others as we survey the various classes of subordinate clause. In §§3–5 we examine in turn the three major classes of finite subordinate clauses, relative, comparative and content, before taking up non-finites in §6 and the minor category of verbless clauses in §7.

2. Subordinators

The two most central subordinators in English are *that* and *whether*. They differ on the dimension of clause type (Ch. 9), with *that* introducing declaratives or jussives, *whether* interrogatives (more specifically, closed interrogatives):

(2) i   [*I believe*] *that she can do it*   Declarative
     ii [*I insist*] *that she do it*   Jussive
     iii [*I wonder*] *whether she can do it*   Interrogative

These are all content clauses; *that*, but not *whether*, can also appear in relative clauses, as in [*I've found the address*] *that she was looking for*.

A general definition of the term subordinator is that it applies to a grammatically distinct closed class of words whose primary role is to mark a clause as subordinate. Typically, subordinators are but one of a variety of structural markers of clause subordination. Thus (2i) has subordinator *that* as the sole marker of subordination, [*They don't understand*] *what he is doing* has no subordinator but differs from main *What is he doing?* in respect of the order of elements, and [*He hasn't yet decided*] *whether to accept the offer* is marked as subordinate both by the subordinator *whether* and by the non-finiteness and missing subject.

Subordinators form one of the four closed primary word classes we have recognised for English. Of the others, determinatives are sharply distinct by virtue of their function in NP structure, and coordinators will be discussed in Ch. 13; here we will accordingly concentrate on the contrast between subordinators and prepositions.

(a) Subordinators are not analysable as head of the construction they enter into. The main reason is that *that* is often omissible – a variant of (2i) for example, is [*I believe*] *she can do it*, where the subordinate status of *she can do it* is not marked in its own structure. *Whether* is not omissible, for it is needed to mark the clause as interrogative – the fact that the subordinator is omissible in (i) but not (iii) is one indication of the 'marked' status of interrogative on the clause type dimension. Notice, however, that although *whether* is not omissible in closed interrogatives, it does not appear at all in open interrogatives, where the clause type is marked by the initial interrogative phrase, as in [*I wonder*] *where she is.*

(b) When a PP is functioning in clause structure, it is prototypically an adjunct, but when a clause introduced by a subordinator functions in clause structure it is prototypically complement, as in (2), or subject as in *That she can do it is obvious* or *Whether she can do it remains to be seen.* Thus in clause structure a preposition + clause sequence prototypically resembles an AdvP in function, whereas a subordinator + clause sequence prototypically resembles an NP. Compare [*He'll tell you*] *subsequently/after he's told her* (adjunct) and [*He'll tell you*] *the result/ that she can do it* (complement). (The formulation is in terms of prototypes because PPs can occur in the more nuclear functions, as we have seen, and content clauses occasionally occur as adjunct: see §5 below.)

Besides *that* and *whether* the class of subordinators contains two less central members, *if* and *for*. Both *if* and *for* also belong to the preposition class, and there are clear affinities between their subordinator and preposition uses.

If is an alternative to *whether* as marker of a subordinate closed interrogative clause: *I wonder whether/if she can do it.* The extension of *if* from a conditional to an interrogative marker is not surprising, given the semantic similarity between the constructions. In the conditional *If she can do it,* [*we'll have no need to worry*] I do not assert that she can do it, but merely entertain this as a possibility, with the implication that it is also a possibility that she can't do it; with the subordinate interrogative [*I wonder*] *if she can do it,* I am wondering which of these possibilities, the positive and the negative, is actually the case. As a subordinator, *if* is subject to certain restrictions that do not apply to *whether*. For example, subordinator *if* does not occur in clauses functioning as (non-extraposed) subject: *Whether/*If she can do it remains to be seen*; in this position (one, significantly, where declarative *that* is not omissible), an unambiguous marker is required. And *if* occurs only in tensed interrogatives: *I'm wondering whether/*if to accept it*; this reflects the fact that the preposition *if* takes as complement a tensed clause, not an infinitival one.

The subordinator *for* occurs only in infinitival declarative clauses; it is complementary with *that*, which is restricted to finite declaratives:

(3) i   *That Kim was so late [was infuriating]*
     ii   *For Kim to be so late [was infuriating]*
(4) i   *[He found a knife] that we could cut it with*
     ii   *[He found a knife] for us to cut it with*

The subordinator *for* is not omissible – but it depends for its occurrence on the presence of a subject: if we drop *Kim* from (3ii) or *us* from (4ii) we must also drop the *for*. The complementary relation with *that*, allied to the fact that prepositions do not take declarative infinitivals as complement, provides the justification for classifying *for* with the subordinators. It nevertheless has much in common with the preposition *for* taking an NP complement, as in *They did it for us*. In the first place, a following case-variable pronoun appears in the accusative case: witness the *us* in (4ii). Accusative case is normal for the complement of a preposition but a personal pronoun subject is prototypically nominative. In the second place, subordinate *for* clauses functioning as complement of a superordinate clause tend to occur with just those verbs that take a prepositional *for* phrase complement: compare *He arranged for an inspection/for them to be inspected*, *He called for a review of the procedures/for the procedures to be reviewed*, and so on.

3. Relative clauses

The most frequent type of relative construction is restrictive (cf. 6.8); we deal with this type first and then turn to the non-restrictive and fused constructions.

3.1 Restrictive relatives

Restrictive relative clauses function as modifiers within NP structure. In *I can't find the book which he recommended*, for example, *the book which he recommended* is an NP with *the* as determiner, *book* as head and *which he recommended* as modifier. In this example, the subordinate clause differs from a comparable main clause such as *He recommended the book* in two respects: (α) it contains the special relative word *which*; (β) the *which* phrase is initial in the clause even though it is functioning as object. A second kind of restrictive relative clause has a 'gap', a missing but understood element, instead of the relative word and may or may not be introduced by the subordinator *that*; we will distinguish the two subclasses as **Rel-word relatives** and **Rel-gap relatives**:

(5) i   [*the book*] *which he recommended*   Rel-word relative
     ii [*the book*] (*that*) *he recommended*   Rel-gap relative

The main relative words occurring in the restrictive Rel-word construction are: *who* and *whom* (forms of **who**), *which, whose, where, when, why.* All are anaphoric: the interpretation of *which* in (i), for example, derives from the antecedent *book*. The relative words are then differentiated on two dimensions:

(a) Antecedent. The antecedents of **who** normally denote humans (occasionally animals), those of *which* non-humans (or infants), while *whose* is found with either type: *the woman whose car wouldn't start, the car whose battery had been removed. Where, when* and *why* have antecedents denoting places, times and reasons respectively: *the country where she was born, the day when we will be re-united, the reason why it didn't work.*

(b) Function. **Who** and *which* are pronouns, heading NPs functioning as subject (*a knife which was blunt*), direct object (*a knife which I found on the beach*), complement of a preposition (*the knife with which he cut it* or, with stranded preposition, *The knife which he cut it with*). *Who* and *whom* are respectively nominative and accusative forms but as with the interrogatives, *who* is in informal style found in clause initial position with non-subject function. *Where* and *when* function as complement/adjunct of place or time respectively, *why* as adjunct of reason. Relative words, like interrogative and exclamative words, may also function not directly in the relative clause but within a content or non-finite clause embedded within the relative clause. In [*the minister*] *who they said was responsible for the leak*, for example, *who* is not subject of the relative clause itself but of the content clause *who* [...] *was responsible for the leak*, which functions as object of *said* – compare the function of *the minister* in *They said the minister was responsible for the leak.*

In Rel-gap relatives, the missing element has almost the same range of functions as the relative word in Rel-word relatives: object in (5ii), subject in [*the dog*] *that was barking*, adjunct of reason in [*the reason*] (*that*) *he resigned*, and so on. The main difference is that the missing element cannot be determiner. There is thus no Rel-gap counterpart to *whose* relatives: [*the woman*] *whose son was abducted* but not *[*the woman*] *that son was abducted*. Note also that where the gap is complement of a preposition, the latter will always be stranded: *the knife* (*that*) *he cut it with*; this construction does not involve movement of the relative element to front position, and hence there is no option of moving the preposition too (*the knife with that he cut it*). The subordinator *that* is omissible except where the gap is subject of the relative clause, as in [*the problems*] *that remained*:

there is here greater need for an overt marker of subordination to distinguish the NP construction *the problems that remained* from the clause construction *The problems remained.*[1]

3.2 The restrictive/non-restrictive contrast

In the following pairs, (i) is restrictive ('R'), (ii) non-restrictive ('N-R'):

(6) i   [*The necklace*] *which Elvis had given her* [*was in the safe*]   R
     ii [*The necklace,*] *which Elvis had given her,* [*was in the safe*]   N-R
(7) i   [*Politicians*] *who make extravagant promises* [*are widely distrusted*]   R
     ii [*Politicians,*] *who make extravagant promises,* [*are widely distrusted*] N-R

In speech, the distinction is clearly marked prosodically: non-restrictive relatives are spoken with a separate intonation contour, whereas restrictives are prosodically bound to their antecedent. In writing, non-restrictives are normally distinguished from restrictives by being marked off by commas (or dashes/ parentheses). Semantically, the information encoded in a non-restrictive is presented as separate from, and secondary to, that encoded in the rest of the superordinate clause, whereas this is not so with a restrictive: here the information it expresses forms an integral part of the message conveyed by the superordinate clause as a whole. For example, in (6i) the relative clause is part of the description that defines which necklace is being referred to: the implication is that there is more than one necklace in the context of discourse, but just one that Elvis had given her; (6ii), on the other hand, implies a context where there is only one necklace: the non-restrictive clause simply gives extra information about it. In (7i) the relative picks out a subset of politicians, whereas (7ii) expresses two propositions about the full set of politicians. Thus in both (6i) and (7i) the relative serves to restrict the denotation of the noun head: *necklace that Elvis had given her* and *politicians who make extravagant promises* have a narrower application than *necklace* and *politicians* alone.

It is because this is the most characteristic use of the construction that it satisfies the general definition of the term 'restrictive'. Again, however, it is important to keep in mind the distinction between the general and language-particular levels, for an English restrictive relative is not always semantically restrictive in this sense. In [*She had three sons*] *she could rely on for help* [*and hence was not unduly worried*] there is no implication that she had more than three sons: the most likely reason for using the restrictive construction, and thus presenting the information contained therein as integral to the larger message, is that it is the reliability of the sons that makes her not unduly worried.

---

[1] 'Rel-word relative' and 'Rel-gap relatives' are not standard terms: as noted earlier, traditional grammar normally analyses the *that* introducing relative clauses as another relative pronoun rather than a subordinator and treats examples like [*the knife*] *he cut it with* as involving the ellipsis or omission of the relative pronoun.

Grammatically, the restrictive and non-restrictive constructions differ as follows.

(a) Internal form. Rel-gap relatives are virtually always restrictive. Non-restrictives allow *which* as determinative as well as pronoun: [*I'll be back on Tuesday,*] *by which time the contract will be ready*.

(b) Antecedents. Non-specifics such as *no one, any candidate*, etc., take only restrictives: *No one who met her could fail to be impressed* but not **No one, who met her, could fail to be impressed*. Conversely, proper nouns without a determiner allow only non-restrictives: *John, who had just flown in from Australia, was suffering from jet-lag*. Non-restrictives can take a clause as antecedent: *Liz won the toss, which gave her a great advantage*; here the whole sentence has the form of a clause with *Liz won the toss* as head and the relative clause as peripheral dependent (the kind of structure illustrated in (20ii) of Ch. 4); restrictives cannot take such antecedents as they always function in NP structure.

Restrictive relatives are much more frequent than non-restrictives and it is they that bring this class of clause in English within the scope of the general definition of the term 'relative'. The term is applicable to a grammatically distinct class of subordinate clause whose members characteristically: (α) function as modifier within NP structure; (β) serve semantically to restrict the denotation of the noun head; and (γ) contain an overt or covert element anaphorically related to the noun head. In (6i), for example, *which* is anaphoric to (*the*) *necklace*, whereas in the Rel-gap example *The necklace* (*that*) *Elvis had given her was in the safe* the covert direct object of *give* is likewise understood as anaphoric to the head. In either case, then, we have a semantic analysis along the lines of "Elvis had given her x; x was in the safe – where x = some necklace". This dual role for the x element – one role in the superordinate clause, one in the subordinate clause – provides an important diagnostic for the relative construction.

3.3 The fused relative construction

One final type of relative construction is illustrated in (8i), which may be compared with the structurally more straightforward (ii):

(8)   i   [*He had quickly spent*] *what she gave him*
      ii   [*He had quickly spent*] *the money which she gave him*

In (ii) *which she gave him* is a restrictive Rel-word relative clause functioning as modifier within the NP *the money which she gave him*; the relative word *which* is anaphoric to (*the*) *money*. Semantically (i) is very similar to (ii): both can be roughly analysed as "She gave him x; he had quickly spent x" (with (ii) explicitly saying that x is money). But whereas in (ii) we find separate expressions corresponding to the two x's, (*the*) *money* and *which*, in (i) we do not: they are, as it were, fused together in *what* (= "that which"). We will accordingly call *what she gave him* in (i) a **fused relative** construction. It is not easy to analyse grammatically. There are good reasons for saying that the whole expression is an NP (it corresponds to the NP *the money which she gave him* in (ii), not to the modifying clause *which she gave him*) – but it differs from a normal NP construction in that it cannot be analysed discretely into head + modifier elements, for *what* is simultaneously head of the whole NP and object of the embedded relative clause. This fusion is perhaps even clearer in examples containing *what* as determinative rather than pronoun: *What books they had were buried away in the attic.* Here *what books they had* is subject of the main clause; it is evident from the *were* that it is plural, and this plurality clearly derives from *books.* The subject is thus an NP with the noun *books* as head, but *what books* serves also as object of *had* in the modifying clause.[2]

The major relative words occurring in the nominal fused relative construction are *what* and the *-ever* compounds *whatever, whoever, whichever: Whoever did that must be a lunatic.* The construction does not readily allow *who* or *which:* **Who was speaking had a French accent.* We must also allow for adverbial fused relatives with *where* or *when: I'll leave it where you put it* (roughly "I'll leave it at place x; you put it at place x"), *They stood up when she entered.* Particularly in the temporal case, however, we are here in the boundary area between adverbial and prepositional constructions: compare the last example with *They stood up before she entered,* where *before* is a preposition taking the content clause *she entered* as complement.

4. Comparative clauses

The subordinate clauses in the following examples belong to the comparative class:

(9) i   *The task is easier than it looks*
    ii   *I have more patience than I had in those days*
    iii *She wrote as many pages as you wrote lines*
    iv   *She went to the same school as I went to*
    v   *She's over eighty, as you know*

The sentences as wholes express comparisons between two terms: how easy the task is and how easy the task looks; how much patience I have (now) and how much patience I had in those days; how many pages she wrote and how many lines you wrote; which school she went to and which school I went to; what is the case and what you know. The two terms are distinguishable as 'primary' and 'secondary' by virtue of being associated with the superordinate and subordinate clause respectively. It is not of course necessary for the terms in a comparison to be distinguished in this way (cf. *The two players were equally inexperienced,* where there is no subordination). Here, however, we will confine our attention to constructions where they are, for it is only in such cases that we have comparative clauses. Thus the general term 'comparative clause' is applied to a grammatically

---

[2] Alternative terms for 'fused relative' are 'headless relative', 'free relative', 'nominal relative'; the construction is commonly analysed as a clause.

distinct class of clause whose members characteristically express the secondary term in a comparison – the 'standard of comparison'. In (i), for example, the comparative clause is *it looks*, not the main clause which forms the sentence as a whole.

In English, comparative clauses function as complement to the prepositions *than* or *as*. *Than* is always correlated with a comparative inflectional form of an adjective or adverb (or determinative *few*), or with *more* or *less* – or, in some dialects only, with *different*. *As* may be correlated with another *as*, or with *so*, *such*, or *the same*, or else it may be used non-correlatively, as in (v).

Syntactically, comparative clauses are structurally incomplete vis-à-vis main clauses. For example, in (i) *it looks* lacks a predicative and in (ii) *I had in those days* lacks an object. Similarly *you wrote lines* in (iii) lacks a determiner for the NP object; the fact that one is in some sense understood explains why we cannot add an overt determiner (**She wrote as many pages as you wrote ten lines*). The closest main clause analogues of the above comparative clauses contain a deictic element such as *that*: *It looks that easy*; *I had that much patience in those days*; *You wrote that many lines*; *I went to that school*; *You know that*. This is not to say of course that the latter have the same meaning as the comparative clauses: their value is in bringing out the nature of the structural incompleteness of the comparative clauses vis-à-vis main clause constructions.

The minimum incompleteness is illustrated in example (iii), where it is only the implicit determiner to *lines* that is missing. If the comparison were between how many pages she wrote and how many pages, rather than lines, you wrote, then the head of the object NP would be omitted too: *She wrote as many pages as you wrote*. This much omission is normally obligatory, but ellipsis of further recoverable material is optional: in (iii) we would not normally have *you wrote pages*, but either *you wrote* or just *you* is possible.[3] The latter then illustrates the maximum incompleteness, with the comparative clause reduced to a single element. Where, as in this example, the single remaining element is subject, a case-variable pronoun will appear as nominative in formal style (*She's taller than I*) but as accusative in informal style (*She's taller than me*).

The construction where a comparative clause is reduced to a single element is to be distinguished from that where the complement of *than* or *as* is simply an NP: [*She is taller than*] *6ft*. Unlike *I/me*, *6ft* is not subject of a reduced clause: there is here no ellipsis. One special case of this latter construction common in certain non-standard dialects is that where the NP complement of *than/as* is a fused relative construction: *She is taller than what Max is*.

5. Content clauses

Content clauses, for the most part, depart less from the structure of main clauses than do relative and comparative clauses: they represent the unmarked category

---

[3] The qualification 'normally' is needed because *pages* can be retained if contrastively stressed in a correction of what has just been said: [⟨A⟩ *She wrote as many pages as I wrote sentences.* ⟨B⟩ *No,*] *she wrote as many pages as you wrote ''pages.*

of finite subordinate clause. Like main clauses, they enter into contrasts of clause type:

(10) i   [*They know*] (*that*) *it is a sound investment*   Declarative
     ii [*They require*] (*that*) *it be a sound investment*   Jussive
     iii [*They wonder*] *whether it is a sound investment*   Interrogative
     iv [*They realise*] *what a sound investment it is*   Exclamative

With declaratives, the major mark of subordination is of course the subordinator *that*: the main clause counterpart of (i) is simply *It is a sound investment. That* is obligatory when the content clause is subject of the superordinate clause (*That it is a sound investment is obvious*), otherwise it is normally optional – but see 8.3 for its occurrence after prepositions.

The subordinator *that* also occurs in jussive content clauses – again optionally except under the above conditions. As noted in 9.3, jussive main clauses fall into two major subclasses, imperative (*Look at the Queen!*) and non-imperative (*God save the Queen!*); jussive content clauses, however, are limited to the non-imperative subclass. The subordinate construction is productive, but the non-imperative jussive main clause construction is not, so that there is no main clause counterpart to (ii): **It be a good investment* (or **Be it a good investment*). The structure of jussive content clauses is thus more straightforwardly described by reference to declarative content clauses than to jussive main clauses. The crucial difference, as illustrated in (10), is that the first verb of a jussive is a base form. This means that there is no tense – and hence no possibility of backshifting: changing the superordinate verb *require* to *required* in (ii) has no effect on the subordinate clause.

Jussive clauses normally have what we have called a 'deontic' component of meaning. We saw in our discussion of main clauses that such a component of meaning can be expressed by jussive clause type or by an appropriate modal catenative verb – compare *Come in at once!* and *You must come in at once*. The same applies with content clauses, the modal catenative usually being *should*: compare jussive (ii) with declarative [*They require*] *that it should be a good investment*. Alternatively the deontic meaning may not be overtly expressed in the content clause itself, being implicit in the context provided by the superordinate clause predicator or predicative: compare jussive [*It is essential*] *that he tell her* with declarative (and non-modal) [*It is essential*] *that he tells her*. With these alternatives available, many speakers make little use of the jussive construction.

The major differences between interrogative content clauses and their main clause counterparts are: (α) the rule of subject-operator inversion normally applies only in main clauses; (β) closed interrogative content clauses are introduced by one or other of the subordinators *whether* and *if*. Compare

(11)   Main   Subordinate

Open   i   *Why do they want it?*   iii [*I realise*] *why they want it*
Closed ii *Do they want it?*   iv   [*I wonder*] *whether/if they want it*

(When the interrogative phrase is subject there will of course be no difference: *Who wants it?* ~ [*I know*] *who wants it*.)

With exclamatives, main and subordinate versions are normally the same whatever the function of the exclamative phrase – the exclamative in (10iv), for example, could stand alone as a main clause. A minor difference is that subject-operator inversion is excluded in subordinate exclamatives – a minor difference because such inversion so rarely applies in main clauses.

Content clauses are found in a considerable variety of function, as seen in (12) (where the content clause is underlined):

(12)		Function	Construction
i	*That he is guilty is obvious*	Subject	⎫
ii	*You'll be disappointed, whichever one you*	Periph-Dep	⎬ Clause
	choose		⎭
iii	*I know that he likes them*	Complement	⎫
iv	*He had invited his mother, that she might*	Modifier	⎬ VP
	see the situation for herself	(of purpose)	⎭
v	*[He rejected] the suggestion that he should*	Complement	⎫
	resign		⎬ NP
vi	*This suggestion, that he should resign,*	Periph-Dep	⎭
	[was outrageous]		
vii	*[I am] sure that it is impossible*	Complement	⎫ AdjP
viii	*[It was] so loud that I decided to leave*	Modifier	⎭
ix	*[I can't do it] unless you help me*	Complement	PP

In functions (iii), (v–vi) and (vii) the range of clause type depends on the verb, noun or adjective on which the content clause is dependent. For example, *know* allows a declarative, interrogative or exclamative (but not a jussive), *believe* just a declarative, *inquire* just an interrogative, and so on. Similarly for function (i), where it depends on the head word of the predicator or predicative: *depend* takes an interrogative as subject, *matter* a declarative or interrogative, *please* a declarative. Prepositions mainly take declaratives as in (ix); some, such as *of* and *on*, take interrogatives provided the head of the larger construction containing the PP allows it: *the problem of who we should send* or *It depends on whether you finish on time*, where *problem* selects *of* + interrogative as complement, *depend* selects *on* + interrogative. Only declaratives appear in (viii), or in similar phrases of other classes containing *so* or *such* as premodifier – cf. the AdvP *[They were talking] so loudly that I decided to leave*. In (iv) we again find only declaratives – but of a very limited kind (normally containing modal *should* or *might*). Finally (ii) involves 'concessive' interrogatives; in this construction the interrogative word in the open type is always an *-ever* compound and the closed type always contains an overt *or* coordination (*She's going with us, whether you like it or not*).

6. Non-finite clauses

Non-finite clauses likewise occur in a wide range of functions:

(13)		Function	Construction
i	*To sell now would be a mistake*	Subject	} Clause
ii	*To judge by her expression, the news was bad*	Periph-Dep	
iii	*I want to see it*	Complement	} VP
iv	*He left at six to catch the early train*	Modifier	
v	[*He was impressed by*] *her will to win*	Complement	} NP
vi	[*It was*] *a time to relax*	Modifier	
vii	[*I am*] *glad to hear it*	Complement	} AdjP
viii	[*She is*] *very young to go to school*	Modifier	
ix	[*He left*] *too soon to hear the result*	Modifier	AdvP
x	[*She rejected the idea*] *of giving up*	Complement	PP

There is not space to examine all these constructions: in the following sections we will thus take up a selection of them, concentrating in particular on the catenative construction, a special case of that where the non-finite is complement to a verb. First, however, we will deal briefly with one more general issue, concerning the subject, actual or 'understood', of non-finite clauses.

The majority of non-finite clauses have no subject element in their structure: they consist of just a VP. Semantically, however, the VP stands in the predicate relation to what we may call an understood subject. This understood subject can usually be derived from the larger construction in which the non-finite is embedded. In *Selling the land* [*was John's first big mistake*], for example, we understand it to be John who sold the land. [*Everyone*] *passing this test* [*will qualify for the final exam*] we interpret as, roughly, "Every person x such that x passes this test will qualify ..." (it does not say that everyone will pass the test): the understood subject may thus be quite abstract. Where one non-finite is embedded in another, deriving the understood subject may involve a sequence of steps. Thus in *Tom had been wanting to see her* the understood subject of *to see her* is recovered from that of *wanting to see her*, which in turn is the same as that of *been wanting to see her*, which, finally, derives from the actual subject of *had been wanting to see her*, namely *Tom*. Under quite restricted conditions, the understood subject is not derivable from the larger construction in this way: it may be recovered, rather, from the context of discourse, as in *Selling the land* [*was a big mistake*], where the seller will be whoever owned the land, or else it may simply be the generic "one", as in *Eating people* [*is wrong*].

Where a non-finite does contain an overt subject, its form may differ from that of a kernel clause subject. In certain constructions, present-participials may, in relatively formal style, take possessive expressions as subject: [*He resented*] *my being given a second chance*. Elsewhere, case-variable pronoun subjects normally appear in the accusative instead of the nominative found in finite clauses: [*He resented*] *me being given a second chance*, [*He arranged*] *for me to see her*.

6.1 The catenative construction

Constructions involving a non-finite as complement of the predicator exhibit a great deal of diversity and complexity; they present formidable problems for the analyst – and it is not surprising that widely varying accounts are to be found in the literature. One problem is this. The prototypical complement is an NP, which is why we speak of the occurrence of non-finites in complement function as involving nominalisation. But, as observed in 6.12, we find different degrees of nominalisation; where there is a relatively high degree of nominalisation we can assign the non-finite to one of the more specific types of complement that are more characteristically filled by NPs. Two places where this is so were mentioned in 4.7. One involves the object, or extraposed object, in the complex transitive construction, as in [*This made it important*] (*for her husband*) *to accompany them* or [*She considered*] *his/him attempting it a waste of time*. The other involves the predicative in the identifying **be** construction: [*The best solution would be*] (*for you*) *to resign*, [*All/What he did was*] *remove the wrapping*, [*The first mistake was*] (*John's/John*) *inviting the boss*.

For the rest, however, non-finites are not so similar, functionally, to NPs and are best analysed as a distinct type of complement – what we are calling a catenative complement. All four kinds of non-finite are found in the catenative construction; they are illustrated in (14), where they are the sole complement of the catenative verb, and in (15), where they follow an NP complement (object):

(14) i   [*Ed wanted*] *to revise the brochure*   *To*-infinitival
      ii   [*Ed didn't dare*] *revise the brochure*   Bare-infinitival
      iii [*Ed enjoyed*] *revising the brochure*   Present-participial
      iv   [*The brochure got*] *revised*   Past-participial
(15) i   [*Liz advised Ed*] *to revise the brochure*   *To*-infinitival
      ii   [*Liz watched Ed*] *revise the brochure*   Bare-infinitival
      iii [*Liz caught Ed*] *revising the brochure*   Present-participial
      iv   [*Liz had the brochure*] *revised*   Past-participial

Specification of the complementation of a catenative verb must indicate which of these eight constructions it can occur in – and not just these eight, for the catenative complement may also combine with a PP (*They prevailed upon him to reinstate us*), a particle (*He turned out to be a cousin of hers*) and so on. As far as the choice among the four kinds of non-finite is concerned, only a relatively small number of catenatives take bare-infinitivals or past-participials – the former are found mainly with the modal operators, **can**, **may**, etc. and sensory perception verbs, **see**, **hear**, and with just a few others such as **help**, **let**, **make**, while past-participials occur with perfect **have** and, as passives, with **be**, **get**, **have** (as in (15iv)), **want**, **order**, **see**, etc. Much the most usual are thus the *to*-infinitival and the present-participial. The choice between them is neither fully predictable from the meaning nor completely random. The most important contributory factor of meaning involves modality: there is a tendency (not just in catenative constructions but more generally) for the present-participial to be associated with actuality, factuality, the infinitival with non-actuality, non-factuality. Compare, for example, *He hoped to read it* and *He enjoyed reading it*: the latter entails *He read it*, whereas the former clearly does not. Or, to take examples with the same catenative, but in somewhat different senses, *I'll try to clean it* and *I'll try cleaning it*: in the first I may well be unable to clean it but my being able to clean it is not an issue in the second, where it is a matter of seeing what happens when I do clean it. *She remembered to lock it* and *She remembered locking it* both entail *She locked it* but note that in the negative, *She didn't remember to lock it* and *She didn't remember locking it*, the first strongly implies that she didn't lock it while the second is as readily usable in a context where she did as in one where she didn't; with the present-participial, unlike the infinitival, the locking is prior to the remembering, so that the meaning difference is here temporal as well as modal. With a few verbs the difference is one of active vs passive voice: compare *He wants to shoot* and *He wants shooting*. Here the present-participial is covertly passive, "He wants/needs to be shot" – covertly because normally a passive has the verb in the past participle form (note, however, that the construction allows an agent *by* phrase, as in *This wants checking by the editor*, which shows that it must certainly be analysed as belonging to the passive construction). With sensory perception verbs (which, as we have noted, take a bare- and rather than *to*-infinitival) there is an aspectual-type meaning difference between infinitival and present-participial. Thus the difference between *I saw her swim across the river* and *I saw her swimming across the river* matches that between the main clauses *She swam across the river* (non-progressive) and *She was swimming across the river* (progressive).

One semantic distinction that applies with some generality to the catenative construction is illustrated in

(16) i   *Kim happened to find the letter*
      ii *Kim managed to find the letter*

where *Kim* is in both cases syntactically subject of the catenative verb. In (ii) there is clearly also a semantic relation between **manage** and *Kim* as well as a syntactic one: **manage** here implies effort on Kim's part. In (i), by contrast, there is no direct semantic relation between **happen** and *Kim*: it says that the event of Kim's finding the letter took place and suggests that it did so by chance, without design – but it is not a matter of design specifically on Kim's part. The lack of direct semantic relation between **happen** and *Kim* is more immediately obvious in *It (so) happened that Kim found the letter*, which is a paraphrase of (i) – more obvious because here there is no direct syntactic relation between **happen** and *Kim* either. Because *Kim* belongs semantically in the **find** clause but appears syntactically in the **happen** clause, (i) is commonly called a 'raising' construction, and **happen** a raising catenative: it is as though *Kim* had been raised out of the subordinate clause into the superordinate one.

The distinction between the raising and non-raising constructions is reflected in their interaction with various thematic processes, notably passivisation (see 12.2) and existential formation (12.5). Thus (16i) stands in the same relation to *The letter happened to be found by Kim* as active *Kim found the letter* does to passive *The letter was found by Kim*. But (16ii) does not have as a thematic variant *The letter managed to be found by Kim*: this is anomalous because it attributes intention, effort to the letter. (And *Kim managed to see Pat* and *Pat managed to be seen by Kim* differ clearly in meaning.) Similarly *A friend of mine happened to be present* stands in the same relation to *There happened to be a friend of mine present* as unmarked *A friend of mine was present* does to existential *There was a friend of mine present*, but *A friend of mine managed to be present* has no existential counterpart **There managed to be a friend of mine present*: **manage** does not allow existential *there* as subject.

The raising/non-raising contrast extends also to clauses having an NP complement as well as the non-finite one:

(17) i   *Pat intended Kim to find the letter*
     ii *Pat asked Kim to find the letter*

Kim is the first complement, *to find the letter* the second. Whereas in (16) the difference was a matter of whether there was a direct semantic relation between the catenative and the SUBJECT (with **happen**, no; with **manage**, yes), in (17) it is a matter of whether there is a direct semantic relation between the catenative and the OBJECT. With **ask** there is: Kim is the one to whom the request is addressed. But with **intend** there is not: **intend** simply expresses Pat's mental attitude towards the potential situation of Kim's finding the letter. Again the finite construction shows the semantic relations more transparently: compare (i) with *Pat intended that Kim should find the letter*. Grammatically, however, *Kim* is object of the catenative in (i) just as in (ii) – note, for example, that in both it can become subject through passivisation: *Kim was intended/asked by Pat to find the letter*. As with the **happen–manage** pair, we find differences in the way **intend** and **ask** interact with passivisation (of the non-finite clause) and existential formation. Thus (17i) has as thematic variant *Pat intended the letter to be found by Kim* but (ii) is not a variant of the anomalous *Pat asked the letter to be found by Kim*. And **intend** allows existential *there* as object, whereas **ask** does not: *Pat intended/*asked there to be a guard on duty*.

I have illustrated the raising/non-raising contrast with *to*-infinitival complements, but it applies also to bare-infinitivals and present-participials:

(18) i   *Kim needn't sign the petition*   Raising
     ii *Kim daren't sign the petition*   Non-raising
(19) i   *Ed heard the guard beating the prisoner*   Raising
     ii *Ed caught the guard beating the prisoner*   Non-raising

In (18) *The petition needn't be signed by Kim* is a thematic variant of (i) whereas *The petition daren't be signed by Kim* is anomalous, and **need**, unlike **dare**, allows *there* as subject: *There needn't/*daren't be any fuss*. The deontic modality in (i) applies to the whole situation of Kim's signing the petition, whereas **dare** in (ii) is predicated directly of Kim. Similarly in (19) **hear** expresses a relation between Ed and the whole situation of the guard beating the prisoner whereas the guard is directly a participant in the **catch** situation.

Catenatives taking a past-participial complement, alone or in combination with an object, belong to the raising class. This is easiest to see with perfect *have*: *Kim has signed the petition*, for example, has *The petition has been signed by Kim* as a thematic variant. In other cases the past-participial is already passive – but often there will be a variant with a different kind of non-finite, as in the pair *Ed saw the exhibition vandalised by the twins* and *Ed saw the twins vandalise the exhibition*.

All the non-finite clauses considered so far in this section have lacked a subject. Usually the understood subject derives from the closest preceding NP in the superordinate clause. Thus in (15) the understood subject of the non-finite derives from the object of the main clause (*Ed* in (i)–(iii), *the brochure* in (iv)), whereas in (14), where there is no NP object, it derives from the subject of the main clause (again, *Ed* in (i)–(iii) and *the brochure* in (iv)). The same principle applies in (16)–(19). But there are exceptions to it. In the first place, there are cases where the understood subject derives from the superordinate clause subject even when an object intervenes. Thus *Liz promised Ed to revise the brochure* is interpreted differently from (15i), *Liz advised Ed to revise the brochure*. With the latter it is a matter of Ed revising it (in accordance with the above principle) but in the former it is a matter of Liz doing so. In the second place, there are cases where no element in the superordinate clause provides the source from which the understood non-finite subject derives: in *Ed said not to wake him till noon* we clearly do not derive the subject of *wake* from main clause *Ed*, but rather from the context. These and similar details have to be catered for in any comprehensive account of the properties of the individual catenatives.

Some catenatives also take a non-finite complement with an overt subject. Such verbs as *arrange*, *call*, *hope*, *long*, *wait* take an infinitival clause introduced by *for*: *He arranged for them to call at six*. Others, such as *deplore*, *enjoy*, *like*, *regret*, *resent*, etc., take a present-participial clause with a possessive expression or (in more informal style) an NP as subject: *Liz resented his/him getting a second chance*. Note that this differs from the raising construction exemplified in (19i), for here *his/him* functions grammatically as subject of the subordinate clause, not object of the superordinate one, as in (19i). One reflection of this difference is that it cannot become subject through passivisation of the superordinate clause: **He was resented by Liz getting a second chance* vs *The guard was heard by Ed beating the prisoner*.

6.2 Non-finites as dependent in AdjP structure

The contrast between the raising and non-raising constructions applies also to the infinitival complements of what we may call catenative adjectives:

(20) i   *Ed was likely to win the race*   Raising
      ii *Ed was eager to win the race*   Non-raising

In (i), unlike (ii), there is no direct semantic relation between the grammatical subject and the catenative adjective: what was likely was the whole situation of

Ed's winning. Note again the paraphrase relation between (i) and *It was likely that Ed would win the race* or *The race was likely to be won by Ed*. In the raising construction the non-finite clause cannot have its own subject: *Ed was eager/ *likely for Max to win the race*. Only a handful of catenative adjectives follow the pattern of **likely**: *certain*, **sure**, *bound*, etc.; the *eager* class is somewhat larger: **glad**, **happy**, **keen**, *reluctant*, **sorry**, etc.

To-infinitivals dependent on an adjective often have the direct object or the complement of a preposition missing but understood from the superordinate clause. Thus in *The proofs are ready for you to check* or *Ed is easy to get on with* we understand "for you to check the proofs", "to get on with Ed". This construction is found in the complements of a few adjectives such as **ready**, **easy**, **simple**, **hard**, etc., but also in modifiers (especially in construction with *too* or *enough*): *The water was too cold to swim in.*

6.3 Non-finites as dependent in NP structure

Non-finites can function as complement or modifier in NP structure. In complement function we find *to*-infinitivals, and the noun head is usually morphologically derived from a catenative verb or adjective: *her/a desire to return to Australia* (with the noun *desire* derived from the verb), *Max's/such eagerness to win*. In addition to such nouns we also find a few which, like the adjectives **ready** and **easy**, etc., take *to*-infinitivals with a missing object or complement of a preposition: *The book was a joy to read.*

In modifier function we find *to*-infinitivals and participials:

(21) i   [*Here is a knife*] (*for you*) *to cut it with*   To-infinitival
     ii [*He wasn't among those*] *consulting the boss*   }
     iii [*He wasn't among those*] *being consulted by the boss* } Present-participial
     iv [*He wasn't among those*] *consulted by the boss*   Past-participial

All of these have affinities with relative clauses. Infinitivals may indeed contain a relative word, always head of an NP functioning as complement to a preceding preposition: [*Here is a knife*] *with which to cut it*. We must therefore extend the class of relative clauses to include some non-finites and since this last example differs from (21i) in the same way as Rel-word relatives differ from Rel-gap relatives, we will also analyse *to*-infinitivals like (21i) as relative clauses. In this example the gap is complement of a preposition; in [*I found some errors*] *to correct* it is object, in [*He's not the one*] *to do the job* it is subject, and so on.

Participial modifying clauses cannot be related to the noun head by means of a relative word and we will regard them as falling outside the boundaries of the class of relative clauses. They never contain an overt subject: the understood subject is derived from the head they modify. The difference between present- and past-participials is a matter of voice (active vs passive) or aspect. Past-participials are passive – but covertly so inasmuch as they do not contain the passive catenative **be** (compare (21iv) with the finite relative [*He wasn't among those*] *who were consulted by the boss*). Present-participials may be active or passive depending on the absence or presence of the passive catenative *be*, as in (ii) and (iii) respectively. Passive present-participials are understood as progressive, although they do not contain the progressive catenative *be* (compare (iii) with finite [*He wasn't among those*] *who were being consulted by the boss*). Thus (iv) contrasts with (ii) as passive vs active, and with (iii) as non-progressive vs progressive.

Participial modifiers are to be distinguished from the peripheral dependents of, say, [*Bill,*] *facing ruin/charged with conspiracy,* [*fled the country*]. The participials here are set apart intonationally like non-restrictive relative clauses, but unlike the latter they are positionally quite mobile – they could, for example, occur initially, preceding *Bill*. For this reason they are better analysed as peripheral dependents in clause structure than in NP structure.

7. Verbless clauses

Verbless clauses may arise through the anaphoric ellipsis of the verb, as in *Kim took the long route, Pat the short*, where the missing verb in the second clause is recoverable from the first. Here, however, we shall be concerned with constructions where we cannot retrieve the missing verb anaphorically:

(22) i   [*He stood with*] *his hands behind his back*
      ii [*Although*] *very upset,* [*she performed remarkably well*]

Such constructions can be related to main clause predications with *be*: *His hands were behind his back, She was very upset*. Copulative clauses differ from others in that the verb is much less a prototypical head. As we observed in 4.3, the copula *be*, in some uses at least, has little semantic content, having a primarily syntactic role of linking the complement to the subject. One grammatical reflex of this is that *be*, unlike non-copulative verbs, does not have the property characteristic of heads of determining what kinds of subject can occur in the clause. The fact that in *It worried the guard* we can replace the NP subject *it* by a subordinate clause, whereas we cannot do this in *It decapitated the guard* is due to the properties of the verbs *worry* and *decapitate*, whereas the possibility of such replacement in *It was strange* but not *It was short* is due to the properties of the adjectives *strange* and *short*. And a second point is that *be* is, under certain conditions such as obtain in (22), omissible.

The absence of a verb makes examples like (22) quite peripheral to the clause category. The distance from the prototype is greater in (ii) than in (i). In (i) there are two constituents in a subject–complement relation: *his hands behind his back* is clearly not a single NP with *behind his back* a modifier of *hands*. This is evident from the fact that *his hands* could not be replaced by a proper noun – *Kim*, say: *Kim behind his back* is not a possible NP. In (ii), by contrast, the clause is reduced to a single element, a predicative: not only is the predicator missing, but so is the subject (though the latter is anaphorically retrievable). Such structures fall at the very limit of the clause category, and it is not always easy to decide when an AdjP should be analysed as the sole element in a verbless subordinate clause rather than being allowed to function directly in the larger construction as an AdjP.

Note, for example, that we have not postulated verbless clauses in *That counts as wrong, I regard it as very important* or *She considered them useless*. The same problem arises with other phrase classes that can function as complement to *be* – NPs, PPs, AdvPs: cf. *[Although] a novice/in great pain, [she performed remarkably well]*.

Verbless clauses commonly occur as complement to a preposition, as in (22): *with* and *without* take subject + complement structures, *although, if, unless, when, while* the subjectless construction. The former type is also found without prepositions: *The meeting over, [everyone went straight home]* ("when the meeting was over, ...").[4] These prepositions can also take participial clause complements – compare *[He stood with] his feet just touching the line, [Although] working under difficult conditions [she performed remarkably well]*. Since participial clauses also function as complement to *be* (cf. *His feet were just touching the line, She was working under difficult conditions*), there is a clear affinity between the verbless and participial constructions.

EXERCISES

I. Finiteness

Classify the unbracketed clauses in (23)–(31) as finite or non-finite, and if non-finite as infinitival, present-participial or past-participial. Identify the type of construction of which they are an immediate constituent, and identify their function within that construction. Thus the answer for (23) is that *living in Sydney* is a non-finite, present-participial, clause functioning as modifier within the NP *people living in Sydney*.

(23) *[People] living in Sydney [have many advantages]*
(24) *Why she did it [is a mystery]*
(25) *[It was unable] to walk*
(26) *[He kept] ringing me up in the middle of the night*
(27) *[The idea] that it might be dangerous [had never occurred to her]*
(28) *[They're very keen] for her to have a second chance*
(29) *[He succeeded in] alienating both parties*
(30) *[You're going to be in trouble,] whatever you do*
(31) *[He had it] checked by the editor*

II. Classification of finite subordinate clauses

Identify the finite subordinate clauses in (32)–(37) and classify them as restrictive relative, non-restrictive relative, comparative or content.

(32) *The money he hadn't spent he was allowed to keep*
(33) *The fact that he was only sixteen didn't really matter*
(34) *The boss, who had arrived at eight in the morning, was still at her desk at midnight*
(35) *The film was longer than it should have been*
(36) *She's coming back at six, by which time the report should be ready*
(37) *I'm glad that you were able to meet her*

---

[4] Some grammars also allow the subjectless type too, analysing *Angry at this revelation, [John stormed out of the room]* and the like as verbless clauses.

III. Relative clauses
(a) Change the Rel-gap relatives in (38)–(41) to the Rel-word type.

(38) *All those she consulted thought she should make a formal complaint*
(39) *Do you remember the time we took her to Aunt Agatha's?*
(40) *The reason he gave seemed pretty unconvincing to me*
(41) *The reason he didn't seek re-election was that he wanted to have more time to devote to research*

(b) Convert the second clause in (42)–(46) into a restrictive relative and embed it as modifier within the appropriate NP in the first. Comment on the semantic effect of the embedding, making use of the concept of 'scope' introduced in Ch. 10 and applying it to quantifiers and definite determiners as well as negatives.

(42) *The book was unobtainable; she recommended the book*
(43) *Nothing is going to make me change my mind; he says nothing*
(44) *He gave me two photographs; he had taken two photographs*
(45) *Everyone had to spend the night at the airport; they retained everyone's passport*
(46) *One of the kids had a knife in his belt; I was talking to the kids*

(c) Some of the relative clauses in (47)–(52) can be construed as either restrictive or non-restrictive, whereas others allow only one construal. (The examples are presented without punctuation: assume that commas can be added where appropriate.) For those that allow both, comment on the difference in meaning between the restrictive and non-restrictive construals, and for those that allow only one say what grammatical factors exclude the other.

(47) *They were living in McAnally Drive which was just round the corner from the school*
(48) *One has to differentiate between the full-time staff who are paid monthly and the part-time staff who are paid weekly*
(49) *He may have seen you in which case we're in for trouble*
(50) *Anyone who thinks that must be mad*
(51) *She was wearing a dress which I'd never seen before*
(52) *She was wearing a beautifully-tailored ankle-length gown of cream silk which I had never seen before*

IV. Comparative clauses

Give main clause analogues containing deictic *that* for the comparative clauses in (53–58):

(53) *She looks thinner than she used to be*
(54) *I made the same mistake as you*
(55) *He has more money than he needs*
(56) *I'll visit them as often as possible*
(57) *Liz won easily, as we'd all expected*
(58) *They arrived late, as usual*

V. Content clauses

For each of the verbs **assume**, **doubt**, **expect**, **hope**, **insist**, **know**, **order**, **realise**, **remember**, **say**, **tell**, **wonder**, say whether it can take as complement a content clause that is (α) declarative, (β) exclamative, (γ) interrogative, (δ) jussive; give an example for each 'yes' answer.

VI. Content clauses and relatives

Is the unbracketed expression in (59)–(64) a content clause, a relative or ambiguously either? If it can be either, explain the ambiguity; if it can be only one, explain why.

(59) [*The idea*] *that he had proposed* [*was preposterous*]
(60) [*The book*] *that he had recommended* [*was out of print*]
(61) [*I can buy*] *what she asked for*
(62) [*I can guess*] *what she asked for*
(63) [*He knows*] *who did it*
(64) [*Do you remember*] *what she taught you* [*?*]

VII. The catenative construction

Examine and illustrate the complementation patterns of the catenatives **attempt**, **avoid**, **enjoy**, **forget**, **hate**, **hear**, **intend**, **like**, **make**, **need**, **prefer**, **remember**, **require**, **try**, **watch**. Can they appear in: (α) intransitive clauses with an infinitival complement; (β) intransitive clauses with a present-participial complement; (γ) transitive clauses with an infinitival complement; (δ) transitive clauses with a present-participial complement? For those that can appear in both (α) and (β) or in both (γ) and (δ), discuss the difference in meaning between the two kinds of non-finite construction.

12

Thematic systems of the clause

1. Thematic variation

The thematic systems of the clause are those where corresponding members of the contrasting classes (such as active *My father wrote the letter* and passive *The letter was written by my father*) are prototypically thematic variants. Thematic variants have the same propositional content, but differ in the way it is 'packaged' as a message. We select one rather than another from a pair or larger set of thematic variants depending on which part(s) of the message we wish to give prominence to, on what we regard the message as being primarily about, on what parts of it we assume the addressee already knows, on what contrasts, if any, we wish to make, and so on.

The general definition given above makes reference to prototypes because the corresponding clauses are not invariably thematic variants. For example, active *The Head willingly made Kim convenor* and passive *Kim was willingly made convenor by the Head* are not thematic variants because the passive, unlike the active, allows an interpretation where it is a matter of willingness on the part of Kim rather than the Head.[1] But such cases are relatively exceptional: normally the switch from active to passive leaves the propositional meaning intact, and similarly with other thematic systems.

Not all thematic variation is attributable to differences between the terms of a grammatical system. *He blames everything that goes wrong on his wife* and *He blames his wife for everything that goes wrong*, for example, are thematic variants not associated with a grammatical system: it is simply a matter of the verb **blame** allowing variation between two patterns of complementation, $NP_x + on\ NP_y$ and $NP_y + for\ NP_x$. Analogously for *He gave the key to his wife* ($NP_x + to\ NP_y$) and *He*

---

[1] More problematic are pairs like *Many of them didn't accept it* and *It wasn't accepted by many of them*. Passivisation here changes the order of *many* and the negative, which affects the salient interpretation of their relative scope: the salient interpretation of the active has *many* outside the scope of the negative ('There were many of them who didn't accept it'), and conversely for the passive ('There weren't many of them who accepted it'). We have noted, however, that the scope of a negative is affected by prosodic properties, and for many speakers at least the active and passive versions can here each sustain both interpretations.

173

gave his wife the key (NP$_y$ + NP$_x$), where we have treated both variants as kernel clauses: cf. 4.5.[2]

Much thematic variation, indeed, is due to prosodic differences between utterances of a single sentence. For example, I might say *She's staying at home so that she can finish her assignment* with a single intonation group (with nuclear stress most probably on the second syllable of *assignment*) or I might say it with two, one for *She's staying at home* (typically with nuclear stress on *home*), and one for the rest (with nuclear stress again on *-sign-*, let us assume). The first presents the whole as a single piece of information, while the second divides it into two. The potential significance of this distinction is reflected in the fact that only the first would be appropriate in a context where it has already been established that she is staying at home: the second, by allotting a separate intonation group to *She's staying at home*, presents this part of the message as new, as something of which the addressee is being informed.

Such prosodic differences fall outside the scope of grammar in the sense we are giving to that term in this book. Before leaving them, however, it will be helpful to comment briefly on the question of nuclear stress placement because of its relevance to grammatical contrasts between different sequential arrangements of constituents.

The placement of nuclear stress helps identify the **new** or **focal** information in the message, as opposed to **given** or **non-focal** information. Suppose we have a context where it is given, i.e. already assumed common ground between speaker and addressee, that someone phoned the matron. I might then say *"Pat phoned the matron/her*: the nuclear stress indicates that *Pat* is a focal constituent, i.e. that the focal information crucially involves Pat ("Pat did it"). But in a context where it is given that Pat communicated with the matron and new that the means of communication was by phone then the natural place for the nuclear stress will be *phoned*. The least explicit indication of focal information is provided by *Pat phoned the "matron*: this is equally consistent with a context where none of the information is given (e.g. in response to *What happened next?*), one where it is given that Pat did something (*What did Pat do?*) and one where it is given that Pat phoned someone (*Who did Pat phone?*). The reason why this gives the least explicit indication of focus is that the nuclear stress prototypically falls within the last open-class word of a focal constituent: there are three constituents having *matron* as the last open-class word, the object *the matron*, the predicate *phoned the matron*, and the whole clause *Pat phoned the matron*; *Pat* and *phoned* by contrast, are each the last open-class word in only one constituent, the subject and predicator respectively. The specification 'open-class word' is needed because *Pat "phoned her*, where *her* is a closed-class word, allows any of the constituents *phoned*, *phoned her* and *Pat phoned her* to be associated with focal information. And the qualification 'prototypically' is needed because there are cases where the

---

[2] The distinction between systematic and non-systematic differences is not completely clear-cut, and a considerable number of grammars do in fact attribute this latter type of variation to a system, treating the ditransitive construction as non-kernel, derived from the prepositional one by a process sometimes called 'dative shift'.

nuclear stress falls before the last word of a focal constituent: this happens most readily when there is a strong association between subject and predicator, as in *The "kettle's boiling*, where the whole clause can be a focal constituent.

In the following sections we will examine in turn six thematic systems of the clause. Five of them (§§2–5, 7) crucially involve differences in the sequential arrangement of constituents, and it will be convenient to conclude this introductory section by mentioning three of the thematic factors that may influence the selection of one order in preference to another among a pair of thematic variants (whether or not they contrast in a grammatical system).

(a) There is a tendency for focal constituents to come towards the end of the clause, as observed in the above remarks on nuclear stress placement. Suppose, for example, you ask, *What did your mother do?*: I might then naturally reply with the answer *She sent a letter of protest to the manager*. In the context for my response the information that my mother did something is given: what is new, focal, is that what she did was send a letter of protest to the manager. The sequential arrangement in the grammar matches the given–new ordering of information: *she* in subject function (here correlating with actor role) precedes *sent a letter of protest to the manager*. Notice that it would be very unnatural in this context to use the passive *A letter of protest was sent by her to the manager*. But in response to *What happened to your mother?* a passive such as *She was taken away by one of the guards* would be completely natural: in this context my mother's involvement in a 'patient' ('undergoer') role in some action or event is given, non-focal, and this matches the grammatical arrangement with *she* appearing early as subject in a passive construction. Or consider the contrast between *I gave the even-numbered ticket to Angela* and *I gave Angela the even-numbered ticket*. A context where it is given that I disposed of the even-numbered ticket and new that the recipient was Angela will favour the first, whereas one where it is given that I gave Angela something (or some ticket) and new that it was the even-numbered ticket will favour the second.

(b) The phrase identifying the primary topic tends to come at the beginning of the clause. This is likely to be the major factor influencing the choice between, say, *Kim married Pat* and *Pat married Kim*: if I am talking primarily about Kim I'm likely to prefer the first, and if I'm talking primarily about Pat the second. Similarly with an active/passive pair such as *Max has just beaten your brother in the quarter-finals* vs *Your brother has just been beaten by Max in the quarter-finals*: other things being equal, the first is likely to be construed as being primarily about Max, the second about your brother.

(c) There is a tendency for long and complex constituents of the clause to occur late. For example, *It is unfortunate that he decided to change the time of the meeting without consulting the bus timetable* is likely to be preferred over *That he decided to change the time of the meeting without consulting the bus timetable is unfortunate*, for it has the long subordinate clause in final rather than initial position in the main clause. (The version with the subordinate clause initial might be used, in accordance with point (a) above, if the content of the subordinate clause is given.)

These factors are not unrelated. The primary topic will very often be someone or something that is quite salient in the context of discourse: it will then normally be identifiable by a relatively short expression (*she*, *the letter* or the like), and this earlier positioning will be favoured by topic-prominence and shortness together. Similarly the given information in the message will often involve the topic (as in *She sent a letter of protest to the manager* in response to *What did your mother do?*), so that topic-prominence and non-focal status will work together in favouring an early position. But there is no necessity for the three factors to match up like this.

2. Voice

An elementary example of the contrast between active and passive voice is given in (1):

(1)   i   *The guard pushed Tom aside*   Active
      ii *Tom was pushed aside by the guard*   Passive

At the general level the terms **active** and **passive** apply to grammatically distinct clause constructions differing in the way the syntactic function of the subject matches up with its semantic role. The terms are defined by reference to the normal association between subject and semantic role in clauses expressing an action: in active voice the subject normally corresponds to the actor (the active participant), and in passive voice it normally corresponds to the patient/undergoer (the passive participant). The grammatical distinction between the clause constructions prototypically includes some difference in the verb.[3]

The contrast exemplified in (1) clearly satisfies these conditions. The guard is the actor, the performer of the action, while Tom is the patient, the undergoer of the action, and the subject is *the guard* in (i), *Tom* in (ii). In a pair like *The guard disliked Tom* and *Tom was disliked by the guard* there is no action expressed (to dislike someone is not to do something to them), so that the roles of actor and patient have no place in the semantic description; the clauses are nevertheless classifiable as active and passive respectively because by virtue of their language-particular grammatical properties the first belongs with (1i), the second with (ii).

If we take the active as basic, we can derive the passive by applying the following operations:

(2)   i   Change the function of the subject (*the guard*) so that it becomes complement of the preposition *by*; the function of the resultant *by* phrase we will call 'agent'.

---

[3] To the extent that this is a matter of distinct inflections or auxiliaries, active and passive will be verbal as well as clausal categories. Thus those grammars that analyse the *be* of (1ii) as an auxiliary will apply the terms active and passive to *pushed* and *was pushed* in (i) and (ii) respectively.

ii   Change the function of the object (*Tom*) so that it becomes subject.

iii Add the catenative verb *be* as superordinate to the original verb; put the latter into the past participle form and transfer its original inflectional properties to *be* (except for any person–number properties: these will be determined by agreement with the new subject).

This operation can be applied to the great majority of transitive active clauses, but not all. One construction where passivisation is not possible is that where the object is obligatorily reflexive, as in *Kim perjured herself* (cf. 6.11.2).[4] Other restrictions are unsystematic, involving particular verbs or, rather, particular grammatical or semantic uses of certain verbs. Examples are *have* in most uses (*Kim has three sons* ~ **Three sons are had by Kim*), *equal* in the sense "be equal to" (*3^2 equals 9* ~ **9 is equalled by 3^2*), the catenative use of *want, like, hate*, etc. (*Everyone wanted Kim to win* ~ **Kim was wanted to win by everyone*), and so on. There are also two or three verbs, e.g. *say* and *rumour*, which are excluded from the active transitive catenative construction but appear in the corresponding passive (**His brother said him to be an alcoholic* ~ *He was said by his brother to be an alcoholic*).

The above account handles the most prototypical passive construction, but needs extension to cover the full range of passives. The term 'passive' is applicable derivatively to de-participial adjectives like *broken* in *The vase was already broken*, inasmuch as the semantic relation between the predicative adjective and the subject derives from that between the verb *break* and its object in a kernel clause such as *He broke the vase* (cf. 7.3). Here, however, we will confine our attention to clausal passives, the main additional constructions we need to consider being as follows:

(a) Agentless passives. The *by* phrase agent is an optional element, and indeed agentless passives like *Tom was pushed aside* are very much more frequent than 'agented' ones like (1ii).

(b) Passives of ditransitive actives. Where the active clause has two objects, as in *The biology teacher gave the kids too much homework*, we have to ask which is made subject by operation (2i). Normally it is the indirect object, giving (3i), but in some dialects it can (with a few verbs) be the direct object, giving (3ii):

(3) i   *The kids were given too much homework by the biology teacher*
     ii *Too much homework was given the kids by the biology teacher*

(c) Passives with stranded prepositions. The element that is made subject by passivisation is not always the object of the verb: it can be the complement of a preposition, as in

(4) i   *The management looked into the matter*
     ii *The matter was looked into by the management*

---

[4] Where the object is optionally, contrastively reflexive, as in *Kim taught herself* (contrasting say with non-reflexive *Kim taught me*), passivisation is unlikely but not ungrammatical. The form, however, is of course *Kim was taught by herself* not **Herself was taught by Kim*, for the pronoun cannot here precede its antecedent.

This type of passive is usually found with prepositional verbs, thus in constructions where the preposition is lexically determined by the verb. The close lexical tie between verb and preposition (***look*** + *into*, ***refer*** + *to*, etc.) makes it comparable to a single verb: the complement of the preposition is then treated, for purposes of passivisation, like a direct object. The lexically related elements normally have to be syntactically adjacent: there cannot, for example, be an object between them (cf. *The secretary referred us to the treasurer* ~ **The treasurer was referred us to*).[5] The construction is not, however, restricted to prepositional verbs, witness examples like *This glass has been drunk out of*, *The bed had been slept in*. Yet even here there is a strong semantic tie between the verb and preposition(s). Drinking out of a glass is readily thought of as affecting it in some significant way (so that it needs washing before it can be used again), and analogously for sleeping in a bed. The unnaturalness of, say, *The post office was walked towards* stems from the difficulty of imagining how walking towards a post office could affect it in any comparable way.

(d) ***Get*** passives. An alternative to (1ii) has ***get*** rather than ***be*** as the superordinate catenative:

(5)   *Tom got pushed aside by the guard*

There are three principal factors influencing the choice between ***be*** and ***get***. Firstly, ***be*** is normally preferred in formal style. Secondly, ***get*** is for the most part excluded when the corresponding active belongs to the transitive catenative construction: *It was/*got assumed to be impossible*. Thirdly, ***get*** tends to be preferred when the subject referent is not a purely passive participant, as in *I'm getting vaccinated tomorrow* (where the speaker is quite likely to have taken some initiative); for this reason ***get*** is favoured in imperatives and other constructions where some measure of responsibility or intention is attributed to the understood subject-referent: *Don't get run over*, *Get lost!*, *I persuaded her to get vaccinated*.

(e) Passives without (intransitive) ***get*** or ***be***. In (5) and (1ii) *pushed aside by the guard* is a past-participial clause functioning as complement to the intransitive catenatives ***get*** and ***be***, but such past-participial clauses occur in certain other constructions as well. One is as complement to a handful of transitive catenative verbs, ***see***, ***hear***, ***have***, ***get***, ***want***, ***order***, etc., as in

(6)   *I saw Tom pushed aside by the guard*

In accordance with the usual rules for the catenative construction (cf. 11.6.1), the understood subject of the participial clause is recovered from the superordinate clause: from the subject in intransitive (5) and (1ii), from the object in transitive (6). A second construction has the participial clause as modifier in NP structure: *The guy pushed aside by the guard* [*was furious*]. Here the understood subject is

---

[5] In some cases adjuncts seem to be not wholly excluded: *The matter had been looked carefully into by the management* (though ... *carefully looked into* ... or ... *looked into carefully* ... would be more likely).

recovered from the rest of the NP (*the guy*). In addition, the clause may be less closely related to the head, having the status of a peripheral dependent, in NP or clause structure: *Tom, pushed aside by the guard, dashed out of the room* (cf. 6.8).

It remains to take up briefly the thematic factors involved in choosing between active and passive constructions. In the prototypical case with which we began, illustrated in (1), passivisation reverses the sequential arrangement of the two NPs, and here the choice will be influenced by the thematic considerations mentioned in §1 above – the tendency for focal and complex constituents to come late in the clause, and for the phrase identifying the primary topic to come early. Moving beyond the prototypical case, there are two further points to add. One is that the agent element in the passive is syntactically optional, as observed in (a) above, whereas the corresponding element in the active, namely the subject, is obligatory (except in imperatives and non-finites). One reason for choosing a passive, therefore, is that it enables us to omit what would have to be included in an active: we can say *The house was built in 1964* but not **Built the house in 1964*. And there are a variety of reasons for omitting the agent. The identity of the agent-referent might be irrelevant (as in this example, if the issue is how old the house is); it might be unknown or too obvious to need specifying; or one might simply wish to conceal it. The second point is that in constructions where the subject is missing, it very often has to be recoverable from an element in a superordinate clause – in *Ed tried not to offend Liz*, for example, the understood subject of the *offend* clause is recovered from the subject of the *try* clause. By providing a choice between alternative subjects (actual or understood) the voice system offers a convenient way of matching the understood subject of the subordinate clause with the superordinate element. Compare, for example, *She tried not to intimidate him* and *He tried not to be intimidated by her*, with "she" the potential intimidator and "he" the potential victim: we need an active in the first and a passive in the second in order for the understood subject to match the superordinate *she* and *he* respectively.

3. Subject-complement switch with identifying *be*

Passivisation does not apply to copulative clauses: *Kim was a genius*, say, has no passive counterpart **A genius was been by Kim*. And clearly there is a semantic basis for this difference in syntactic behaviour between transitive and copulative clauses. Prototypically the object is semantically comparable to the subject in that they both pick out participants in the situation: the voice system then allows a choice as to which participant-role is associated with the subject. Thus in (1), as we noted, there are two participants and either of the corresponding NPs can be made subject. The prototypical predicative, on the other hand, is semantically quite different in that it gives a property ascribed to the subject-participant. In *Kim was a genius* there is only one participant, Kim, and hence only one of the NPs, *Kim*, is a candidate for subject function.

The verb *be*, however, has a variety of uses, and in particular we can distinguish the ascriptive use of *Kim was a genius* and the identifying use illustrated in *The best place to park is opposite the post office*. This expresses an identifying relation between two terms, the identified ("the best place to park") and the identifier ("opposite the post office"). We have noted (4.3) that an identifier complement is not a prototypical predicative but has significant syntactic affinities with an object: it can be a personal pronoun (*The only one they didn't ask was you*), it may allow a contrast of number (*What we want is another patrol/more patrols*) – and it can be reassigned to subject function:

(7) i   *The best place to park is opposite the post office*
     ii *Opposite the post office is the best place to park*

Note that the syntactic difference between these is not the same as that in (8), where we are concerned not with identifying the toy shop, but with ascribing a location to it:

(8) i   *The new toy shop is opposite the post office*
     ii *Opposite the post office is the new toy shop*

The process deriving (ii) from (i) in (7) reassigns the syntactic functions, but in (8) it merely reorders them (cf. §7 below). Thus in (7ii) *opposite the post office* is subject, as is evident from the fact that the closed interrogative counterpart is *Is opposite the post office the best place to park?* – but in (8ii) *opposite the post office* is a locative complement, just as it is in (i), and this is why we cannot have **Is opposite the post office the new toy shop?*.

The identified term is always expressed by an NP – including a fused relative construction, as in *What I said was that I would give it some thought*. The identifier, on the other hand, may have a variety of forms: an NP (*The cause of death was heart failure*), a content clause (*The problem with that suggestion is that you'll never get the boss to agree*), a non-finite clause (*The best thing to do is to start again*), a PP (7i), an AdjP (*What he is is stupid!*), an AdvP (*The only way to drive here is very, very slowly*), and so on. We take as basic the version where the identified term is expressed by the subject, as in (7i), for the other version is an exceptional clause construction precisely by allowing such a range of subjects – it is the only one, for example, where we find AdjPs or AdvPs as subject. (7ii) thus derives from (i) by a process which reassigns the syntactic functions and which accordingly bears some similarity to passivisation. It does not, however, effect any change in the verb or introduce the preposition *by*, so that the marked and unmarked versions are nothing like as clearly distinct from each other as are passive and active clauses. Nor indeed is it always so easy to tell whether a given occurrence of *be* is identifying or ascriptive. Nevertheless, the distinction between (7) and (8) is very clear, and there is no doubt that the semantic distinction between identifying and ascriptive *be* is to a significant extent grammaticalised in English.[6]

---

[6] There are, however, many grammars that do not make this distinction and which do not therefore have a grammatical system contrasting (7i) and (ii).

4. Extraposition

The general term **extraposition** is applied to a syntactic process which characteristically moves a subordinate clause subject to the right, to a position beyond the main predicate; depending on the type of language concerned, it may or may not involve the addition of a dummy pronoun to take over the vacated subject function. In English the term applies to the process deriving (ii) from (i) in such pairs as

(9)   i   *That he had been lying was obvious to everyone*
     ii   *It was obvious to everyone that he had been lying*
(10) i   *(For you) to change your mind now would be a mistake*
     ii   *It would be a mistake (for you) to change your mind now.*

The subordinate clauses *that he had been lying* and *(for you) to change your mind now* are moved to the right of the main clause predicate and *it* is inserted to take on the subject function: English is a language where the subject is an obligatory element in declarative main clauses and hence one where extraposition adds a dummy pronoun to satisfy that requirement.

Except under very restrictive conditions that we needn't go into here, the extraposed element is obligatorily (not just characteristically) a subordinate clause in English. Thus if we replace *that he has been lying* in (9i) by, say, *his guilt*, extraposition is no longer possible: **It was obvious to everyone his guilt.*[7] The subordinate clause may be finite, as in (9), or infinitival, as in (10). Subjectless present-participial clauses are sometimes extraposed over short predicates (*It's been nice meeting you*), but for the most part they resist extraposition: this is one indication that they are more highly nominalised than finites and infinitivals (cf. 6.12).

There are some restrictions on the predicate over which a clause may be extraposed. Most obviously it cannot contain another clause as complement: *That he hasn't replied shows he's not reliable* but not **It shows he's not reliable that he hasn't replied.* Nor can it contain an identified complement, a further indication of the grammaticalisation of the ascriptive/identifying distinction with ***be***: extraposition is possible with *Why she didn't tell us is a mystery* (ascriptive) but not with *Why she didn't tell us is the important question* (reversed identifying construction). For certain other kinds of predicates, by contrast, extraposition is obligatory, namely with such verbs as ***appear***, ***seem***, ***chance***, ***happen*** (finite clause subjects), ***remain*** and the passive of ***hope***, ***intend*** (infinitival subjects): *It seemed that we'd been misled, It is hoped to avoid such errors next time*, but not **That we'd been misled seemed, *To avoid such errors next time is hoped.*

Although extraposition prototypically applies to move a clause out of subject position, it can also move one out of object position, over another complement:

(11) i   *He found being able to talk things over with her a great help*
     ii   *He found it a great help being able to talk things over with her*

---

[7] *It was obvious to everyone, his guilt* differs from the extraposition construction in punctuation/ intonation and also in its thematic motivation. Its primary use would be in a context where there has been prior mention of his guilt, so that this occurrence of *his guilt* would have only a clarifying role: it would not provide the sole indication of what *it* refers to.

Usually, though not invariably, the relation between the object and the complement over which it is moved is comparable to that between a subject and a predicate in a simpler construction (cf. *Being able to talk things over with her was a great help ~ It was a great help being able to talk things over with her*), so that this application of extraposition is clearly analogous to the prototype. Where the subordinate clause is finite or infinitival, however, extraposition is obligatory: *He made it known that he was dissatisfied* (not **He made that he was dissatisfied known*), *They hadn't intended it to be so easy to get away* (not **They hadn't intended to get away to be so easy*). This is a special case of a broader restriction: when finite or infinitival clauses are functioning in the structure of a larger clause they are virtually excluded from medial position (i.e. a position which is neither initial nor final).[8]

The thematic motivation for extraposition is that it puts a subordinate clause in final position, in keeping with the tendency noted in §1 above for heavy, complex material to come late. In (9), for example, (ii) is easier to process in that we are not kept waiting for the main predicate – and the greater the length and complexity of the subordinate clause relative to the main predicate, the greater the likelihood that the extrapositioned variant will be preferred. Extraposition also results in a structure to which subject-operator inversion can apply. Thus we can form an interrogative from (ii) but not from (i) in (9) and (10) – inverting (i) would put the subordinate clause in medial position. One circumstance that may, by contrast, favour the selection of the unmarked, non-extrapositioned, version is when the content of the subordinate clause is given information; this is not likely to arise very often, however, for if the content were given it would tend to be expressed by means of a pronoun, say, rather than a clause – *That was obvious to everyone* rather than (9i).

5. The existential construction

In this section we will be concerned with a second construction involving a dummy pronoun as subject, this time *there* rather than *it*. It is illustrated in the marked member of the following pair:

(12) i   *Some friends of hers were on the committee*
     ii *There were some friends of hers on the committee*

(ii) belongs to what is called the **existential construction**. At the language-particular level, this is defined by the presence of dummy *there* as subject. At the general level, it is defined as a grammatically distinct construction including among its most salient uses the expression of existential propositions – propositions that such-and-such exists. The English construction with *there* as subject satisfies this general definition by virtue of its use in examples like [*Are you sure*] *that there is a god* [*?*] ("that (a) god exists"), *There undoubtedly are people who think like that* ("People who think like that undoubtedly exist"); it must be emphasised, how-

---

[8] Adjuncts can follow, however, provided the subordinate clause is relatively short (and the adjunct is reasonably long): *I predicted it wouldn't work as long ago as last Christmas.*

ever, that this is only one of its uses, that there are others – one is exemplified in (12ii) – which do not lend themselves to paraphrase with "exist". Existential propositions can of course be expressed by means of clauses of the form 'NP *exists*', but this does not represent a grammatically distinct clause construction: *exist* is simply an intransitive verb, not differing grammatically from numerous others.

Dummy *there* derives historically from the locative *there* of *Don't put it over there* and the like, but in Modern English they are clearly distinct semantically, phonologically and grammatically. Locative *there* means "to/at/in that place" and contrasts with *here* – it is interpreted either deictically (*Look over there*) or anaphorically (*He went to Paris in 1910 and stayed there* [= "in Paris"] *for ten years*); dummy *there*, on the other hand, has no identifiable meaning of its own, and it can combine with either locative *there* or *here* (*There's a mistake there/ here*). Phonologically, locative *there* is stressed and has the vowel /ɛə/, while dummy *there* is unstressed and the vowel is commonly reduced to /ə/. Grammatically, locative *there* is an adverb, while dummy *there* is a personal pronoun (though a marginal member of the class: see 6.11.1). As we are concerned in this section with the existential construction, *there* is to be interpreted in what follows as dummy *there*, not locative *there*.

There normally occurs in subject function.[9] It is not, however, a prototypical subject: in the existential construction the usual subject properties are shared between *there* and the post-verbal NP (i.e. *some friends of hers* in (12ii)). Nevertheless *there* behaves like a subject in most respects. Note in particular that its position is that of a subject: before the verb in declaratives, after the operator in interrogatives (*Were there some friends of hers on the committee?*). *There* does not inflect for case, but if the post-verbal NP has the form of a case-variable personal pronoun it will normally be accusative, an indication that this NP is not subject ([⟨A⟩ *Who was left?* – ⟨B⟩] *There was only me*). What is non-prototypical about *there* is that it does not determine the person–number inflection of the verb: *were* in (12ii) agrees with *some of her friends*.[10]

Many existential clauses have no non-existential counterpart, but we will look first at those that do. (12) provides an example of this kind. We here derive the existential variant from the non-existential by moving the initial NP from subject to post-verbal complement position and inserting *there* as the new subject. This process of 'existential formation' can apply only under very restrictive conditions; the main types are as follows.

(a) *Be* + locative complement: *A jacaranda tree was in the front garden* ∼ *There was a jacaranda tree in the front garden*. Locative is to be interpreted broadly – so as to include (12), for example.

---

[9] It appears as object only in the transitive catenative construction that involves 'raising', as in *I expect there to be some friends of hers on the committee* (cf. 11.6.1); we will confine our attention in this section to the more basic construction where it appears as subject.

[10] Traditional grammar tends to recognise only the agreement property, and thus to analyse *some of her friends* as subject. It is interesting to note, however, that examples like *There's some people outside*, with the verb agreeing with *there*, are common in informal style.

(b) **Be** + predicative: *No doctor was present* ∼ *There was no doctor present.* The predicative is normally an adjective like *present, absent, available, eligible, ill*, etc., that relates to the immediate more or less transitory situation, rather than one denoting a relatively permanent property (cf. **There was no doctor Australian*). Note, for example, that *Is there anyone tall enough to reach that apple?* would become unacceptable if we dropped *enough to reach that apple.*

(c) Catenative **be** + present- or past-participial clause complement: *Children were playing on the road* ∼ *There were children playing on the road.*

(d) Intransitive verbs other than **be**: *Many problems remain* ∼ *There remain many problems.* Only a few verbs are found here: **appear, arrive, arise, exist, follow, occur** and the like.

Existential clauses without a non-existential counterpart are illustrated in

(13) i   *There are lots of people like that*
    ii   *There was an explosion (at the chemical factory)*

The predicate has **be** as verb and usually a single complement with the form of an NP (and optionally various adjuncts). The absence of a non-existential counterpart reflects the fact that in kernel clauses **be** does not normally occur without some kind of complement. The process of existential formation thus applies here obligatorily, instead of optionally – just as extraposition applies obligatorily with such verbs as **appear** and **seem**.

The NP complement in existential clauses is normally indefinite, more precisely one with a determiner like *a, some, enough, several, many*, or a cardinal numeral, one with no determiner at all, but not one with a determiner indicating proportion, such as *most* or *all*. Definites certainly cannot be excluded altogether, however, especially in the obligatorily existential construction of (13) – [⟨A⟩ *Who do you suggest for secretary?* – ⟨B⟩] *Well, there's Tom*; *There's always the possibility she'll change her mind.*

Looked at from a thematic point of view, the effect of the process of existential formation is to move out of subject position an NP which clearly does not express the topic (even in those cases where it is definite), an NP which moreover very often introduces a new entity into the context of discourse. And these are of course thematic properties which, other things being equal, favour non-subject position.[11]

6. The cleft construction

The cleft construction is illustrated in (14ii–iv), which are all thematically marked counterparts of (i):

[11] Many grammars refer to the existential construction as the '*there* construction' (and to existential formation as '*there* insertion'); we find similar constructions in other languages, however, so that a general term is much to be preferred.

(14) i   *Becker beat Lendl in the Wimbledon final*
    ii   *It was Becker who beat Lendl in the Wimbledon final*
    iii *It was Lendl that Becker beat in the Wimbledon final*
    iv   *It was in the Wimbledon final that Becker beat Lendl*

At the general level the **cleft construction** is definable as a grammatically distinct construction whose members are characteristically derivable from more elementary clauses by dividing – 'cleaving' – them into two parts, one of which is highlighted, while the other is subordinated in the form of a relative clause having the highlighted element as antecedent. Often (as in English), the highlighted element functions as complement to the verb "be". (14ii), for example, derives from (i) by dividing it into a highlighted element *Becker* and a residue *beat Lendl in the Wimbledon final*: the highlighted element is made complement of *be* in a main clause, while the residue appears in a subordinate relative clause with *Becker* as antecedent.

In English the highlighted element functions as complement to *be* with the dummy pronoun *it* as subject. As is often the case with non-kernel constructions, the structure of cleft clauses is somewhat problematic: it is not easy to see just where the relative clause belongs in the constituent hierarchy. Although it has the highlighted element as antecedent, the two do not form a constituent together: in (ii), for example, *Becker who beat Lendl in the Wimbledon final* does not behave as a single unit. A more plausible analysis is to take the relative clause as an immediate constituent of the sentence as a whole, a dependent of the *be* clause:

(15)

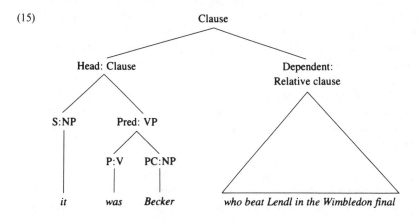

The ambiguity of an example like *It's the hat your mother bought at Myer's* will then be reflected in a difference in constituent structure. In one interpretation this is a cleft version of *Your mother bought the hat at Myer's*, but there is another interpretation in which *it*, rather than being a dummy pronoun, refers to some entity in the context of discourse which the clause goes on to identify as the hat your mother bought at Myer's – it might serve as answer to a question like *What's that over there?*, and *it* is here replaceable by other NPs such as *that, that strange object over there*, and so on. In the first interpretation, the structure is like that shown in (15); in the second, *the hat your mother bought at Myer's* is a constituent, an NP with the relative clause functioning as modifier to *hat*. The two interpretations would tend to be distinguished prosodically, with the main stress falling on *hat* in the first and within the relative clause, most probably on *Myer's*, in the second.

As we see from (14), there is a range of elements that can be selected for highlighting: subject in (i), object in (ii), adjunct in (iii). The restrictions on what can be highlighted are partly a matter of function, partly a matter of class. As for function, we cannot select the predicator nor, for the most part, the predicative: **It's cunning/an agnostic that he is*. And the indirect object resists highlighting as it does other kinds of relativisation: ?**It was Kim I gave the book*. Much more natural would be *It was Kim I gave the book to* or *It was to Kim I gave the book*, which derive not from the ditransitive construction (*I gave Kim the book*) but from the one with object + PP complement (*I gave the book to Kim*). As for class, the highlighted element is usually an NP or a PP. Subordinate clauses are not wholly excluded, at least in subject position: compare ?*It's that he was so apologetic that surprised me* (subject) and **It's that she would reconsider her decision that she said* (object).

The internal form of the relative clause is largely the same as that of a restrictive relative – see 11.3.1. The main difference has to do with the range of elements that can be relativised: most notably, the cleft allows much greater freedom in relativising PPs, as in *It was from Peter that I heard it*, *It was to me he was referring*. A second difference is that the Rel-gap type is strongly preferred in the cleft construction unless the relative word is *who* (and perhaps *whom* or *whose*): if, for example, we add *which* before *your mother* in our ambiguous sentence *It's the hat your mother bought at Myer's*, the cleft interpretation becomes unlikely or is lost altogether. And, thirdly, in the cleft construction *that* is omissible in informal style even when the relativised element is subject: *It was John did it*.

We have said that the superordinate clause has *it* as subject, *be* as predicator and the highlighted element as complement. Other properties, however, can be selected in essentially the same way as in an ordinary clause. In addition to (14ii), for example, we could have *It was surely Becker . . .*, *It wasn't Becker . . .*, *It may have been Becker . . .*, *It is Becker . . .*, and so on. Thus although it is illuminating to describe the cleft construction in terms of a process operating on a more elementary, non-cleft structure, this provides only a partial description: such a derivation yields as it were a skeleton clause which can be fleshed out in a variety of ways in accordance with the ordinary options available for copulative clauses.

The cleft construction gives thematic prominence to the complement of *be* at the expense of the relative clause – which is why I have been speaking of the former as the highlighted element. Prototypically the information contained in the relative clause is assigned subordinate status because it is assumed to be known to the addressee, or readily inferrable from what is known. The extreme case is where it is given in what has just been said, and here the relative clause can be omitted: [⟨A⟩ *Who broke that vase?* – ⟨B⟩] *It wasn't me* (*who broke it*).

Very often the thematic priority accorded the highlighted element is reinforced prosodically, so that it carries the main stress and the content of the relative clause is presented as non-focal information. This will arise when the highlighted element is contrastive and/or the content of the relative is more or less given in the context of discourse. The effect when the relative clause information is given is then similar to that achieved in speech by nuclear stress placement alone: compare "*Peter broke the vase* and *It was "Peter who broke the vase*; in writing stress is generally not indicated and the cleft is thus here particularly useful as a means of giving thematic prominence to an element. This is not to say that the effect is exactly the same as that achieved by stress placement: the cleft construction also carries an implication of uniqueness/exhaustiveness. Compare, for example, *She likes "Peter* and *It is "Peter she likes*: the latter implies that she does not like others (in the context of discourse).

The highlighted element does not have to carry the main stress. When it does not, the informational content of the relative clause will have focal status: it will be new information. This does not mean that it is not known to the addressee, but that it is new with respect to the current context of discourse. Thus I might say *It was Callaghan who devised the appeals procedure that was introduced last year* in a context where there has been no mention of the appeals procedure. In this case, however, it is more than likely that there will have been mention of Callaghan: Callaghan will have very clear topic status, with prominence given to his or her role in devising the appeals procedure as opposed to the fact that someone devised it, which may be taken for granted. Another example might be *It's only recently that I've discovered how this thing really works*. This differs from the last in that *only recently*, unlike *Callaghan*, is not likely to be repeated from what has just been said, but the highlighting indicates that I am treating the recency of my discovery as the significant information: the discovery itself is presented as not being at issue.

The systems discussed in §§2–5 all crucially involve differences in the sequential arrangement of elements (effected by a reassignment of functions). Cleft formation may also change the sequence but it does not necessarily do so – compare (14iii, iv) with (ii); the crucial change effected by this process concerns, rather, the hierarchical arrangement of elements. Such a difference in hierarchical arrangement is likewise found in such pairs of thematic variants as

(16) i   *He needs a little discipline*
     ii *What he needs is a little discipline*

In (i) *he, needs* and *a little discipline* all belong to the same clause, whereas in (ii) *he* and *needs* are assigned to a subordinate clause, *a little discipline* to a superordinate one. As with the cleft construction, the content of the subordinate clause is presented as being not at issue. (16ii) is, however, not quite equivalent, thematically, to the cleft construction *It is a little discipline that he needs*: (16ii) is more likely than the latter in that it can be used in contexts where the information that he needs something is non-focal without being strictly given: it's simply not very newsworthy, something presented as uncontroversial even though not explicitly established.

(16ii) illustrates what is commonly called the **pseudo-cleft construction**. This term is suggestive of the fact that in spite of apparent resemblances to the cleft construction it should not be described in an analogous way. Thus (16ii) will not be derived from (i) by a process of cleft formation, and we will not regard (i) and (ii) here as terms in a grammatical system. There are two reasons why this is so. In the first place, we find examples with the form of (16ii) which could not be derived from a more elementary structure like (i): *What I like about her is that she is so thoughtful and considerate* (cf. **I like about her that she's so thoughtful and considerate*), *What is wrong with the proposal is that it doesn't provide a proper appeals procedure* (**That it doesn't provide a proper appeals procedure is wrong with the proposal*), and so on. Secondly (16ii) is an instance of the identifying *be* construction with *what he needs* as the identified term, and as such it is to be related to examples like *All he needs/The thing he needs/The other thing he needs/One of the things he needs is a little more discipline*: there is no reason to give a fundamentally different treatment to the case where the identified term happens to be a fused relative than to those where it is an NP of some other form.

7. Thematic reordering

Most elements of clause structure have an unmarked or basic position – the position they occupy unless there are special grammatical and/or thematic reasons for putting them elsewhere. We have already noted a number of non-kernel grammatical constructions where elements are moved from their basic position – interrogatives, exclamatives and Rel-word relatives; in this section we will be concerned with departures from the basic order that are triggered by purely thematic factors.

In view of the limited space available, we will confine our attention to two kinds of thematic reordering: the movement of an element to the front of the clause or to the end. These reordering processes allow for a variety of elements to appear in first and last position, the thematically most important positions in the clause.

Thematic fronting is illustrated in

(17) i   *The next day he was in Paris*
     ii   *Her sister I quite liked*
     iii *Selfish he's not*
     iv   *[She said she would invite them and] invite them she did*

In (i) the fronted element is an adjunct, in the others a complement of various kinds. Note that the complement may be one created by existential or cleft formation: *And serious implications there certainly were, Kim it was who did most of the work*. In addition, the fronting process may apply to an element within a subordinate clause: *The others I know will be there* (where *the others* has been moved from subject position within the clause complement of *know*), *some of the papers he hadn't even read* (where *some of the papers* originates in object position in the non-finite *read* clause), and so on.

The thematic motivation for moving an element to the front may be to give it topic status. (i) and (ii), for example, are readily interpreted as being about "the next day" and "her sister" respectively. Another reason, not inconsistent with the first, may be to provide a cohesive link with what has gone before. The link may be achieved by contrast: in *Liz herself didn't appeal to me but her sister I quite liked*, for example, we have a contrast between "her sister" and "Liz herself". Or the link may be a matter of repetition, as in (iv), the effect being then to bring given material to the front, leaving the new for final, typically focal, position.

Different kinds of element vary with respect to the ease with which they can be fronted. Adjuncts can in general be moved more readily than complements. Thus the fronting of a complement is usually of questionable acceptability outside of declarative main clauses – compare *When she introduced him, why did you pretend you didn't know him?* (fronted adjunct) and ?*The others, why didn't you check more carefully?* (fronted complement). The greatest restriction applies to (17iv): the non-finite complement of a catenative operator can be fronted only in the case of repetition.

Movement to final position has applied in

(18) i   *Even more worrying is the disappearance of the file*
    ii   *On top of the wardrobe was a battered old trunk*
    iii *A friend of hers turned up whom I'd never met before*
    iv *She explained to us the reasons for her decision*
    v   *He brought in the washing*

The element moved to the end is subject in (i) and (ii), a post-head dependent in the structure of the NP subject in (iii), and object in (iv) and (v).

Movement of the subject to the end is usually accompanied by the fronting of a complement or adjunct, as in (i) and (ii); note that these involve ascriptive, not identifying *be*: they are structurally comparable to (8ii) above, not to (7ii). In (i) the fronting of the predicative provides a link with what has gone before, this time by means of comparison, and the end-positioning of the subject is conducive to its receiving prosodic prominence as the focal part of the information. In (ii) the marked order likewise serves to put into a more prominent position the main new entity being introduced, "a battered old trunk". In (iii) the subject as a whole, *a friend of hers whom I'd never met before*, cannot be end-positioned (for *up*, being part of an idiom *turn up*, cannot be fronted). Instead, just the relative clause is moved: the effect is again to put complex material at the end, and more particularly to avoid the imbalance of a long subject followed by a short (and not very newsworthy) predicate. The basic position for the object in a monotransitive clause is just after the predicator, but where it is significantly longer than a second complement or an adjunct it can be moved to the right, as in (iii) and (iv), in accordance with the tendency mentioned earlier to have long and complex elements at the end. The longer and more complex the object is, the greater the likelihood of its appearance in final position. Movement of the object is most frequent when the second complement is a particle, as in (iv) – here we can even move a personal pronoun object provided it is contrastively stressed (*They didn't take in "me*).

EXERCISES

I. Voice

(a) Do (19)–(26) have a passive counterpart? If yes, what is it? If no, why?

(19) *The Emperor presented the victor with a gold medal*
(20) *Your wife asked the waiter to close the windows*
(21) *The prosecutor clearly demonstrated that they had an excellent motive*
(22) *Some of them resented his behaviour*
(23) *She seemed a decent enough sort of person*
(24) *They called five times*
(25) *Her husband spent whatever she gave him*
(26) *Her husband grumbled, whatever she gave him*

(b) We noted in 11.6.1 that intransitive raising and non-raising catenatives interact differently with the voice of the non-finite complement, inasmuch as in the raising construction (27), but not in the non-raising (28), (i) and (ii) effectively stand in the same relation as in (1):

(27) i   *Kim happened to find the letter*   (= (16i) of Ch. 11)
      ii *The letter happened to be found by Kim* (thematic variant)
(28) i   *Kim managed to find the letter*   (= (16ii) of Ch. 11)
      ii *The letter managed to be found by Kim*   (anomalous)

Construct comparable pairs (varying the content of the infinitival clause) for the catenatives **appear**, **begin**, **continue**, **expect**, **fail**, **have** (as in *Kim has to check the proofs*), **intend**, **like**, **ought**, **remember**, **tend**, **try**, **use** (*He used to interview them*). Which belong to the raising class?

(c) Similarly for the transitive construction:

(29) i   *Pat intended Kim to find the letter*   (= (17i) of Ch. 11)
      ii *Pat intended the letter to be found by Kim* (thematic variant)
(30) i   *Pat asked Kim to find the letter*   (= (17ii) of Ch. 11)
      ii *Pat asked the letter to be found by Kim*   (anomalous)

Construct such pairs for the catenatives **advise**, **believe**, **challenge**, **persuade**, **prefer**, **prove**, **remind**, **teach**, **think**, **urge**. Which belong to the raising class, like **intend**?

(d) Suggest plausible motivations for the selection of the agentless passive construction in (31)–(34).

(31) *The book was published in 1933*
(32) *[The enemy opened fire] and five of our men were killed instantly*
(33) *The specimens were examined spectroscopically*
(34) *The delay in attending to this matter is regretted*

II. Extraposition

(a) Can extraposition apply to (35)–(38)? If so, give the non-kernel clause that results from applying it, and if not explain why.

(35) *Why he did it remains unclear*
(36) *Why he did it is what we've got to find out*
(37) *The reason why he did it hasn't been revealed*
(38) *For you to mention it to her would be a big mistake*

(b) Give the unmarked, non-extrapositioned, counterpart of those among (39)–(42) which have one – in the others extraposition is grammatically obligatory.

(39) *It makes me mad to see them behave like that*
(40) *I find it extraordinary that no one thought of consulting us about it*
(41) *It is to be hoped that things will be better next year*
(42) *It is more than likely that I shan't be here next year*

III. The existential construction

(a) Is the *there* in (43)–(46) the locative adverb or the dummy pronoun – or ambiguously either?

(43) *There he is*
(44) *There goes our last chance of saving the match*
(45) *There's Peter*
(46) *There's me.*

(b) Give existential counterparts for those among (47)–(51) which have one, and say why the others do not.

(47) *Several of his students were among the injured*
(48) *Only a few of them knew why he had gone*
(49) *One of them was a paraplegic*
(50) *A long digression on dreams followed*
(51) *A long digression on dreams followed this analysis of the poem*

(c) We noted in 11.6.1 that intransitive raising catenatives like **happen** allow existential *there* as subject (provided the non-finite complement is compatible), whereas non-raising catenatives do not: compare *There happened/*managed to be a friend of mine present*. Examine the catenative verbs listed in Exercise I(b) above and show with examples that this criterion yields the same assignment to the raising and non-raising classes as the voice criterion. Similarly take the transitive catenative verbs from Exercise I(c) and show that only the raising ones allow *there* as object – compare *Pat intended/*asked there to be a guard on duty* from 11.6.1.

IV. The cleft construction

(a) Give the unmarked, non-cleft, counterpart of the following:

(52) *It was because she was ill that she stayed away*
(53) *It's next week that they are arriving*
(54) *Is it me you are referring to?*
(55) *Why is it always me who has to clear up?*

(b) Which elements in *Kim had given the key to George the day before* can be made the high-lighted element in the cleft construction? Give examples to justify your answer.

(c) Can cleft formation apply to (56)–(61) with the underlined phrase as the highlighted element? If so, what is the result? If not, why?

(56) *I gave George the key*
(57) *I gave George the key*
(58) *She sang the aria too slowly*
(59) *That he was apparently so cheerful made me suspicious*
(60) *She told him that he ought to resign*
(61) *Tom was particularly unpleasant yesterday*

V. Constructions with *it*

Do (62)–(66) belong to the extrapositioned construction, the cleft construction or neither?

(62) *It's incredible that he didn't check the brakes*
(63) *It is undoubtedly the best one to buy*
(64) *It's a nuisance, this rain*
(65) *It was Tom who was responsible*
(66) *It was unclear who was responsible*

13

Coordination

A compound sentence, we have said, contains two or more main clauses:

(1) *Her daughter was a dentist and her son was studying law*

This illustrates the most central and frequent compound sentence construction, that where the main clauses are coordinated, and this chapter will be concerned with investigating coordination, as it applies both to main clauses and to other kinds of expression. But it is worth noting before we embark on that investigation that coordination is not the only possible constructional relation between clauses other than subordination: the clauses may be simply 'juxtaposed'. Thus other kinds of compound sentence are illustrated in *It hurts, doesn't it?*, where an interrogative tag is juxtaposed to a declarative (cf. 9.6) or *The more you look into it, the fishier it seems*, the correlative comparative construction, and so on.

1. Basic coordination

We will speak of *her daughter was a dentist* and *her son was studying law* in (1) as the 'coordinated elements' in the construction. They are coordinated here by means of *and*, but in terms of constituent structure the *and* belongs more closely with the second element, so that a partial structure is as follows:

(2)

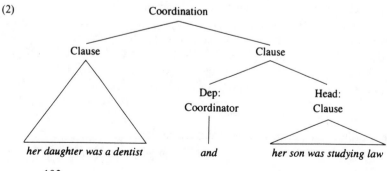

This is thus another case where we have one clause functioning as head of another (cf. 4.9) – and where a more sophisticated analysis might make further discriminations of class.

The term 'coordination' implies that the elements are of equal syntactic status; subordination by contrast involves inequality, a relation between a dependent (the subordinate element) and a head (the superordinate one). Precisely because coordinate elements are of equal syntactic status, no functional labels are given to the immediate constituents of the coordination in (2). The same applies when the coordination occurs lower in the constituent hierarchy:

(3)   *The Governor, the Premier or the Mayor could open the Exhibition*

(4)

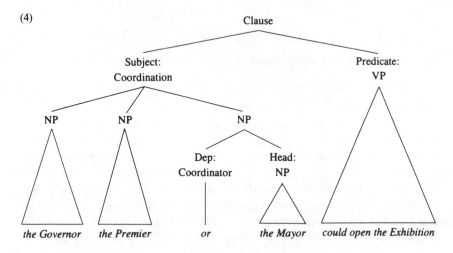

The subject position is filled by *the Governor, the Premier or the Mayor* as a whole, but we do not assign functions within the coordination construction to the three NPs which are its immediate constituents.

For the rest, (1) and (3) lend themselves fairly straightforwardly to analysis in terms of constituent structure, classes and functions. But this is not so for all coordination. In (5), for example,

(5)   *Ed has written, and I am about to write, a long letter of protest*

and does not introduce an element that would form a constituent in the related kernel clause *I am about to write a long letter of protest*. We will accordingly make a distinction between **basic coordination**, which can be described directly, and **non-basic coordination**, which will be described indirectly, in terms of its relation to the more elementary type. Thus (1) and (3) will be described directly, while (5) will be related to a basic coordination such as *Ed has written a long letter of protest and I'm about to write a long letter of protest*. In this first section, only basic coordination will be considered.

The coordination construction is definable, at the general level, as one which characteristically has the following properties applying to the most central instances of it; not all properties will necessarily be found in every language (hence the qualification 'characteristically') and any given property will not necessarily hold in a particular language for all instances of coordination (hence the qualification 'most central instances').

(a) Coordinators. A coordination prototypically contains one or more special markers assignable to a distinct class of words, coordinators. The most basic semantic role of coordinators is to express the logical relations of conjunction and disjunction, corresponding approximately to English *and* and *or* respectively. If we join two propositions "p" and "q" by conjunction, the resultant compound proposition "p and q" will be true if both component propositions are true, and false otherwise. For example, "Her daughter was a dentist and her son was studying law" is true provided "Her daughter was a dentist" and "Her son was studying law" are both true: if either is false (or if both are), then the compound proposition is false. Conversely, if we join "p" and "q" by disjunction, the resultant "p or q" will be true if either component proposition is true, and false if both of them are false. Thus "Tom has missed the train or the train is late" is true if either of "Tom has missed the train" and "The train is late" is true, but false if both are false. The coordinators *and* and *or* correspond most closely to these logical links when they join (declarative main) clauses, but coordination of smaller units than clauses is very often logically equivalent to conjunctive or disjunctive coordination of clauses: *Ed and Pat know the answer* is logically equivalent to *Ed knows the answer and Pat knows the answer*, while *She told Ed or Pat* is logically equivalent to *She told Ed or she told Pat*.

(b) Reducibility to one element. A coordination is prototypically replaceable by any one of the elements on its own. Thus (1) can be syntactically reduced either to *Her daughter was a dentist* or to *Her son was studying law*; (3) can be reduced to *The Governor could open the Exhibition*, to *The Premier could open the Exhibition* or to *The Mayor could open the Exhibition*; and so on.

(c) Order change. Prototypically, the order of elements can be changed without affecting the propositional meaning of the sentence. This reflects the fact that the logical conjunction "p and q" is equivalent to "q and p" and the logical disjunction "p or q" to "q or p". Thus (1) is equivalent to *Her son was studying law and her daughter was a dentist*; similarly in (3) all six of the possible orderings of the three coordinated elements are logically equivalent.

(d) Likeness of class and function. The elements in any one coordination are normally alike in class and (where relevant) in function. The interpretation of 'likeness of class' is straightforward: the elements in (1) both belong to the class of main clauses, those in (3) are all NPs, and so on. Likeness of function is best understood via property (b) above: if we reduce to a single element, its function will be the same, whichever element we choose. Thus if we reduce (3) to *The Governor could open the Exhibition*, the NP *the Governor* will be subject; if we reduce it to *The Premier could open the Exhibition*, the NP *the Premier* will likewise be subject; and so on. Or, to put it another way, it is by virtue of the functional likeness that we can assign a unitary function to the coordination as a whole. The ungrammaticality of *She had eaten some chips and this morning* is due to the functional unlikeness between *some chips* (object in *She had eaten some chips*) and *this morning* (adjunct in *She had eaten this morning*) – contrast *She had eaten some chips and an apple*, where each of the coordinated elements could stand alone as object. Functional likeness does not apply in (1) – hence the qualification 'where relevant'. The reason is that the coordination forms a sentence by itself and thus is not part of any larger syntactic construction within which it could be assigned a function – and if we reduce it to a single clause, that clause would likewise form a whole sentence.

(e) Open-endedness. There is no grammatical limit to the number of elements that can enter into a prototypical coordinative construction. We could expand (1), which has two coordinated elements, to *Her daughter was a dentist, her son was studying law and her cousin was an accountant*, which has three, then add a fourth term, then a fifth, and so on: the only limits are imposed by considerations of coherence, comprehensibility, aesthetics, not of grammaticality.

(f) Range of occurrence. Coordinations can occur in most places in the syntactic structure of a sentence. In (1) the sentence itself has the form of a coordination; in (3) the coordination is subject; in [*He*] *wrote and directed* [*the play*] it is predicator; in [*She had eaten*] *some chips and an apple* it is complement; in [*I'll do it*] *this morning or this afternoon* adjunct; and so on: if a given position in a sentence can be filled by an expression of class X it is usually also possible for it to be filled by a coordination of Xs. For this reason it has not been necessary to refer to coordination in earlier chapters when giving the functions of the classes discussed. When we say that an NP can function as subject, object, complement of a preposition, etc., it is to be understood that it can also function as one element in a coordinative subject, object, complement of a preposition, etc. And similarly, when a subordinate clause is defined as a clause having a dependent function within a larger construction that is itself a clause or a constituent of one, this is to be understood as allowing also for the case where the dependent function is filled by a coordination of subordinate clauses. A detailed description of coordination would need to specify the exceptions, but for the regular cases a single statement is sufficient: the possibility of replacing an X by a coordination of Xs does not need mentioning for each different value of X.

One case that is worth drawing attention to here, however, is that a coordination may occur as an element within a larger coordination. In [*I'll invite*] *Tom and Mary or Bill and Liz*, for example, we have a structure where at the first layer *or* coordinates *Bill and Liz* with *Tom and Mary*, and each of these then contains a second layer of coordination. Or rather that is the structure in one interpretation, for the example is in fact ambiguous. In the interpretation just considered, I'm going to invite two people, but there is another interpretation where I'm going to invite three: Tom, Liz and either Mary or Bill. In the latter interpretation, the first layer of coordination has three elements, the NP *Tom*, the coordination *Mary or Bill* and the NP *Liz*.

We will now turn to an outline of basic coordination in English, presenting it under the above six headings.

(a) Marking by coordinators. Most coordinations are explicitly marked as such by the presence of one or more coordinators, as in all the examples so far. They are not, however, a requirement of the construction, being absent from the special type known as **asyndetic** coordination, as in [*She is*] *honest, hard-working, intelligent* or [*We need*] *bananas, apples, oranges, pears*. Semantically these are interpreted as though *and* were present. The syntactic unity of the construction derives from the functional likeness of the elements, property (d): *honest, hard-working, intelligent* as a whole functions as predicative. As there is no such functional unity in *Tom laughed, Liz chuckled, Pat grinned*, we have no comparable basis for saying that the three clauses belong to a single syntactic construction: from a syntactic point of view, it is questionable whether what we have here is a single sentence rather than a sequence of three separate sentences.

The two most central coordinators are *and* and *or* – most central in that they figure in constructions that are most distinctively coordinative with respect to properties (e), open-endedness, and (f), range of occurrence – see below. In coordinations of three or more elements, they usually introduce only the final element, as in (3). It is also possible, however, to have them before all elements other than the first, as in *The Governor or the Premier or the Mayor* [*could open the Exhibition*]: the effect is to emphasise the coordinative relation between the elements. When it coordinates declarative main clauses, *and* expresses logical conjunction, as illustrated earlier. Very often some further relation between the clauses beyond mere conjunction will be implied: *Ed was late and she was furious*, for example, will generally convey that her being furious was a consequence of Ed's being late. Such implications are not to be attributed to the meaning of *and*, however, for they can appear as readily when the clauses are merely juxtaposed: *Ed was late; she was furious*.

In the most elementary cases, coordination by *and* of smaller units is logically equivalent to coordination of clauses – *She was young and energetic*, for example, is equivalent to *She was young and she was energetic*. The possibility of such a paraphrase is, however, subject to two important limitations, illustrated in

(6) *One teacher was young and energetic*
(7) *Ed and Kim solved the problem*

In (6) the properties "young" and "energetic" are ascribed to the same teacher, whereas in *One teacher was young and one teacher was energetic* they are not. (The implication of the latter is that the young teacher and the energetic teacher are different, but they do not have to be: the crucial point is that they are not stipulated to be the same, as they are in (6).) In (6) the coordination is within the semantic scope of the quantifier *one*, but when we switch to clausal coordination the scope relations are changed, with a consequent difference in meaning. The same phenomenon is found in examples like *Many of them were young and energetic, They weren't young and energetic, Who was young and energetic?*, where the coordination falls within the scope of the quantifier, negative and interrogative respectively. Although such considerations of scope prevent a paraphrase with clausal coordination, the meaning of *and* in (6) can be related indirectly to conjunction – we can give a rough semantic analysis along the lines of "There was one teacher x such that x was young and x was energetic", where "and" again represents conjunction.

(7) differs from *Ed solved the problem and Kim solved the problem* in that the latter involves two acts of solving whereas in the former there may have been just one, with Ed and Kim working together. Where *and* joins NPs the coordination normally enumerates members of a plural set – and what holds for a set as a whole does not necessarily hold for the members as individuals. (7) may be contrasted on the one hand with (8i), on the other with (8ii):

(8) i *Ed and Kim are a pair of crooks*   Combinatory
     ii *Ed and Kim are Australian*   Segregatory

Being a pair of crooks necessarily applies to Ed and Kim in combination: we will say then that *Ed and Kim* in (8i) receives a 'combinatory' interpretation. Being Australian, however, applies separately to Ed and Kim as individuals: the coordination in (8ii) receives a 'segregatory' interpretation. (7) then allows either a combinatory interpretation (they reached a joint solution) or a segregatory one (they each solved it). The distinction between combinatory and segregatory interpretations applies not just to *and* coordinations of NPs but also to non-coordinate plural NPs – we could replace *Ed and Kim* by *the twins, they* or whatever without affecting the point. What makes it particularly relevant to coordination is its bearing on the relation between phrasal and clausal coordination: only where the combinatory interpretation is excluded will there be logical equivalence, as between (8ii) and *Ed is Australian and Kim is Australian*. The meaning of *and* in NP coordination is thus not reducible to logical conjunction: we need a broader, additive meaning of which conjunction would then be a special case. Compare also its use in linking interrogatives, as in *Who are you and what do you want?*; this would characteristically be used to ask two questions: the *and* adds the second to the first.

Examples like (6), (7) and (8i) make it clear that we should not regard phrasal coordination as derivative from clausal coordination: it is for this reason that what we are calling 'basic coordination' is not restricted to the coordination of clauses.

Consider now the meaning of *or*. Our initial account was in terms of logical disjunction: the compound proposition expressed by, say, *Tom has missed the train or the train is late* is true if either of the component propositions (the 'disjuncts') "Tom has missed the train" and "The train is late" is true. We can distinguish two kinds of logical disjunction, exclusive and inclusive. Exclusive disjunction excludes the possibility of more than one disjunct being true, while inclusive disjunction allows it. Thus salient interpretations of

(9) i   *You can have peach melba or you can have plum pudding*
     ii *You can get one from Cole's or you can get one from Woolworth's*

are respectively exclusive and inclusive. Thus (i) is likely to be construed exclusively – i.e. as excluding the possibility of your being able to have both peach melba and plum pudding – in a context where the issue is the choice of dessert in a fixed-price meal or in a social milieu where it would be considered a breach of etiquette to have two desserts. (ii), on the other hand, is likely to be construed inclusively – i.e. as allowing that the item in question is obtainable both from Cole's and from Woolworth's – in a context where I am leaving it to you to choose which shop to get it from: you will have such a choice only if both shops stock it.

The choice between exclusive and inclusive interpretations here depends on the semantic content of the disjuncts together with background knowledge and context. Similarly *The letter was posted on Tuesday or Wednesday* will normally be interpreted exclusively because letters are normally posted only once, whereas the earlier *Tom has missed the train or the train is late* will normally have an inclusive interpretation because the likely context is one where I'm advancing reasons for Tom's absence, and if he missed the train I have no evidence as to whether it is late or not. Sometimes, however, there are linguistic indicators. One can, for example, make it explicit that two disjuncts are not mutually exclusive by adding *or both*: *You can have peach melba or plum pudding or both*, and one can of course likewise explicitly rule out the inclusive interpretation by adding *but not both*. *At least* in the second disjunct, as in *Ed did it himself, or at least he said he did* rules out the case where the first disjunct is true and the second false, but it allows that where both are true and thus leads to an inclusive interpretation of the disjunction. Prosodic properties of the utterance may also be relevant: in particular, nuclear stress on *or* will tend to favour an exclusive interpretation because of an implied contrast with *and*. Recall, further, that we noted in 9.4 that an interrogative like *Does she speak French or German?* can be used, depending on the intonation, as a closed question of either the yes/no type ("Does she speak one of these languages or not?") or the non-yes/no type ("Does she speak French or does she speak German?"): in the first reading there will be a rise on *German*, in the second a rise on *French* together with a fall on *German*. In the first the disjunction is quite incidental to the question but in the second it is crucial: it is the focus of the question. And in this second reading the disjunction always receives an exclusive interpretation: I assume she speaks just one of the languages and ask which it is; *She speaks both* is, of course, a possible response, but it is not an answer in the sense of 9.4, precisely because it rejects the assumption built into the question that she speaks only one.

Phrasal coordination with *or*, as with *and*, is often equivalent to clausal coordination, but again not always. *Or* does not yield the combinatory interpretations found in (7) and (8i) above, but the scope factor may apply with *or* as much as with *and* to block equivalence between clausal and phrasal coordination. For example, *Most of them were from Sydney or Melbourne*, where the coordination is within the scope of the quantifier *most*, is clearly not equivalent to *Most of them were from Sydney or most of them were from Melbourne*. Similarly

(10) *He hadn't seen Tom or Bill*

is not equivalent to *He hadn't seen Tom or he hadn't seen Bill*. The disjunction in (10) is within the scope of the negative: it is the negative of *He had seen Tom or Bill* (which is equivalent to *He had seen Tom or he had seen Bill*). A disjunction within the scope of a negative is normally interpreted inclusively, so that the negative denies the possibility of both disjuncts being true, as well as that of either one alone being true; in this interpretation (10) is equivalent to *He hadn't seen Tom and he hadn't seen Bill*: a negated inclusive disjunction is logically equivalent to a conjunction of negatives. However, with contrastive stress on *or* the disjunction can be interpreted exclusively (as observed above) and the negation will then be taken as denying the possibility that the disjuncts are both false: in this highly marked interpretation (10) implies *He had seen Tom and he had seen Bill*. (Compare *You don't need qualifications in linguistics "or philosophy: you need them in both.*)

Besides *and* and *or* the coordinator class includes: (α) *but*, as in *I asked him but he refused*: (β) *both*, *either* and *not* when correlative with *and*, *or* and *but* respectively: *Both Kim and Pat* [*witnessed the accident*], [*We could meet*] *either this afternoon or tomorrow morning*, [*They finally went*] *not by plane but by car*; (γ) *neither* and *nor* when correlative with each other: [*They*] *neither knew nor cared*. We will look at them briefly in turn, noting in passing that all these words belong to other classes as well as to the coordinator class.

But means essentially "and yet" – it expresses contrast overlaid on conjunction. This feature of contrast excludes it from NP coordination with a combinatory interpretation: *All the girls but only one of the boys solved the problem*, unlike (7), has only a segregatory reading. As well as being a coordinator, *but* can be a preposition with the meaning "except, besides", as in *She'll talk to anybody but you*. Here *but you* is a dependent to the head *anybody* – *you* and *anybody* are not of equal syntactic status.

Both and *either* correlate with *and* and *or*, serving to emphasise the coordinative relation between the elements. In NP coordination, *both . . . and* normally has a segregatory interpretation – *both* would be out of place, for example, in (8i). *Either* favours an exclusive interpretation of the disjunction: *Tom or his brother will be there* allows more readily for them both being there than does *Either Tom or his brother will be there*. But we certainly cannot go so far as to say that it actually expresses exclusive disjunction, for it is not inconsistent to add *or both*: *You can have either peach melba or plum pudding or both*. And note that *either* could be added to (10), where the equivalence to *He didn't see Tom and he didn't see Bill* depends on the disjunction being taken inclusively. *Both* and *either* also belong to the determinative class (*both parents*, *either parent*), while *either* can be a connective adverb appearing in negative clauses such as *Kim didn't like it either*: these uses are easily distinguished from the coordinator one.

The primary use of *not* is as an adverb, as in *They are not going by plane*. It remains an adverb, of course, in *They are not going by plane but by car*. In *They are going not by plane but by car*, however, the *not* is indissolubly tied to the coordination (witness the ungrammaticality of **They went not by plane*): in this construction, then, *not* and *but* act together as a pair of correlative coordinators syntactically comparable to *both . . . and* or *either . . . or*.

Finally correlative *neither . . . nor* simply results from the incorporation of a negative into *either . . . or*: compare *He hadn't seen either Tom or Bill* and *He had seen neither Tom nor Bill*. *Neither* can also be a determinative (cf. *neither parent*), and both *neither* and *nor* can be connective adverbs: *They didn't like it and neither/nor did I*. In this use they are not correlative, but variants. The crucial syntactic difference between their connective and coordinator uses is that in the former they can combine with *and*, as in the example given: contrast the coordinator use, as in **[They] neither knew and nor cared*. Thus any one element can be coordinated by no more than one coordinator, though coordinative linking can be accompanied by the looser type of linking effected by connective adverbs. Note that examples like *I saw Tom but neither Kim nor Liz* do not violate this rule, for we have two layers of coordination here, with *but* and *neither* coordinating different elements: *neither* coordinates *Kim* to *Liz*, while *but* coordinates *neither Kim nor Liz* to *Tom*.

(b) Reducibility to one element. In the most straightforward cases a coordination is syntactically reducible to any one of the elements on its own. Such reduction may not be possible, however, when we have a coordination of NPs that is related by agreement to some other expression in the sentence, as in (11i), or is antecedent to an anaphor requiring a plural antecedent, as in (ii):

(11) i *Ed and Kim have arrived*
     ii *Ed and Kim had known each other for five years*

In these examples reduction of the coordination to a single element involves replacement of a plural by a singular and hence leads to ungrammaticality: **Ed have arrived*, **Ed had known each other for five years*. In (i) it is a simple matter to adjust the agreeing forms (*Ed has arrived*), but we cannot do this in (ii) because reciprocals inherently require a plural antecedent.

One further qualification is necessitated by the fact that reciprocal constructions are not always overtly marked as such. Thus *Ed and Kim met for lunch*, for example, is covertly reciprocal in that "each other" is understood though not expressed; reduction to a single element is no more possible here than in the overt reciprocal (11ii). This constraint is related to the phenomenon of combinatory interpretations, for *Ed and Kim* here allows only a combinatory reading; since the elements are singular, reduction to one will then be inconsistent with this required reading. Reduction in the earlier (8i) is then blocked for the same reason.

(c) Order change. Again in the most straightforward cases, the order of coordinated elements can be reversed, as illustrated above for (1) and (3). The main inhibiting factor here – a quite frequent one – is where one coordinate element is or contains the antecedent for an anaphorically interpreted expression or ellipsis in a following element, as in *Tom's passport was out of date and this forced him to withdraw*. In the natural interpretation *this* is anaphoric to the first clause (being interpreted as "the fact that Tom's passport was out of date") while *him* is anaphoric to *Tom*. We cannot switch to *This forced him to withdraw and Tom's passport was out of date* without changing the interpretation of the pronouns: in coordination a pronoun normally has to follow its antecedent. Analogously in *Pat had left before the end and we had too*, where the ellipsis is anaphoric: "we had left before the end too".

In these examples the anaphoric relation is explicit, evident from the pronoun, or the ellipsis. Elsewhere the anaphoric relation may be merely implied, but such an implication will likewise block a change in the order of elements: *She went home and had a bath*. Besides the conjunctive meaning, there is here an implication that the events occurred in the order in which they are expressed, an implication of "then" in the second element: if we reverse to *She had a bath and went home* we change the implied order of events. *And* and *or* can both be used with an implied conditional relation between the elements: *Come early and you'll be able to see the boss* ("If you come early you'll be able to see the boss", "Come early and then/in that case you'll be able ..."), *Come early or you won't be able to see the boss* ("If you don't come early you won't be able to see the boss", "Come early or otherwise you won't be able to see the boss"), and such implications of consequence likewise serve to prevent a change in order.

We should also note that for many high frequency coordinations, one particular order is conventionalised: *ladies and gentlemen, men and women, bread and butter, fish and chips, buy and sell, up and down*. Reversing the order here leads not to ungrammaticality, but to a relatively unidiomatic expression.

(d) Likeness of class and function. In all the examples so far the coordinate elements have been alike in class and, where relevant, in function too. There are places, however, where the like class condition may be relaxed provided the like function requirement is met. The two most frequent such cases involve, on the one hand, the predicative and, on the other, adjuncts or complements of time or place:

(12) i [*She is*] *interested in people and a good judge of character*
     ii [*We could do it*] *immediately or after lunch*

In (i) we have a coordination of an AdjP and an NP, either of which could stand alone in PC function, and in (ii) a coordination of an AdvP and a PP, either of which could function alone as time adjunct. Likeness of function is thus here sufficient to permit the coordination, but a difference of class is not always so readily allowed. A tensed declarative clause, for example, can often appear in the same function as an NP, but coordination of such expressions is much less natural than that of like classes: ?*That he was lying and his contempt for the whole procedure must have been obvious to everyone*.

(e) Open-endedness. The coordinators *and* and *or* clearly allow an indefinite number of coordinate elements, whereas *but* is normally restricted to two-element coordinations. Correlative *both* likewise occurs only with two elements; some speakers have the same restriction for *either/neither*, but others allow more than two, as in *You can have either tea or coffee or cocoa.*

(f) Range of occurrence. *And* and *or* can coordinate elements at almost any place in the structure of sentences. The other coordinators, by contrast, are subject to such restrictions as the following. (α) *Both, not* and – for many speakers – *neither* cannot coordinate main clauses: **Both Kim liked it and Pat did too.* (β) *Either* cannot coordinate interrogative or exclamative main clauses: **Either was it a hoax or was it genuine?.* (γ) *But* does not readily coordinate NPs: **I saw Kim but Ed*; there must be a contrast in polarity (*I saw not Kim but Ed*), of quantification (*I saw all the dogs but only a few of the cats*), and so on. Such restrictions do not diminish the significance of this property, particularly in combination with (d), for the distinction between coordination and subordination. Compare, in this connection,

(13) i   *Kim was a friend of his but she refused to help him*
    ii *[Kim,] who was a friend of his but who refused to help him, [must bear a heavy responsibility]*
(14) i   *Kim refused to help him although she was a friend of his*
    ii *[Kim,] who refused to help him although she was a friend of his, [must bear a heavy responsibility]*

In (13) *but* coordinates two main clauses in (i), two relative clauses in (ii); the co-ordinate (equal) status of the elements related by *but* is reflected in the fact that when (i) is relativised to become (ii), both undergo the same change (*Kim* is replaced by *who* and so is *she*). In (14), by contrast, *Kim refused to help him* and *she was a friend of his* are of unequal status, the former superordinate (head), the latter subordinate, and this is reflected in the fact that relativisation affects only the first (*Kim* is replaced by *who* but *she* is not).

2. Non-basic coordination

Non-basic coordination involves: (a) discontinuity, (b) bound ellipsis or (c) restructuring.

(a) Discontinuity arises where the second coordinate element is brought forward to appear as an interpolation within the first, instead of following it – compare (15i) and (ii):

(15) i   *Kim – and she's a disinterested witness – says he is innocent*
    ii *Kim says he is innocent and she is a disinterested witness*

(ii) is an example of basic coordination, with a structure of the kind shown in (2). In (i), by contrast, the first element is discontinuous, being interrupted by the interpolated second element. The motivation for this departure from the basic order is typically to bring a pronoun (here *she*) closer to its antecedent (*Kim*).

(b) **Bound ellipsis** contrasts with **free ellipsis** as illustrated in:

(16) i *Liz ordered a martini and Bill a beer*   Bound ellipsis
     ii *Liz ordered a martini but Bill didn't*   Free ellipsis

We understand "Bill ordered a beer" in (i), "Bill didn't order a martini" in (ii). The ellipsis in (ii) is free in the sense that it applies without restriction on the kind of clause concerned: in (16ii) *order a martini* is omitted from a coordinated main clause, in *Liz ordered a martini but those who didn't were given one anyway* it is omitted from a relative clause, in *Liz always ordered a martini if Bill didn't* it is omitted from a content clause complement of *if*, in ⟨A⟩ *Did Bill order a martini?* ⟨B⟩ *No, he didn't* it is omitted from a simple sentence, and so on. (16ii) can thus be analysed as an instance of basic coordination: the coordinate elements do not differ in form from non-coordinate clauses. The ellipsis in (i), by contrast, is restricted to certain constructions, primarily coordination: we could not omit *ordered* in, for example, *Liz ordered a martini but those who ordered a beer were served first*, *Liz ordered a martini if Bill ordered a beer*, and so on. The form of the second clause here is thus to be accounted for in our description of non-basic coordination.

The particular type of bound ellipsis found in (16i) is known as **gapping**: it leaves a gap in the middle of a clause. More precisely, a gapped clause contains a subject and at least one complement or adjunct, but has a gap between them. The gap may involve just the predicator, as in (15i), or the predicator together with one or more other elements: *His father gave him some records, and his mother a tie* (predicator + indirect object – *gave + him*), *Liz had ordered a martini, and Bill a beer* (predicator + predicator of non-finite complement – *had + ordered*), and so on. Gapping is just about limited to coordination – including, however, the asyndetic type: *Liz ordered a martini, Bill a beer* (so that in non-basic asyndetic coordination the elements can undoubtedly be main clauses: the ellipsis serves to establish a syntactic relation between the clauses).

A second kind of bound ellipsis (one with no widely used specific name) is found in

(17) *She often went to Melbourne, but never to Adelaide*

We need to recognise ellipsis here because, as it stands, *never to Adelaide* is not comparable, in terms of function or class, with the element to which it is coordinated, *often went to Melbourne*, a predicate with the form of a VP. In the non-coordinate construction *She never went to Adelaide* the *never* and *to Adelaide* do not form a constituent and hence cannot be assigned a function or class: in (17), therefore, *never to Adelaide* is described derivatively, by reference to the full VP *never went to Adelaide*. Note that although we have ellipsis of the predicator, (17) does not belong to the gapping construction, as there is no subject in the second element. This second type of bound ellipsis is characteristic of coordination but not wholly restricted to it: *but* could be replaced by, for example, *although*, a preposition with closer affinities than most to the coordinators. But it is still very clearly not free – cf. *There were two who often went to Melbourne and one who never to Adelaide.*

In (17) both constituents in the second coordinate element contrast with functionally parallel constituents in the first: *never* with *often* and *to Adelaide* with *to Melbourne*. In other cases the second element contains an adjunct which is not overtly contrastive in this way. Thus in *I'm going to Melbourne and if there's time to Adelaide* the conditional *if there's time* contrasts not with a different conditional but with the absence of a conditional: my going to Melbourne isn't subject to conditions but my going to Adelaide is. Similarly in *Pat will be there and perhaps Kim too*: the modal adjunct *perhaps* contrasts with the absence of such an adjunct in the first element.

This type of bound ellipsis may combine with the interpolation mentioned in (a) above: *Pat – and perhaps Kim too – will be there*. Because *perhaps* is an adjunct functioning in clause structure, rather than a dependent in NP structure, we analyse this as involving non-basic coordination of clauses rather than basic coordination of NPs. Note, as further evidence, that if we replaced *will* by *be going to*, the *be* would take the form *is*, not *are*: it would agree with *Pat*.

(c) Restructuring is illustrated in

(18) *Joan has read, and Pat is planning to read, the complete works of Sarah Grand*

When *Joan has read the complete works of Sarah Grand* stands alone as a sentence, we analyse it into a subject with the form of an NP and a predicate with the form of a VP. Instead of a single VP like this, we could have a coordination of VPs: *Joan has read the complete works of Sarah Grand, and believes they are very much underrated*. This fits straightforwardly into our account of basic coordination – a non-coordinative subject is in construction with a coordinative predicate. In (18), by contrast, we have a non-coordinative object (*the complete works of Sarah Grand*) in construction with a coordinative 'pre-object' – it is non-basic because it works as though the immediate constituents of *Joan has read the complete works of Sarah Grand* were *Joan has read* ('pre-object') and *the complete works of Sarah Grand* (object). The term 'restructuring' thus indicates a change from the normal constituent structure – a change that is marked by the clear prosodic break after *to read*.

Restructuring of NPs rather than clauses is found in examples like *one British and one American officer*, where *one British* and *one American* are coordinated even though they do not form constituents in the NPs *one British officer* and *one American officer*.

Restructuring prototypically occurs in coordination, but it is also found in subordination with such prepositions as *whereas, while, although*: *Some people admired, while others deplored, the highly sophisticated humour that she contrived to incorporate into all her speeches*. These prepositions, although distinguishable from coordinators by reference to the properties discussed in §1 above, are clearly closer to them than are prototypical prepositions such as *to, on, of, at*.

EXERCISES

I. Coordinators

(a) Discuss the extent to which the unbracketed words in (19)–(23) have the grammatical properties of coordinators:

(19) [*It was raining,*] so [*we decided to cancel the trip*]
(20) [*We must press on,*] for [*time is running out*]
(21) [*I'd have gone with them,*] only [*I wasn't feeling very well*]
(22) [*It was an efficient*] yet [*rather impersonal organisation*]
(23) [*We invited him,*] although [*we knew he wouldn't come*]

(b) Discuss the interpretation of the disjunction (inclusive or exclusive) in:

(24) *They're selling it for $500 or the nearest offer*
(25) *I bet he marries Susan or Jane*
(26) *He hadn't written to his mother or his father*
(27) *Half of them had already read the novel or seen it on TV*

II. Reducibility to one element

Are the coordinations in (28)–(31) grammatically replaceable by each one of the elements? If not, why?

(28) *Kim and her opponent shook hands amicably*
(29) *Tom and Ed should watch their step next time*
(30) *You and I could finish it together*
(31) *One or other of them is going to have to resign*

III. Order change

Discuss the effect of reversing the coordinated elements in:

(32) *We're meeting Sue and her husband next Tuesday*
(33) *Let me see you round here once more and I'll set the dog on you*
(34) *I overslept and missed the train*
(35) *They've got a black and white terrier*
(36) *They'll be here at six or at least they said they would*

IV. Likeness of function

Construct example sentences containing coordinations of (α) NP + PP; (β) NP + AdvP; (γ) AdjP + PP; (δ) PP + subordinate clause.

V. Range of occurrence

Construct example sentences containing coordinations in the following positions:

(α) NP structure: (i) determiner, (ii) pre-head modifier, (iii) head, (iv) post-head modifier, (v) complement;

(β) PP structure: (i) head, (ii) complement;

(γ) AdjP structure: (i) pre-head modifier, (ii) head, (iii) post-head modifier, (iv) complement.

VI. Clausal and phrasal coordination

Discuss the semantic relation between (37)–(40) and the corresponding clausal coordinations.

(37) *Kim and Pat cycle to work*
(38) *Everyone was drinking tea or coffee*
(39) *No one had anything good to say about Pat or her husband*
(40) *Was he born in Australia or in New Zealand?*

Further reading

The fullest description of English grammar to appear in recent years is *A Comprehensive Grammar of the English Language* by Randolph Quirk, Sidney Greenbaum, Geoffrey Leech and Jan Svartvik (Longman, 1985; 1779pp.). This monumental work, the culmination of some twenty years' collaboration between the authors, is an indispensable reference work for advanced study in English grammar; apart from its detailed treatment of the language itself, it contains a valuable bibliography. Two shorter volumes based on the same collaborative enterprise are *A Grammar of Contemporary English* by the same four authors (Longman, 1972; 1120pp.) and *A University Grammar of English* by Quirk and Greenbaum (Longman, 1973, 484pp.; American edition published under the title *A Concise Grammar of Contemporary English*).

The present book draws heavily on my contribution to the Cambridge Textbooks in Linguistics series, *Introduction to the Grammar of English* (Cambridge University Press, 1984; 483pp.). The latter deals more fully with just about all the topics covered here; it also has more on the linguistic concepts employed and provides a limited amount of bibliographical information.

The three-volume *Linguistic Typology and Syntactic Description* edited by Timothy Shopen (Cambridge University Press, 1985) provides an excellent reference source for those interested in comparing English with other languages with respect to its grammatical categories and constructions.

For readers wishing to look further into the field of linguistics, there are now quite a number of good introductions available. They include: Akmajian, A., Demers, R. A. and Harnish, R. M., *Linguistics: an Introduction to Language and Communication* (MIT Press, 2nd edn, 1984); Crystal, D., *What is Linguistics?* (Edward Arnold, 4th edn, 1985); Fromkin, V. and Rodman, R., *An Introduction to Language* (Holt, Rinehart and Winston, 1974); Hudson, R. A., *Invitation to Linguistics* (Martin Robertson, 1984); Lyons, J., *Language and Linguistics; an Introduction* (Cambridge University Press, 1981); Yule, G., *The Study of Language* (Cambridge University Press, 1985).

Index

interrogative, 3–5, 12, 13, 33, 45, 50, 80, 86,
101, 102, 104–5, 120, 124, 125, 127, 129,
130, 132, 134–8, 139–40, 141, 142, 146, 153,
154–5, 156, 161–2, 171, 182, 183, 188, 198,
199, 203
intransitive, 59–60
inversion, 45, 135, 138, 145, 161–2, 182
irregular lexeme, 17

jussive, 43–4, 132–4, 153, 161–2, 171
juxtaposition, 193

kernel clause, 11–14, 20–1, 22, 28, 35, 44, 49–
68, 129, 135

language-particular definition, 1–5, 6, 22
lexeme, 6–7, 8n, 19, 23
lexical morphology, 17–18, 27, 114
lexicalisation, 126–7
lexicon, 1, 7, 24, 59, 61, 90, 104, 115, 126
locative, 121

main clause, 13, 44, 130, 152, 203
manner adjunct, 64, 65, 120, 122, 134, 147
marked, 14
masculine, 98
mass: *see* count
modal adjunct, 64, 80
modal operator, 28, 38, 46, 50, 71–2, 78–81,
132, 136, 148, 161, 164
modality, 69, 78–81, 164
modifier, 3, 31, 66–7, 85, 92–94, 95, 111, 113,
115, 116, 118, 120–1, 125–6, 155, 162, 163,
168
monotransitive, 57, 59–60
mood, 37, 69, 79–80
morphological process, 16–17, 21, 27
morphology, 1, 16–18

negation, 13, 38, 39, 40, 45, 51, 132, 140,
143–51, 173n, 198, 200, 201
neuter, 98
neutral style, 18
neutralisation, 77
new information, 174, 184, 189
nexus question, 137n
nominalisation, 103–5, 114, 164, 181
nominative, 9, 97–8, 134, 155, 156, 160, 163
non-affirmative, 46, 146–7, 150
non-assertive, 146n
non-basic coordination, 203
non-finite, 43–4, 63, 145, 153, 163–9, 180
non-kernel, 21, 185
non-specific, 91, 158
non-tensed, 28, 40–1
non-verbal, 11
notional definition, 4, 9
noun, 2–3, 5–6, 22–3, 25, 29, 53, 84–107, 108,
111–12, 116, 117, 118, 127, 159, 160, 168–9,
170, 186, 203, 205

number, 5, 29, 38, 39, 44, 54, 84, 85, 87–8, 89,
92, 108, 112, 159, 180
number-transparent, 87–8
numeral, 116–17

object, 29, 50, 53–6, 60, 62, 67–8, 85, 94, 164,
166, 177, 179–80, 181, 186, 189
object complement, 54n
objective case, 98n
objective predicative, 54n, 56–7
obligatoriness: *see* omissibility
oblique, 61–2
omissibility, 25–6, 51, 52, 61, 65, 93, 132, 154,
156, 161, 169, 186
open class, 23–32, 27, 174
open interrogative/question, 5, 134–8, 141
operator, 38, 45–7, 48, 50, 135, 144, 145
optionality: *see* omissibility
order of elements, 153, 175, 188–9, 195,
201–2, 204, 206
ordinal numeral, 117
orthography, 103

paradigm, 6, 28, 38, 47
particle, 28, 40–1, 92, 93, 111, 112–16, 119,
125, 128, 170
particle, 62, 68, 121, 164
parts of speech, 8, 22–36
passive, 13, 17, 41, 51, 53, 54, 56, 57, 58, 59,
67, 113–14, 123, 125, 131, 164, 165–6, 167,
168–9, 173, 175, 176–9, 180, 181, 190
past participle, 27–8, 39, 40–2, 43, 47, 112–14,
164, 167, 168–9, 170, 177, 178, 184
past tense, 27–8, 39, 41–2, 47, 50, 70–2
patient, 55
perfect, 41, 75–8, 83, 113, 167
performative, 131, 141
peripheral dependent, 66–7, 85, 93–4, 95,
120–1, 122, 125–6, 147, 162, 163, 169, 179
person, 38, 39, 44, 97, 132
personal pronoun, 50–1, 91, 97–9, 100, 139,
180, 183, 189
phrasal coordination, 198, 199–200, 207
phrase, 24–7, 34, 92, 103, 111, 115
place adjunct/complement, 60, 62, 65, 120,
202
polar question, 137n
polarity, 13, 40, 45, 139
polysemy, 89
positive, 13
possessive, 29, 33–5, 36, 85, 86, 90, 92, 100–1,
105, 111n, 116, 167
postposition, 123
postpositive, 109, 110, 116
predicate, 9, 26, 49, 51–2, 57, 65–6
predicate nominal, 54n
predicative (complement), 29, 50, 53–6, 56–7,
60, 62, 63, 65, 67–8, 85, 108, 109, 110, 111,
113–15, 116, 117, 134, 179–80, 184, 186, 202
predicative use of adjective, 30, 31